AF334271

Art of Celebration
GEORGIA

Published by

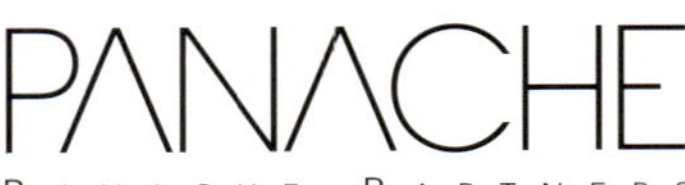

PANACHE

PANACHE PARTNERS

Panache Partners, LLC
1424 Gables Court
Plano, TX 75075
469.246.6060
Fax: 469.246.6062
www.panache.com

Publishers: Brian G. Carabet and John A. Shand

Printed in Malaysia

Distributed by Independent Publishers Group
800.888.4741

PUBLISHER'S DATA

Art of Celebration Georgia

Library of Congress Control Number: 2009939303

ISBN 13: 978-1-933415-86-4
ISBN 10: 1-933415-86-X

First Printing 2010

10 9 8 7 6 5 4 3 2 1

Panache Partners, LLC, is dedicated to the restoration and conservation of the environment. Our books are manufactured with strict adherence to an environmental management system in accordance with ISO 14001 standards, including the use of paper from mills certified to derive their products from well-managed forests. We are committed to continued investigation of alternative paper products and environmentally responsible manufacturing processes to ensure the preservation of our fragile planet.

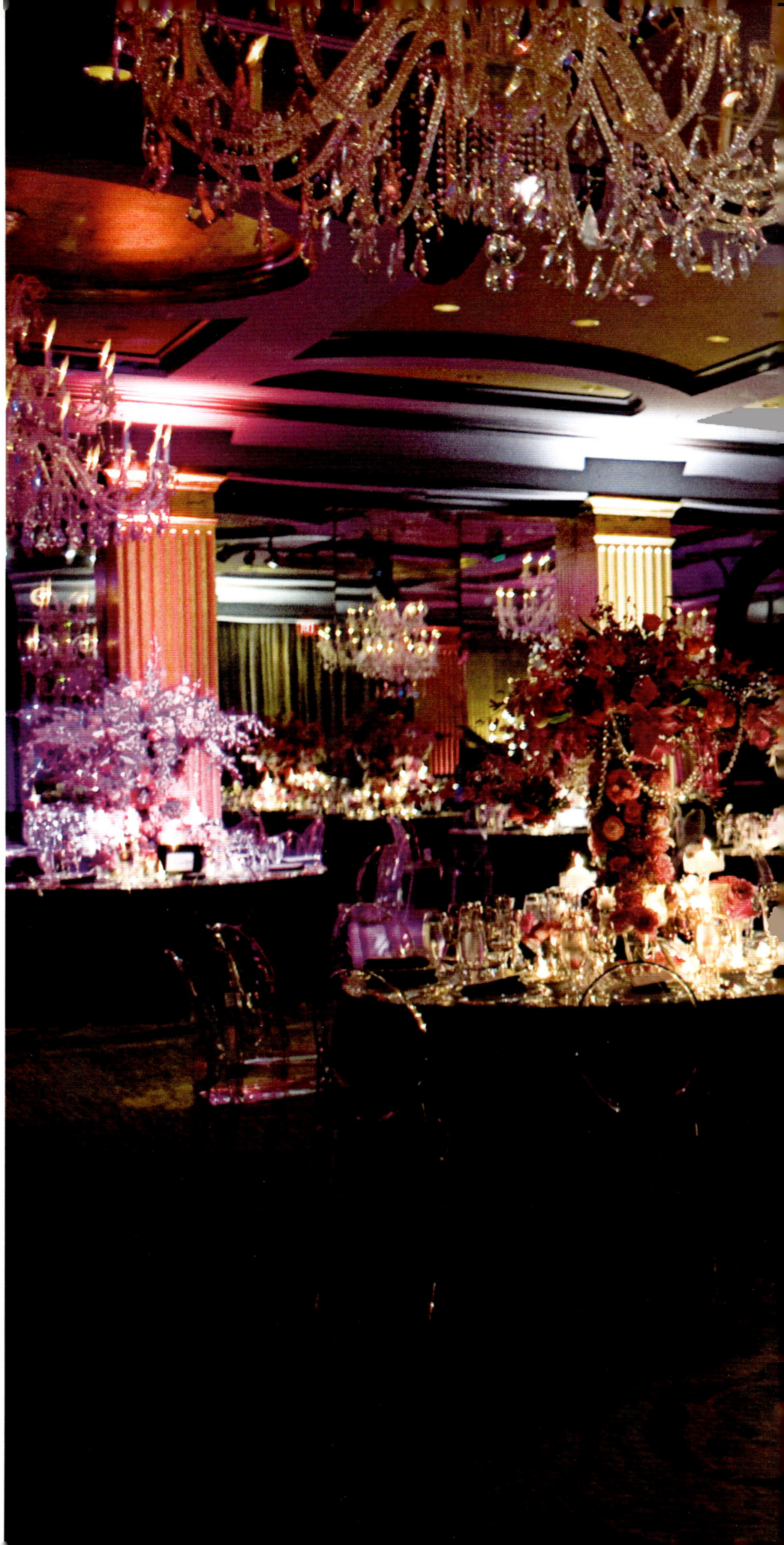

Art of Celebration
GEORGIA

INTRODUCTION

Celebrations are woven into our lives as rituals from the moment we are born; we pave our long and winding road with revelry. How we celebrate milestones, rites of passage, and faith identifies and shapes the culture. Yet because the undertaking of such events requires the visions of a select few, the work of many, and the motivation of all, our celebrations are universal.

In *Art of Celebration Georgia*, we chart modern-day visionaries who mastermind remarkable events. With a rich history of Southern hospitality, the most talented professionals converge with world-renowned venues to create everlasting memories.

The magic of a phenomenal celebration is achieved with great collaboration, which is brilliantly presented in this book through the visually stunning creations and fascinating insights of a variety of experts. We begin this journey with event planners—the directors and producers—who pull it all together, manage, and execute the visions even BEFORE THE MUSIC BEGINS. And because once you've set the date, the next step is LOCATION, LOCATION, LOCATION, we turn our focus to Georgia's most incredible venues, which become inspirational backdrops.

The event, floral, and lighting designers are true visionaries of CREATING AN AMBIENCE; these artists are responsible for endless ideas and boundless efforts and are often the heart and soul of an unforgettable gala. Then EAT, DRINK & BE MERRY in the culinary world of caterers, whose works of art and ingenious creations delight the palate and astound the mind. From there, IT'S ALL IN THE DETAILS. Through the amazing talents of musicians, entertainers, and photographers, CAPTURING THE MOMENT will forever keep alive the experiences of life's ritual—the art of celebration.

Art of Celebration Georgia will inspire, inform, and just might take your breath away!

Phil Reavis,
Executive Publisher

Chapter One—Before the Music Begins

Chapter Two—Location, Location, Location

Chapter Three—Creating an Ambience

CONTENTS

CHAPTER FOUR—EAT, DRINK & BE MERRY

CHAPTER FIVE—IT'S ALL IN THE DETAILS

CHAPTER SIX—CAPTURING THE MOMENT

"An event should lead guests in a journey of the soul by prompting certain emotions throughout the celebration."

—Kimberley Ichter

"Finding the perfect venue is where inspiration begins."

—Marc Nevárez

"Large focal pieces and small custom accents can stretch a budget to create beautiful events."

—Kelly Haywood

"You don't have to be complicated to be fabulous."

—Deb Steege

Before the

Presenting Atlanta
Lounge

Music Begins

Barbara Roos Events

BARBARA ROOS

With an ability to visualize a concept and then meticulously direct all of the pieces into place, Barbara Roos has an exceptional eye for design. After receiving a business degree and working in the event industry, Barbara hit her stride with event designing and she's been nothing but fabulous since.

Numerous event hosts return again and again to Barbara for all of their events—one company for more than 25 years—and a few moments with her quickly explains what keeps them coming back for more. Of paramount importance to Barbara is the guests' comfort; she knows that if guests are uncomfortable, then they won't remember the purpose of the event or her amazing design. She even goes so far as to sit in each seat before the event to ensure a light won't shine in anyone's face or the music won't be too loud.

Working hand in hand with her focus on each guest is Barbara's attention to detail. From the placement of the napkins and the creativity of the table numbers to the efficiency of the bar staff, she wants everything to work in harmony for the best effect imaginable. Of course the resulting ambience is nothing without her vision. Taking cues from all aspects of life, Barbara's inspiration is her guide and often swings her designs in all directions. With no singular style pegged as her preferred look, Barbara's favorite event is the one she's currently planning.

An environmentalist's 70th birthday party at Georgia Aquarium was a monumental occasion. In lieu of gifts, guests donated to the Captain Planet Foundation, which provided the source for the event's nautical theme and slogan: "Don't worry about the wind; Adjust the sails." Waving flags stood as table numbers, various items with a round shape signified bubbles, and succulent plants that were donated to organizations addressed an eco-friendly approach.

Photograph by Harold Alan Photographers

Photograph by Harold Alan Photographers

"New uses for stylish staples—like wearing different accessories with a black dress—can add pizzazz."

—Barbara Roos

Right: At Georgia Aquarium, furniture groupings around the main exhibits encourage conversation.

Facing page: The young birthday girl's favorite color—Tiffany blue—was the inspiration for the "Breakfast at Tiffany's" theme. Despite the potential of a more grown-up ambience, I used satin bows and twinkling crystal on the table to ensure a soft and youthful look.

Photograph by Eric Wittmayer Photography

Left and below: Since pink was the bat mitzvah girl's favorite color—and her birthday was on Valentine's Day—I pulled out all of the rosy décor we could find. To incorporate a creative aspect to necessary elements, I set the place cards in pink rocks and flowers. Guests then pulled on the pink ribbon to find their table number.

Facing page top: The same venue can be completely transformed using the lighting and décor. At a prominent hotel in Atlanta, I achieved a feminine ambience for the Juvenile Diabetes Research Foundation's Mother's Day event and a glamorous, 1920s feel for a wedding.

Facing page bottom: The event host wanted clusters of low table arrangements interspersed with candles; the result was breathtaking.

Photograph by Eric Wittmayer Photography

Photograph by Eric Wittmayer Photography

Photograph by Eric Wittmayer Photography

Photograph courtesy of Barbara Roos Events

"Attitude is everything. Negative thinking leads toward letting something fall through the cracks."

—Barbara Roos

Photograph by Robin Wright

Photograph by Eric Wittmayer

Photograph by Laura Negri Photography

Photograph by Eric Wittmayer

Photograph by Robin Wright

Above and facing page top right: To match the colors of the attendants' attire, I continued with brown and chocolate hues but weaved in cream and pink for softness. I designed handpainted tablecloths, set the table with clear chargers to take full advantage of the linens, and—upon the event host's wishes—placed an edible chocolate menu wrapped in cellophane on the plates, which doubled as a take-home favor.

Facing page top left and bottom: I place a great deal of emphasis on the flowers. Whether we create a magnolia branch canopy with hanging lanterns over the dance floor, a floral-wrapped huppah for a garden ambience, or an airy arrangement at the bottom of a tall centerpiece, the colors, texture, and placement of flowers can have a dramatic impact.

Photograph by Harold Alan Photographers

Photograph courtesy of Barbara Roos Events

"Ensuring the décor is appropriately scaled is like a pair of eyeglasses—it allows you to see all of the right things in all of the right places."

—Barbara Roos

Right: Adding a personal touch to an otherwise undecorated space—like the dance floor—brings a sense of flair.

Facing page top: To give a cleaner look, I like to add a streamlined stage surround instead of the traditional pleated draping.

Facing page bottom: In a cocktail tent at a notable country club, hanging orchids and paper lanterns offer a preview of the main ballroom.

Photograph by Laura Negri Photography

views

An event is all based on trust and confidence. Select people to help you that exude those qualities and rely on them explicitly. Word of mouth and referrals—especially from venue staff—are the key to finding dependable people.

HELENE & COMPANY

HELENE POPOWSKI

When Helene Popowski decided to leave her position as the head of catering at the Ritz-Carlton, Buckhead, people familiar with her work spoke up. They were less than pleased at the idea of losing her talent and just weren't ready to let go of her expertise. After working in upscale hotels for 14 years—including the legendary Plaza Hotel in New York City—Helene established a broad base of clientele that had grown to expect these unforgettable events. With their encouragement, she established a namesake company. Sounds like a happy ending? Well it was just the beginning.

Today, Helene & Company reflects all of the experience, respect, and insight that Helene has acquired over the years. She has a unique gift of being able to step back and see the big picture while simultaneously being able to focus on each and every detail. She dreams big and executes flawlessly. Combining originality, creativity and a side of compulsiveness, each event has her unique stamp on it, but the hosts' personalities always shine through. Gaining inspiration from textiles, colors, and anything that pops, she balances timeless with trendy and goes above and beyond. Her role is to bring an idea to life, and make certain that the hosts feel like guests at their own event.

For a reception that was very close to my heart, I wanted everything to look classically romantic. The bride requested a pink wedding so I maximized the Ritz-Carlton with beauty and color that I knew she would love. Arrangements provided fresh, lush flowers, Creative Tables supplied the linens, and Magnum designed the soft lighting scheme—everything came together.

Photograph by Denis Reggie

Photograph by Eric Wittmayer

Photograph by Eric Wittmayer

Photograph by Eric Wittmayer

Photograph by Eric Wittmayer

Above: Set at the Fernbank Museum of Natural History, a bar mitzvah conveyed personality without disrupting the integrity of the space. We used Andy Warhol-style images of the boy playing sports and displayed them throughout the party without concealing the museum's exhibits and architecture. We worked with EventScapes for the décor, We Rent Atlanta for all the rentals, Bold American for catering, Active Production and Design for lighting, and US Beat Band for entertainment.

Facing page: When the owners of a stunning Atlanta home wanted to celebrate their twins' b'nai mitzvah, I knew that the event had to match their highly tailored taste and showcase the uniqueness of the house. The modern, Italian-villa-inspired home created a unique challenge and opportunity. We had to cater to both children and adults in a separate but cohesive way. Directing adults to the indoors and children to an outdoor tent from Tents Unlimited, we maximized the home's distinct features and matched the level of customization for both children and adults. Elegant seating beneath cabanas highlighted the backyard's South Beach feel, while high-energy entertainment from Lee J. Howard, an amazing ice sculpture by Jim Duggan, and a living fountain statue were elegant conversation pieces. Bold American provided food and décor, Active Production and Design did the lighting, and We Rent Atlanta supplied all of the rentals.

"Good taste is an asset to any event."

—Helene Popowski

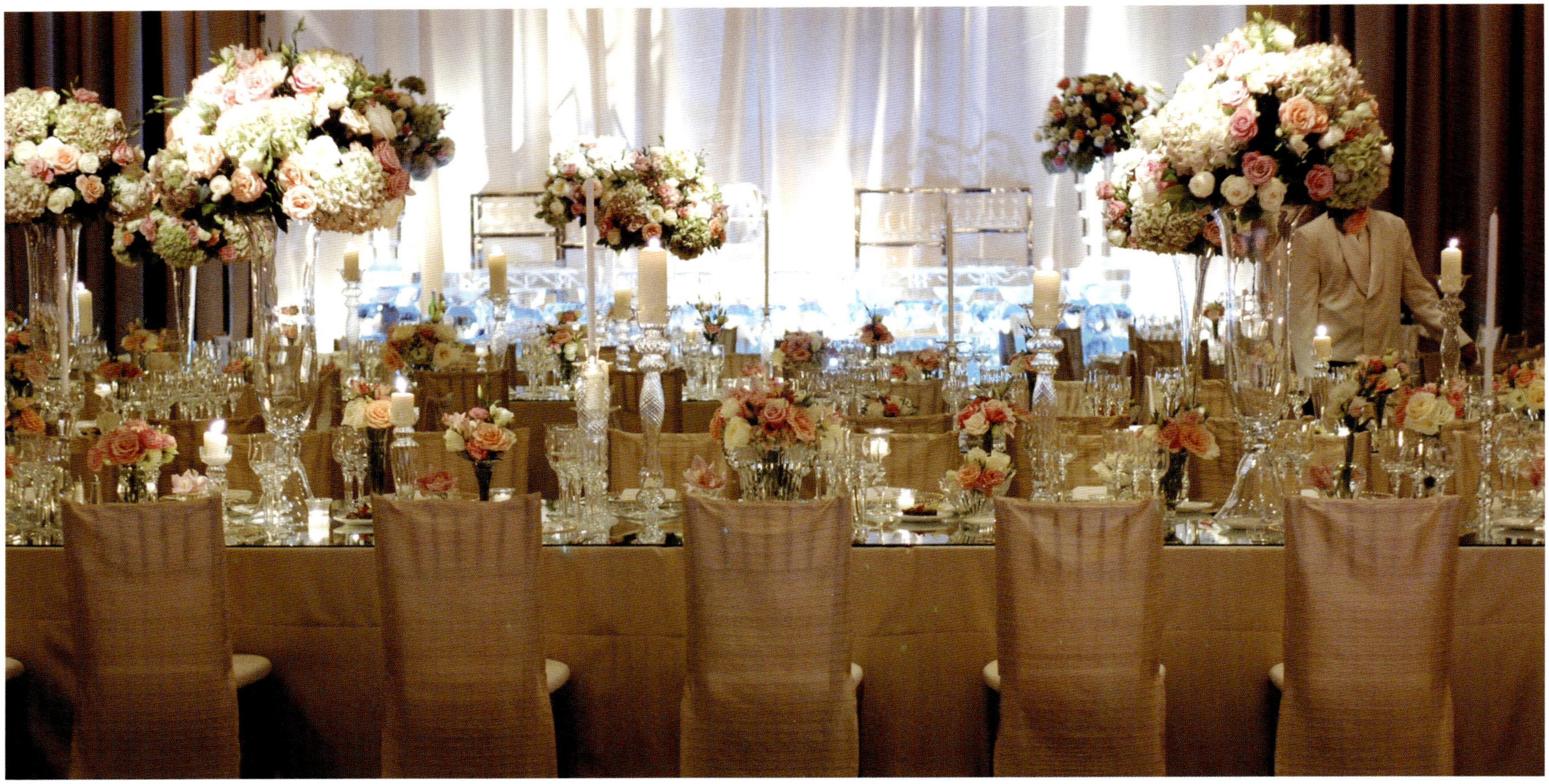

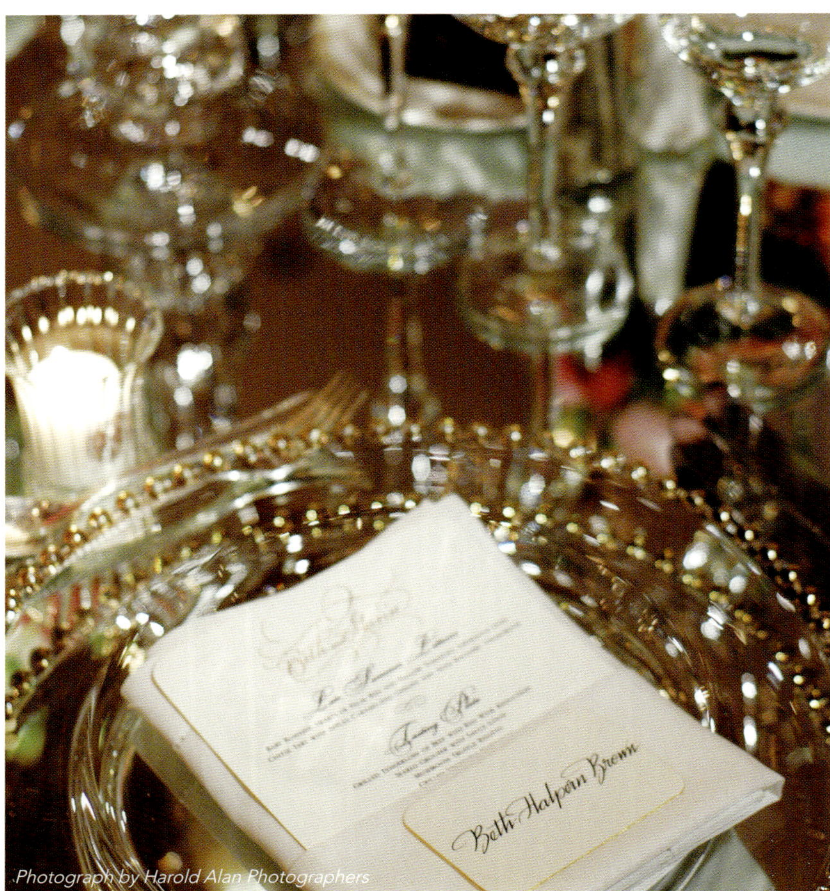

Photograph by Harold Alan Photographers

Photograph by Harold Alan Photographers

Above and left: Set at the InterContinental Buckhead, the wedding was highly emotional and infused with a tremendous spirit. Arrangements, Creative Tables, We Rent Atlanta, and Magnum helped make the event memorable.

Facing page: When I planned a large kosher wedding we designed a phenomenal menu and flew in a fabulous band from New York. What others may see as a challenge, I embrace as an opportunity. I pride myself on being solution-oriented. We collaborated with EventScapes and We Rent Atlanta for the special occasion.

"You should enjoy the food, atmosphere, and entertainment as much as your guests. It's a once-in-a-lifetime event—relish it."

—Helene Popowski

Photograph by Harold Alan Photographers

Photograph by Harold Alan Photographers

Photograph by Eric Wittmayer

Photograph by Eric Wittmayer

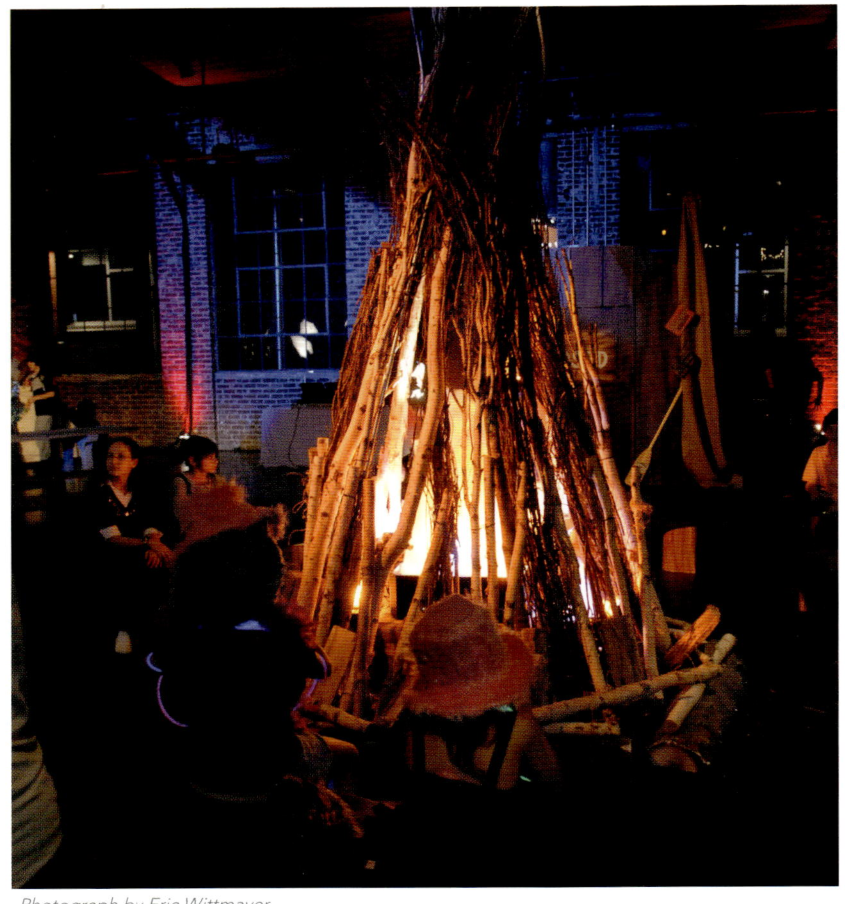

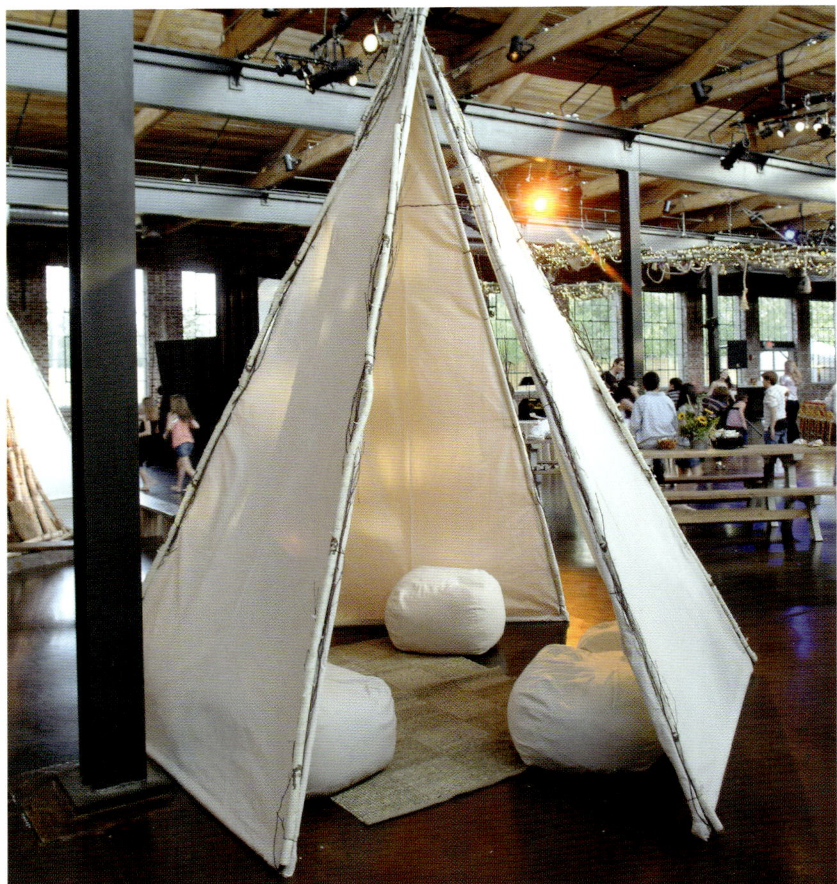

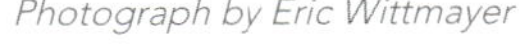

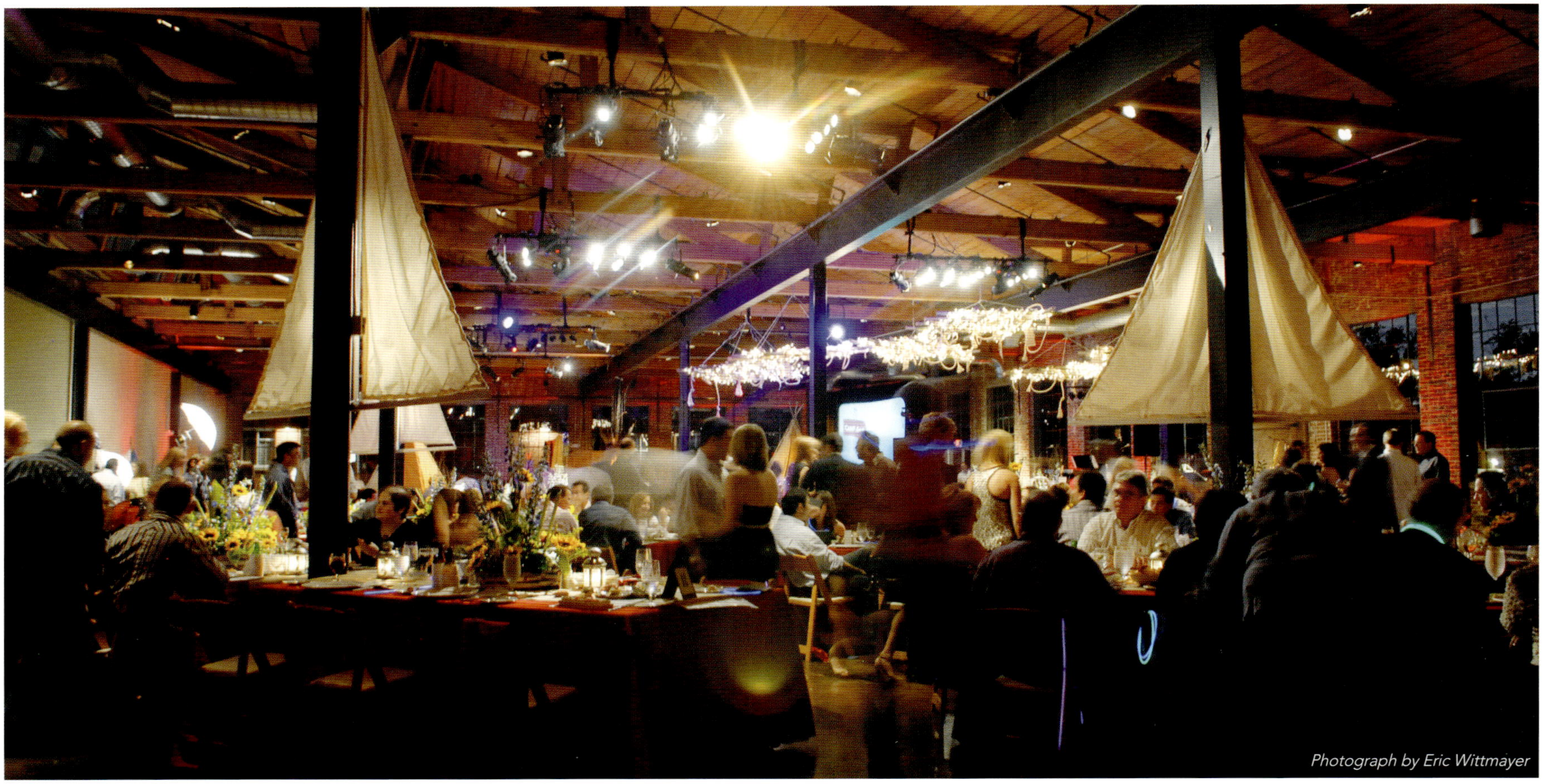

Photograph by Eric Wittmayer

Photograph by Harold Alan Photographers

Photograph by Harold Alan Photographers

Right: College football is a religion in the South—Georgians take college football very seriously—and Georgians have the best tailgate parties. For my son's bar mitzvah, I wanted to capture that spirit and include the University of Georgia's mascot. Celebrating the Bulldogs and using the iconic letter G throughout the event's design, we featured red and black décor throughout the space. Over half of the guests were university alum, making for a very spirited crowd. Dewitt Smith Video Productions provided footage of the event; EventScapes, Active Production and Design, and Let's Celebrate made it all possible.

Facing page: Nothing is more fun than sleep-away camp for two boys who were celebrating their b'nai mitzvah. We turned Atlanta's Puritan Mill facilities into camp grounds for the kids—and adults—to enjoy. Guests sat around traditional campfires and dined on family-style camp food. Butcher paper lined the dinner tables and featured fun, scrawled phrases like "meet me at the flagpole." We collaborated with EventScapes, Active Production and Design, and US Beat Band to create the one-of-a-kind party.

views

If the caterer takes care of the food, the florist oversees the flowers, who designs and pulls it all together and more importantly, who looks after you? That's where the event planner comes in. As an event planner I play a vital role and ensure that the hosting family enjoys the journey. I am respected for my objective advice and ability to negotiate and review contracts. I strive to make my clients feel pampered and well-taken care of throughout the event planning. While there are line item costs, the benefit of working with Helene & Company is priceless.

Juice Studios

KRIS HAMMETT | KRIS SHEA | ANGIE WINCKLER | ELLEN WOODARD

If the name Juice Studios doesn't conjure up images of fresh, fun, innovative spaces, then take one look at an event. Pure energy and raw creativity pours from the room—you can't help but notice there's something different.

As a boutique event management firm, Juice Studios offers a new perspective on meetings, conferences, parties, and destination events. It all began with a founding team of partners who still lead the pack today: Kris Hammett, Kris Shea, Angie Winckler, and Ellen Woodard offer years of wide-ranging experience in production, sales, and operations. This team translates their passion and know-how into events that offer far more than visual stimulation; they create, design, and plan for all of the five senses. And there really is no limit on the possibilities, whether it's a far-off destination event, a marketing video installation, or a massive logistics conference in the heart of Atlanta. Always on the cutting edge, the partners pool their resources and work in markets across the country—New York, California, and Florida—to get constant input and inspiration for the hottest ideas, styles, and products. Step into a Juice Studios event and you'll know that the firm has captured something fun, new, and undoubtedly exciting.

For a tented event called Art in Motion, we highlighted local artists in a number of ways. Projected artwork appeared on the tent's walls, changing with each course throughout the evening. Gorgeous hand-blown vases—also from local artists—made for distinct centerpieces and reflected the city's creative environment.

Photograph by Chris Savas Photography

Photograph by Adam Belanger Photography

Photograph by Adam Belanger Photography

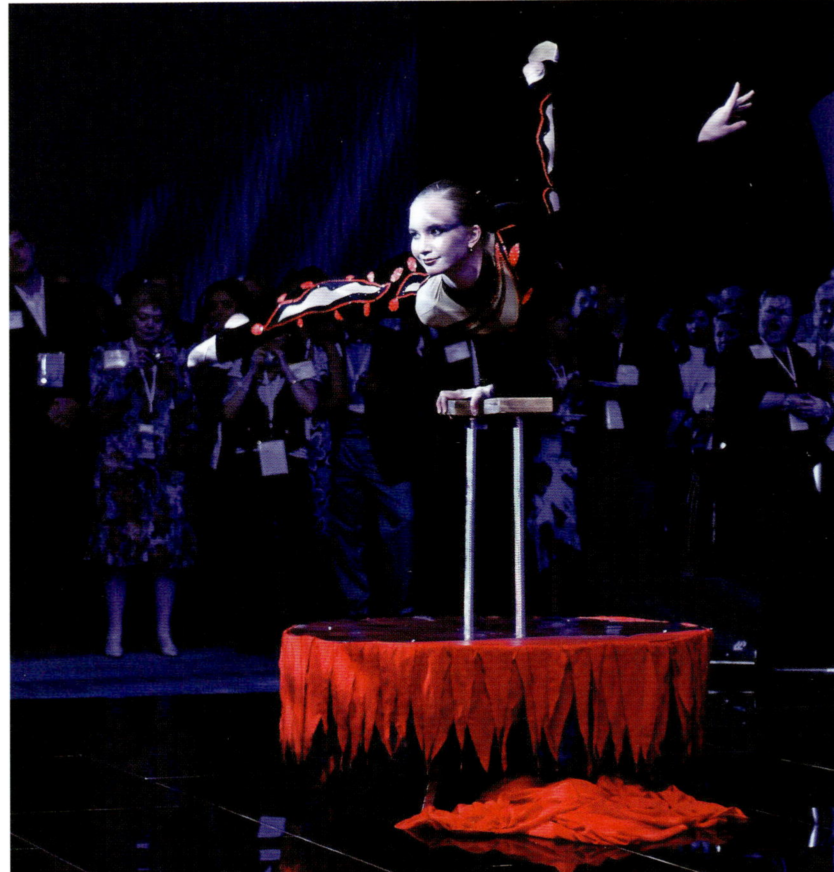

Above and left: Instead of kicking off a corporate incentive program with a subdued cocktail hour, we brought in cirque performers with an ocean theme to entertain guests at Georgia Aquarium. The décor mirrored an underwater fantasy with wave walls, black lights, and berry and white florals.

Facing page: The world-famous CNN Center, situated in a dramatic high rise, provided the perfect backdrop for a product launch. The black and grey tiles of the massive atrium and the red accent in the CNN logo coordinated well with the hosting company's own logo, providing a sense of drama amid modern technology.

"At any hour, details can change. Keeping up with the changes is an exciting challenge."

—Luz Sierra

Photograph by Ross DeLoach, Northlight Photography

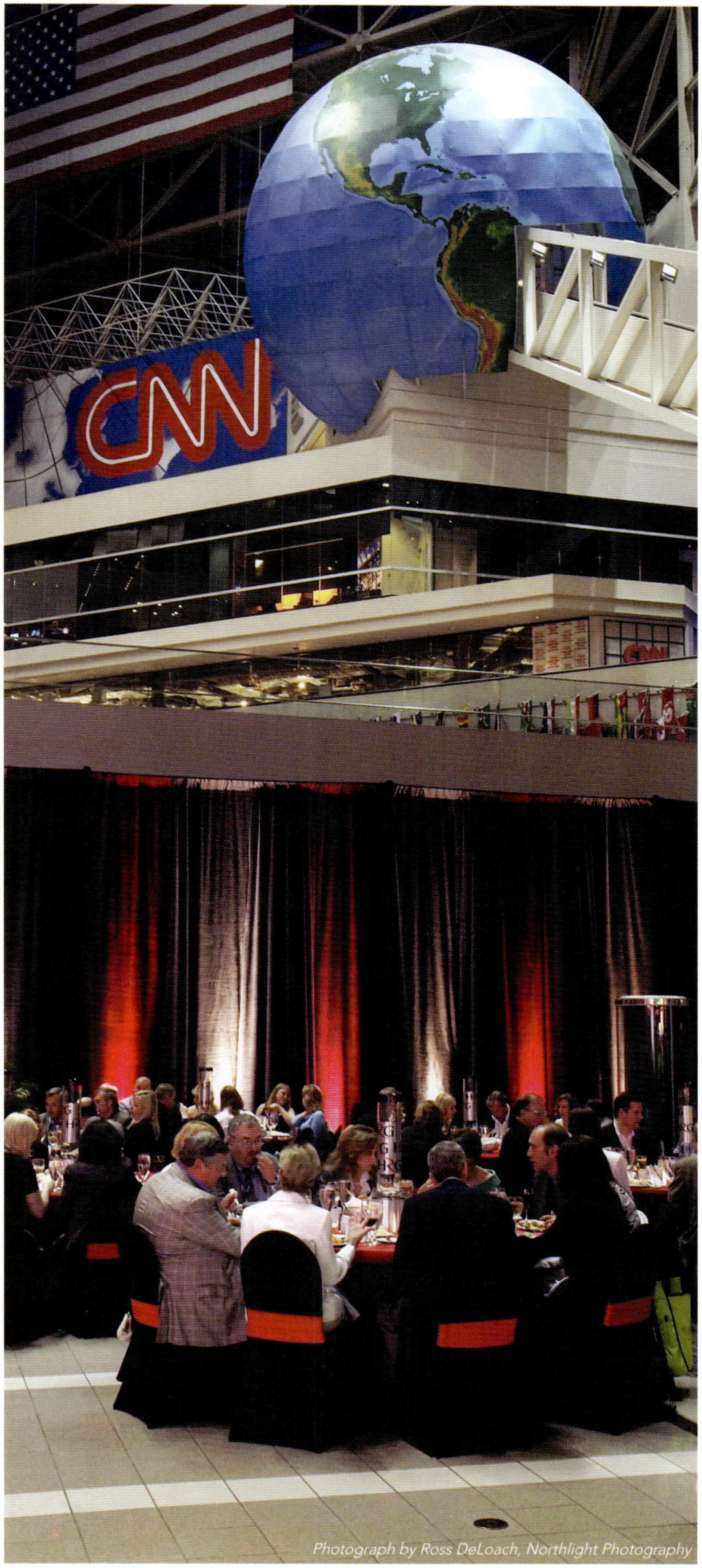

Photograph by Ross DeLoach, Northlight Photography

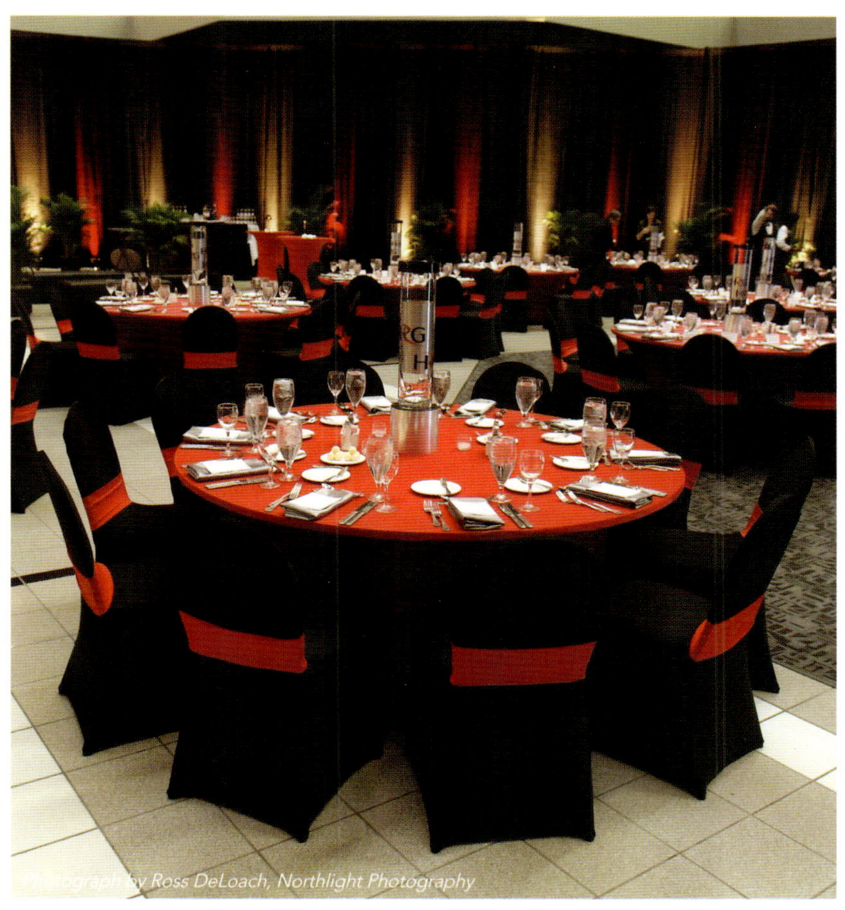

"Reconfirm, reconfirm, reconfirm—
that's the number one rule in
successful event management."

—Brigette Soskin

Above: Focused illumination offers the Fox Theatre, which features Middle Eastern and Egyptian architecture, just the right atmosphere for a holiday event, with white and silver décor to take advantage of the lighting. Snowflakes were created by employees, who were thrilled to see their contributions sprinkled on the tables, and the three-dimensional flakes suspended from the ceiling highlight the holiday ambience but stay mindful of religious diversity.

Facing page top: With attendance growing by the hour for an event at Georgia Aquarium, a tent at Pemberton Park was added as overflow space. By using the clear ceiling panels in the tent, approaching guests were greeted with a lively ambience from the spectacular lighting design and guests inside could see downtown views.

Facing page bottom left: We added excitement to the large dance floor with a creative floor design and intelligent lighting.

Facing page bottom right: In order to fill the Georgia World Congress Center Murphy ballroom with its 40-foot ceilings, we used vertically oriented décor and dropped fabric panels from the ceiling. The modern look was achieved through simple but large elements.

Photograph by Patrick Williams Photography

Photograph by Patrick Williams Photography

Photograph by Patrick Williams Photography

Photograph by Patrick Williams Photography

Photograph by Patrick Williams Photography

"Large focal pieces and small custom accents can stretch a budget to create beautiful events."

—Kelly Haywood

Right: Pianist Bruce Hornsby entertained during an exclusive association board dinner. The ornate architecture of The Ritz-Carlton, Atlanta was complemented by formal textiles and accent lighting to highlight the tables and stage décor.

Facing page: Associated Luxury Hotels International chose Château Élan, a magnificent resort and winery, for a weekend of education and events. One activity, a *Phantom of the Opera* evening, included a luxurious dinner setting of black and white linens and chairs with dramatic red accents and a live performance from the current London *Phantom* cast. A lively afterparty of drinks, dessert, and dancing concluded the evening in the Cask Room, which was transformed into a late-night disco with colorful lighting that reflected off the stainless steel wine casks, bar, and tables.

Photograph by Ross DeLoach, Northlight Photography

views

In the world of events, the phrase "too much information" does not exist. The more information provided by the event host, the better equipped the design team is to create an outstanding proposal that aligns with the host's vision.

Presenting Atlanta

CINDY FOWLER | JIM COX

Cindy Fowler's charitable heart runs deep—and it's no wonder since her involvement with the Junior League was crucial for her success. After working as a tour guide in the 1970s, Cindy realized that many wives didn't attend convention activities but accompanied their husbands anyway. With the help of 13 Junior League friends who became tour bus guides, Cindy opened a tour company that catered to the conventioneers' wives. With her friends' indispensible help, she has since transformed the tour company into Presenting Atlanta, what is now the oldest, single-owner destination management firm in Atlanta.

Over the last 38 years, Presenting Atlanta has managed events for Fortune 500 companies, anxious brides, political candidates, and the entire world during the 1996 Olympic Games. With the 1994 addition of partner Jim Cox, who has worked for Marriott, The Ritz-Carlton, and Merv Griffin, and with the help of Presenting Atlanta's superb staff, there isn't one event that is beyond their scope and expertise. And now, with the addition of a new division called Presenting America, no geographic location is too far for Cindy and Jim and their team.

Since its founding, Presenting Atlanta has truly kept Cindy on her toes, which is just as she prefers. Yet with her success, she has continued her community-oriented attitude by donating time and resources to numerous nonprofit events. Her staff, many who have been with her for more than 10 years, also exude a love for Atlanta, as evidenced through their passionate work and benevolent activities.

Taking inspiration from The Plaza's famous Palm Court, we revolutionized a classical ballroom in an exclusive club into an exciting, sophisticated atmosphere that the cast of *Casablanca* would have envied. Richly draped lounge seating flanked the perimeter of the space and lush palm foliage throughout gave style and texture to the elegant reception. Square and round tables with custom linen tablecloths filled the room's center. Beverage service was a highlight and featured nostalgic cocktails provided by Cuff and Buttons, a New York beverage purveyor, using original recipes from the private bar Milk & Honey.

Photograph by LaCour Photography

Photograph by Ross DeLoach, Northlight Photography

Photograph by Ross DeLoach, Northlight Photography

Photograph by Ross DeLoach, Northlight Photography

Photograph by Jim Fitts

"Even the traditional requires untraditional thinking to keep it fresh."

—Cindy Fowler

Above and right: A sophisticated black and white theme, including swan ice sculptures and stunning white rose centerpieces, gave The Atlanta History Center extra grace and elegance. To add pizzazz, we commissioned a Virginia ironworker to design and fabricate wrought iron chandeliers to replace the existing traditional recessed lighting.

Facing page: At the spectacular Georgia Aquarium, an evening took on an otherworldly quality. We created an aerial framework and rigging that allowed a trained aerialist and trapeze artist to entertain the awed crowd. Nothing like this had ever been attempted at Georgia Aquarium, and the entire night's festivities went without a hitch. By placing tables next to the mesmerizing beluga whale exhibit, we created a stunning background for dinner amidst the dream-like atmosphere.

Photograph by Jim Fitts

Photograph by Presenting Atlanta

Photograph by Burgess Amusements

Above and left: Almost any space, either indoors or out, can be converted into an impressive event with just the right touch. Flexibility, versatility, and creativity are invaluable assets, whether the event is a Southern-themed annual meeting with nearly 3,000 guests and multiple entertainment stages at the Georgia World Congress Center's International Plaza or a grand finale at Centennial Olympic Park for 9,000 young people who were competing in robotics.

Facing page: A well-designed table setting is an essential part of every event plan. This is where the party's style and taste are focused and often where guests will spend most of their time. From a luau-themed, moss-covered serving table to the sheer elegance of an immaculate formal setting, no detail should be overlooked.

Photograph by Ross DeLoach, Northlight Photography

Photograph by Ross DeLoach, Northlight Photography

Photograph by Ross DeLoach, Northlight Photography

Photograph by Ross DeLoach, Northlight Photography

Photograph by Ross Henderson

Photograph by Ross DeLoach, Northlight Photography

Right: To create a lush, natural scheme, we adorned each table with an elegant candelabra and multi-colored peonies. Five-foot-tall white planters containing 10-foot-tall palm trees, all potted in the parking lot, were transported by six-man crews. Flowering gardenia plants around the base of each tree completed the design.

Facing page top: A nightclub-themed event required nothing less than a total transformation of the space from rough and rustic to sleek and sophisticated. The lounge that resulted could have taken South Beach by storm. Reflective floors, white floor-to-ceiling fabric, and contemporary lighting and furniture all combined to create the perfect effect.

Facing page bottom: Originality and meticulous cooperation with the venue manager can help overcome challenges. At the Atlanta Braves' Turner Field, a next-day ballgame required conscientious attention to protecting the field while the hottest day of the year prompted the need to provide air conditioning.

Photograph by LaCour Photography

views

- ❖ Keep up with the current trends. We love the New York Social Diary online.
- ❖ Indulge the guests' senses from the moment they step into the party.
- ❖ People generate heat—lower the thermostat.

MAGNOLIA EVENTS & PLANNING

CHRISTINA ZUBOWICZ | SUZANNE REINHARD

Just as a conductor leads a talented group of musicians in a beautiful concerto, Magnolia Events & Planning founder Christina Zubowicz and partner Suzanne Reinhard have been orchestrating dream events for others while creating a dynamic symphony all their own. With steady hands and passionate hearts, Christina and Suzanne draw on their combined 40 years of experience in hospitality and catering to fulfill the vision for each event.

From its inception in 2004, Magnolia Events was named after the Southern magnolia tree because Christina resonated with its key characteristics of strength, elegance, and charm. By utilizing constructive alliances with fellow event professionals, Magnolia Events collaborates to develop prudent yet luxurious settings that embody the host's dream. The team's positive philosophy further fosters an approach to showcase each professional's role and talent for a powerful synergistic atmosphere.

This ambience of strength and harmony is a trademark for Magnolia Events. Their strategic ability to coordinate large groups of vendors and to have a professional attitude and calm demeanor propels the team to achieve a successful event. The team's desire is for the entertainer, caterer, venue staff, designers, and event host, through fostering exceptional partnerships, to feel enthused to create the event envisioned. While others may appear frazzled before and during an event, Christina and Suzanne employ their conductor mentality and rely upon their unrivaled planning and depth of experience.

Following the old Hollywood glamour with a bit of French design, Tony Brewer & Company's use of clean lines, decadent details, and estate tables offers a nod to the classics in the St. Regis Hotel ballroom. With an interior designer for the host, we followed her desire for opulent beauty with a romantic and sumptuous ambience.

Photograph by LaCour Photography

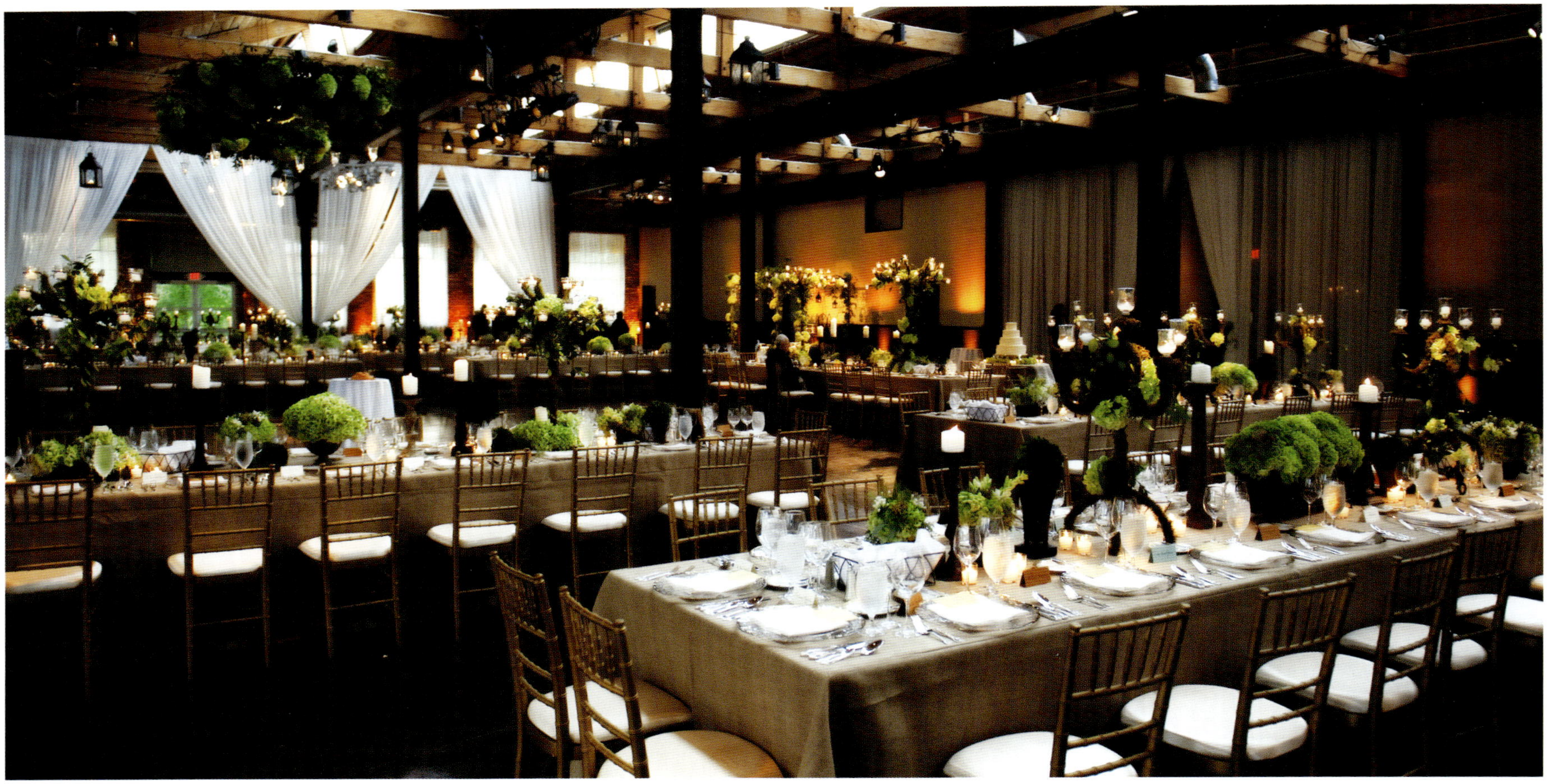

Photograph by Ric Mershon Photographers

Photograph by Ric Mershon Photographers

To accomplish the feel of *A Midsummer Night's Dream* and still maintain modernity, we coordinated an Old World style and fresh, clean décor. Banquet seating, natural colors, centerpieces by Arrangements that mimicked small trees, and an overhead arbor added to the whimsical, lush garden atmosphere. The ambience mixed perfectly with the Puritan Mill's natural wood and large windows. Keeping the lights low and highlighting certain areas with a yellow hue evoked an intimate yet fanciful feel.

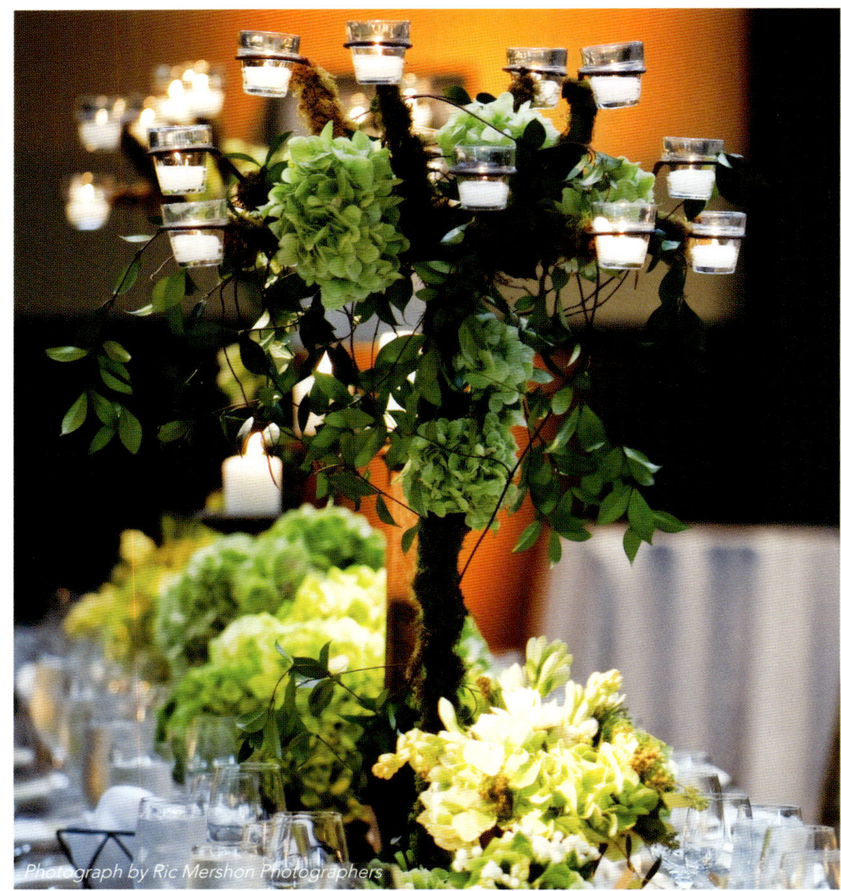

"Forming a strong alliance with families, designers, and vendors creates a seamless event process."

—Christina Zubowicz

Photograph by Ric Mershon Photographers

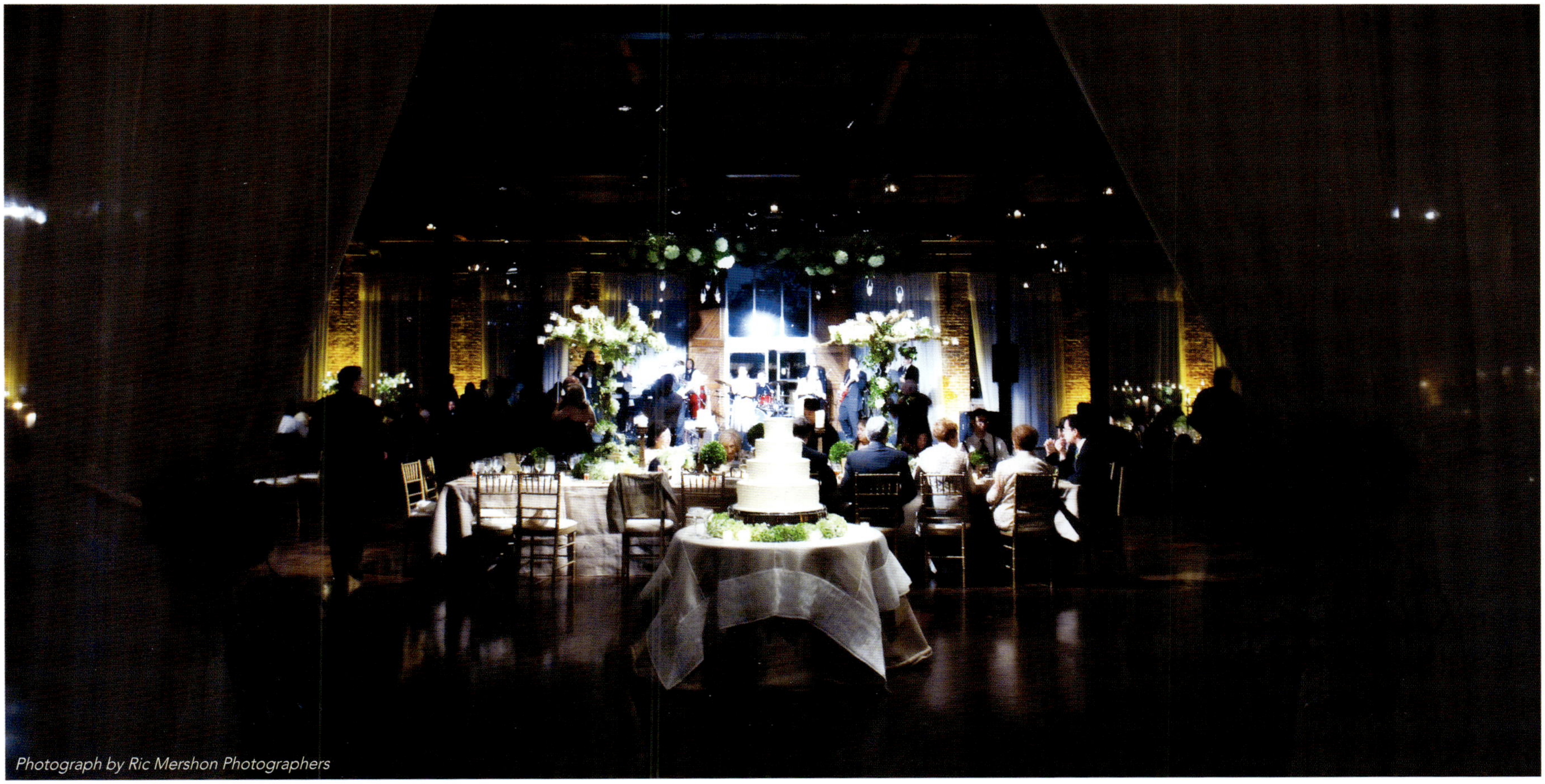

Photograph by Ric Mershon Photographers

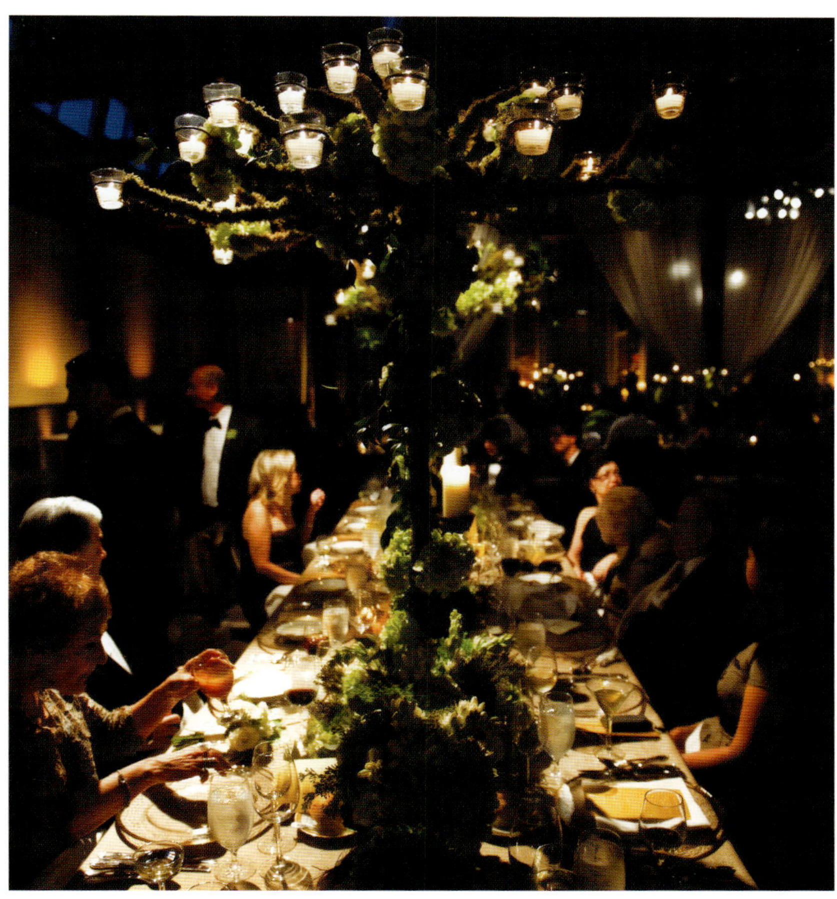

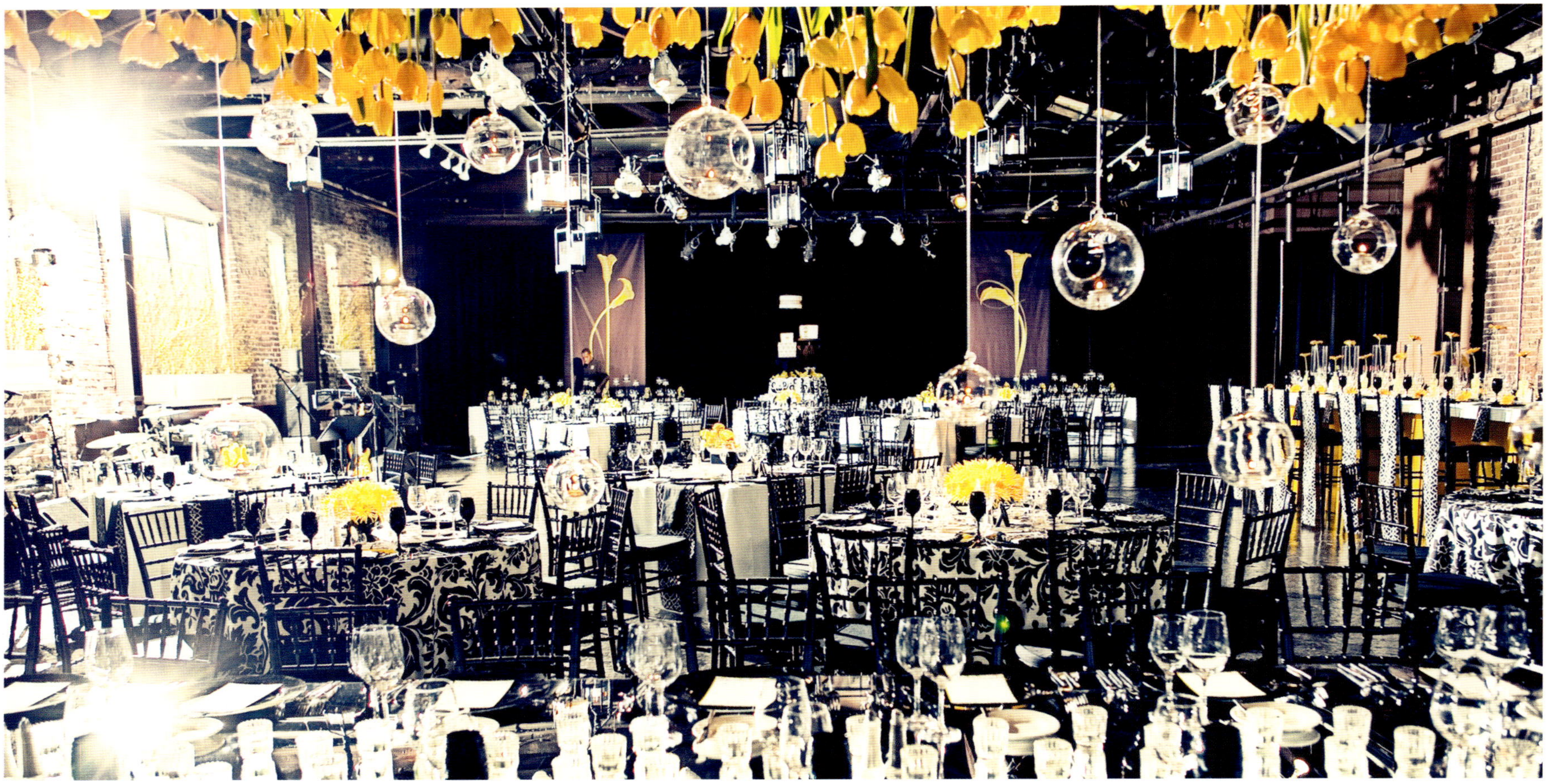

Photograph by Our Labor of Love Photography

Photograph by Our Labor of Love Photography

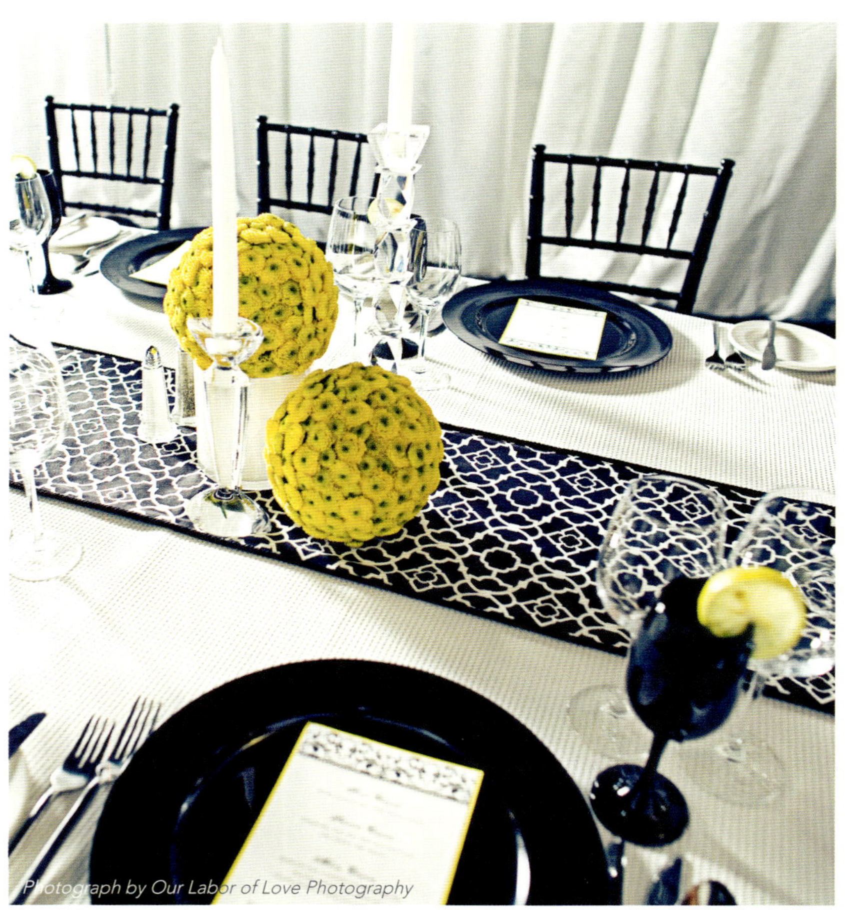

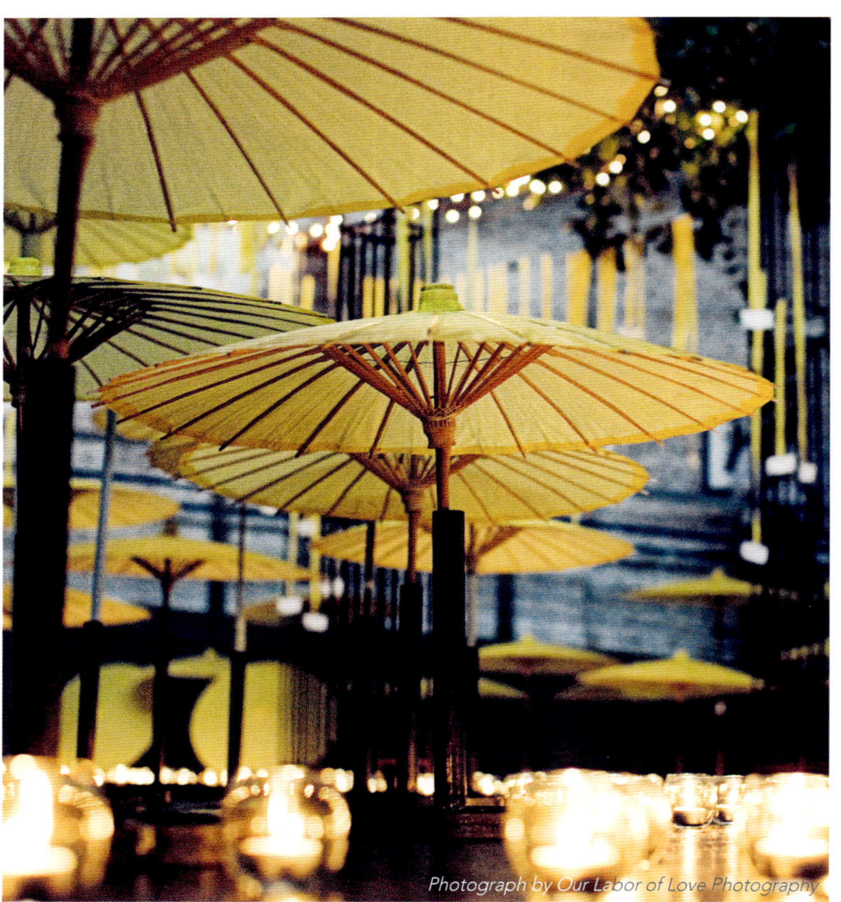

Photograph by Our Labor of Love Photography

"Selecting planners who allow the hosts to enjoy the fruits of their vision without a thought toward the event management is imperative."

—Suzanne Reinhard

The goal was for the guests to have a unique experience from the first moment of arrival at the King Plow Arts Center. Our décor team led by Steve Bales with Bold American, utilized a variety of spaces that all coordinated with each other, from the outside garden area and loft during cocktail hour to a ceremony-in-the-round, from the umbrella garden with a variety of dining tables to the lounge area. To achieve a high impact throughout the space, the designer used numerous monochromatic elements. A single flower color and minimal types of flowers amidst the black and white theme allow each unique area to blend together. A variety of patterns and textures within the black and white tones, upside-down tulips, and cakes hanging from the ceiling added just enough interest and detail to keep the senses engaged.

views

Monochromatic colors can have a significant influence when used correctly. Just a splash of a different hue mixed into the design can assist in highlighting a certain element or area while still maintaining an overall flow among the spaces.

EVENTS WITH GRACE

LAUREN BREWTON

You may think you have a pretty good idea of what event coordinators do; but spend a day with Lauren Brewton and you might be surprised. Sure, the predictable tasks of scheduling, planning, and networking happen on a regular basis—but that's just the tip of the iceberg. When Lauren began Events with Grace in 2001, she took on a much more multifaceted position than she ever could've predicted. Shifting between counselor, financial advisor, confidant, and liaison, Lauren knows what people need before they do and goes above and beyond the call of duty at the drop of a hat. She's ready to lend her ear, her advice, or her strictly professional opinion whenever duty calls.

With a servant's heart and a knack for organization, Lauren pulls from a variety of experiences to create each event. Her background has ties to nearly all event-related industries; dressmaking, catering, floral design, and pastry all have a place in her past. Events with Grace reveals just how comfortable she is with every aspect of the event process, resulting in elegant, classic celebrations that capture the emotion of life's special occasions.

For an April ceremony, we took advantage of the bride's family garden. The lush springtime scenery served as inspiration for the whole event. We used a long, unifying table to give the reception for more than 100 guests an intimate feel and placed enchanting, Old World planters down the length of the dining space. Everything was done with the family's taste in mind; details complemented the home's décor, as if pieces of the interior came to the outdoors. Pintucked linens and custom cushions matched the classic tailoring of the bride's Oscar de la Renta gown.

Photograph by Priscilla Wannamaker

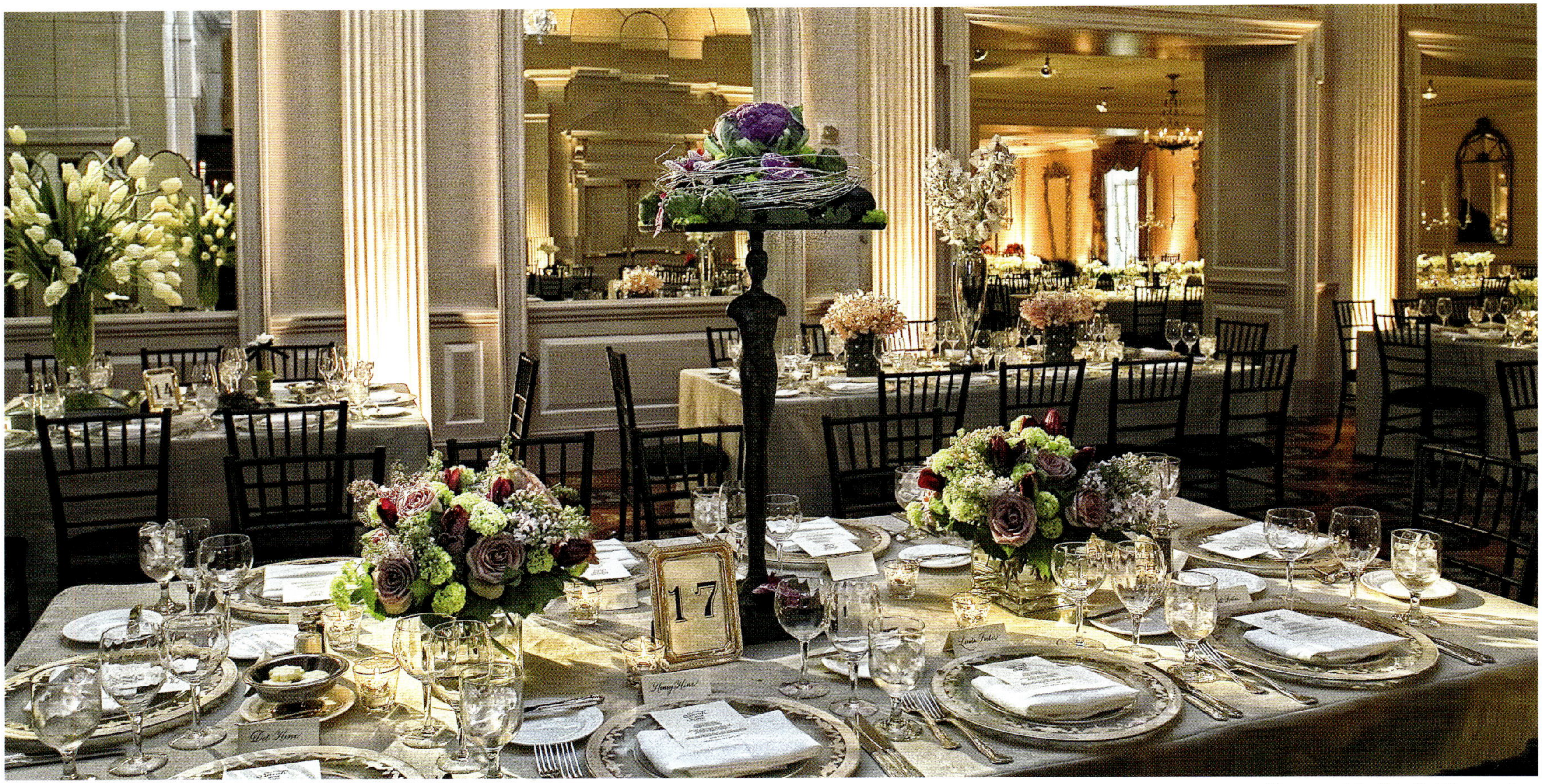

Photograph by Priscilla Wannamaker

Photograph by Priscilla Wan

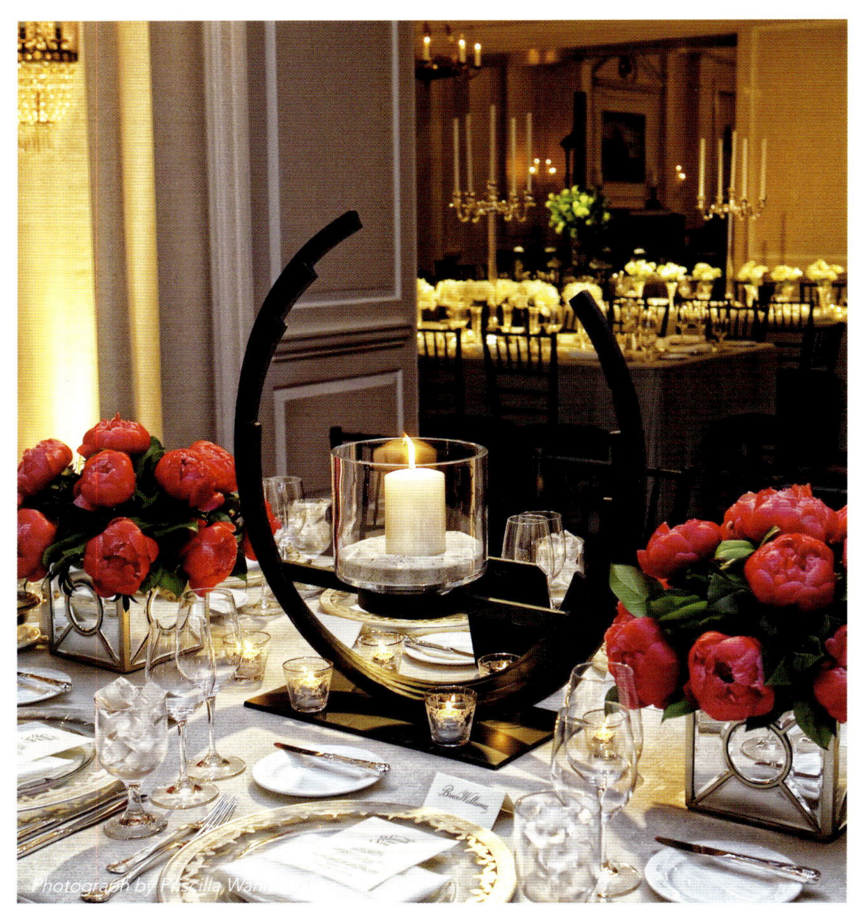

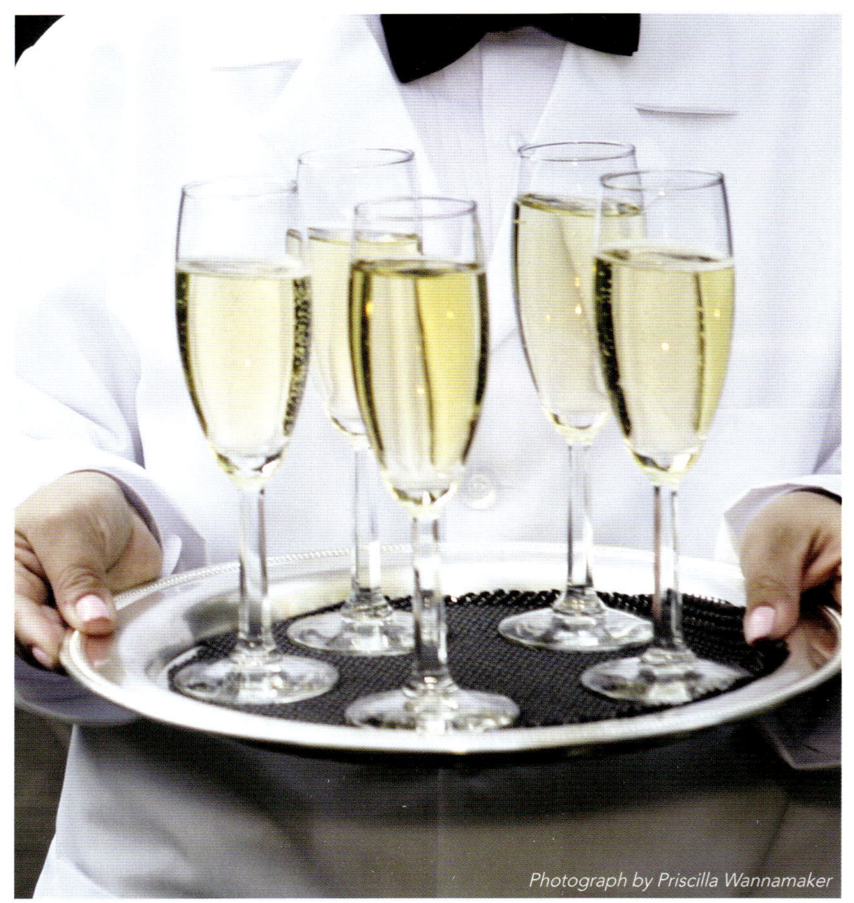

Photograph by Priscilla Wannamaker

"The best events start with a clean slate and an open mind."

—Lauren Brewton

Right: We worked with the pastry chef and the floral designer, Robert Long, to give the cake a straight-from-the-garden feel. Edible gum paste flowers, pea gravel, and organic white tones gave us precisely the look we wanted.

Facing page: All the details count. Lighting, architectural design, and colors came together at a reception in downtown's Capital City Club. Classic and dramatic, each table held a different type of flower, from peonies, orchids, and tulips, to gorgeous mixed arrangements. Because the groom and his family were Australian, we used their nationality in many details of the event, like music, food and drink.

Photograph by Priscilla Wannamaker

views

You don't have to be a millionaire to work with an event planner. Do your research and ask around before assuming anything about specific financial restraints; and don't be afraid to address the topic directly. Elegance isn't reserved just for the ultra rich.

Full Circle Events

SALLY SILVERMAN

Whether guests are eating deep dish pizza at Millennium Park in Chicago, enjoying salmon in Seattle amidst beautiful city and mountain views, or taking in the Big Apple's sights from Stevens Institute of Technology in Hoboken, New Jersey, Full Circle Events is all about an authentic experience designed specifically for each event host. Instead of just another meeting or corporate party, Sally Silverman's ideal events bring out the culture and allow guests to eat, taste, smell, and see the city or region.

To keep the cultural focus in the forefront of every event, Sally's unparalleled team members are well traveled, well educated, and creatively inquisitive—her three essential criteria for inspiring authentic events. Planning always begins with the host's ideas and goals; a brainstorming session with the entire team follows, at which experts in each area research the ideas. Finally, a point person takes over the planning to ensure the event exceeds the host's expectations and projects the desired image.

Paired with Sally's selection of a remarkable team is Full Circle's focus on relationships, both with the event hosts and with other industry professionals. From the first conversation about an event through the cleanup after a meeting, the personal connections make the events worthwhile and bring about the skills and ideas necessary to showcase the local flavor.

Knowing your audience is key in business as well as event planning. For a convention at the Omni, we knew exactly what kind of vibe would appeal to Makita's special clientele. We turned the entertaining area into a masculine lounge framed by impressive 68-foot-long, 18-foot-high branding banners. Guests were blown away that we brought in a sculptor to use Makita's tools to carve a larger-than-life power tool out of ice right before their eyes.

Photograph by Atlanta Event Photography

Photograph courtesy of Full Circle Events

Photograph courtesy of Full Circle Events

Photograph courtesy of Full Circle Events

Photograph courtesy of Full Circle Events

"Finding the new jewel of an attraction or location in the destination city is critical to intriguing the guests."

—Sally Silverman

Right: We hosted an aeronautical company's press conference for a new plane at the Corcoran Gallery of Art in Washington, D.C. Uplit columns, music, and delicious cuisine turned the event into an elegant cocktail party.

Facing page top left: The National Air and Space Museum's Steven F. Udvar-Hazy Center provided the perfect entertainment for guests involved in the aviation industry. Waiters dressed as flight attendants, docents—some who were former pilots—and favors resembling first-class airplane kits completed the flight-inspired evening.

Facing page top right: A desert setting near Phoenix prompted large fire pits, uplit cacti, Native American-costumed entertainment, and s'mores roasted over the fire for dessert.

Facing page bottom left: We highlighted the amazing architecture and a newly revealed collection during an intimate evening at the Pennsylvania Academy of the Fine Arts; a harpist, classical guitarist, and docents provided entertainment.

Facing page bottom right: Nearly everyone knows something about Frank Lloyd Wright; but to learn his history and see how he lived is truly special. Guests were bused in to Taliesin West for cocktails on the front lawn as the sun was setting. Docents assisted in tours of the home; then a dinner under the stars with uplit citrus trees and glowing tables concluded the intriguing evening.

Photograph courtesy of Full Circle Events

Photograph courtesy of Full Circle Events

views

Be honest about the budget. A reputable firm will want to know and work with the real monetary constraints. And don't believe the false assumption that a smaller budget equals a less-than-fabulous event. There are always ways to be creative and achieve an extraordinary event.

It's My Party, Inc.

SHARON FISHER

A self-proclaimed puppeteer of sorts, Sharon Fisher is the person in the background who is directing the production, ensuring each movement is in perfect rhythm with the others. With her friendly personality, a management background, and extensive international travels filled with cultural experiences, Sharon jumped at the chance to merge all of these characteristics into her everyday work.

Nearly two decades ago, a woman who was ill approached Sharon for help in creating a bar mitzvah for one of her children. After transforming what the woman needed into something she never could have imagined—and seeing the joy this brought to the family—Sharon was hooked. It's My Party, Inc. was founded and has grown to encompass planning for all kinds of events, from Jewish celebrations and Indian ceremonies to 50th anniversaries and beyond.

Combining her love of interacting with people with an uncanny ability to see the big picture, Sharon has mastered the art of understanding the host's wishes as well as imparting her own opinion and expertise. Her dedication to working as a team with everyone from the event host and the caterers to the decorator and the event staff enhances her maneuvers as a puppeteer. At each event, Sharon infuses a particular flavor that fits perfectly with the hosts. She is only satisfied when the hosts feel the event encompassed everything they could have wanted.

A young couple's desire was to bring their future children back to the location of their ceremony and reception. Therefore I embraced Georgia Aquarium's ambience with blue and purple hues and warmed the space with a gazebo to feature the cake and twinkling lights on the trees.

Photograph by Ric Mershon Photographers

Right: Decorating for a bar mitzvah offered a unique challenge to be classy, masculine, and trendy. I accomplished a club-like atmosphere with black linens enhanced by metal rings, lit bars, casual seating, and small, lit centerpieces featuring succulents and other nonfloral arrangements.

Facing page top: Tall sparkling centerpieces add grace and whimsy to a young girl's dream party. With a "Breakfast at Tiffany's" theme based on the girl's favorite color, the event took on a sophisticated yet still youthful ambience.

Facing page bottom: Because the host had to settle for an inside reception, we brought the outside in for an earthy ambience. Magnolia branches and lanterns hung above the dance area, a leaf pattern lit the floor, the cake was set on a tree stump, and the centerpieces emanated an upscale woodsy feel. The magnificent effect transformed a normal ballroom into a scene from *A Midsummer Night's Dream*.

Photograph by Eric Wittmayer

Be open to subtle compromises. Even if the available budget isn't in line with the movie-like performance first envisioned, the event can still have plenty of flair and spectacular moments.

Location, Loca

Location, Location

Georgia Aquarium

The Home Depot co-founder Bernie Marcus didn't set out to open an aquarium. But after revolutionizing the home improvement industry, Bernie credited the citizens of Georgia, where The Home Depot was headquartered, with some of his success. So, to touch individual lives and impact the economy, Bernie donated $250 million to open Georgia Aquarium, which remains the world's largest indoor aquarium. With sea creatures swimming through eight million gallons of water among more than 60 exhibits, the galleries tell a global water story with features modeled after the greatest zoos and aquariums in the world.

This majestic setting offers a one-of-a-kind experience with a variety of spaces for all events, including 23,000 square feet of private event space, a generous atrium, and multiple intimate gallery areas. And, although most visitors are originally hooked by the wow factor of the aquarium, event hosts and guests leave amazed by the quality of the food, which should come as no surprise. Chef Wolfgang Puck, who is famous for concepts like mini burgers and smoked salmon pizza, combines world-class cuisine with eco-conscious choices for an incredible pairing. Leading the dining dream team, as Bernie affectionately says, is executive chef Greg Brickman, who trained under Wolfgang Puck in Los Angeles.

Whether awestruck by a beluga whale during an elegant dinner, fascinated by a whale shark while dancing at a lively reception, or tantalized by Wolfgang Puck Catering's mouthwatering fare, Georgia Aquarium guests are certainly influenced because of Bernie's generous spirit.

Located in the center of the aquarium, the atrium provides access to the five galleries, allowing room for up to 5,000 people to mingle between the spaces, including the Oceans Ballroom. With its beautiful floor, neutral colors, and intelligent lighting, the atrium can be transformed into just the right ambience for each event.

Photograph by Patrick Williams

Photograph by Patrick Williams

"Because Atlanta is such an interesting, lively city, we knew the aquarium's ballroom had to be outstanding."

—Bernie Marcus

The Oceans Ballroom provides a dramatic setting for an elegant reception, under a tiled, wave-like ceiling. There is no other place in Atlanta where guests can mingle and enjoy dinner with live art continuously changing. On one side of the ballroom is a view into the Ocean Voyager habitat with whale sharks, hammerheads, groupers, manta rays, and thousands of other fish. The other side offers a look into the beluga whale habitat.

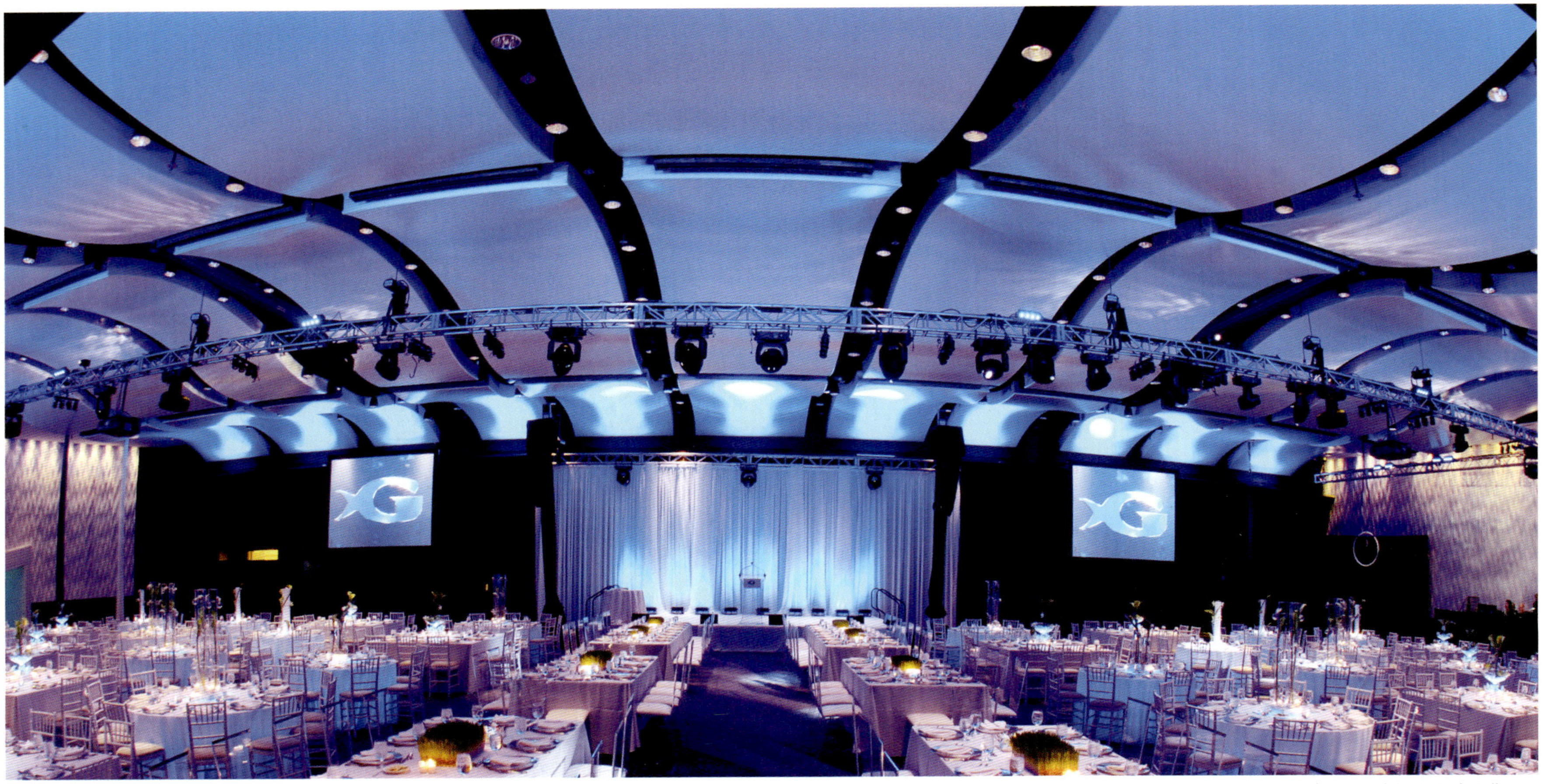

Photograph by Patrick Williams

Photograph by Patrick Williams

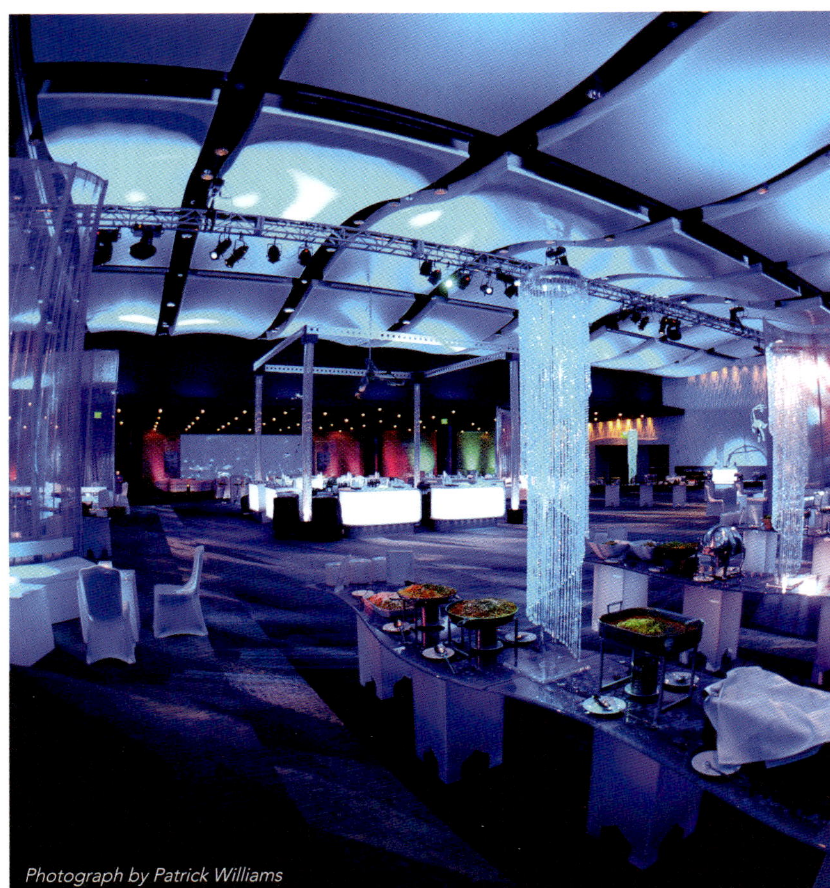

Because of the Oceans Ballroom design, the possibilities are nearly endless. Its separation from the rest of the aquarium allows daytime events to occur, as evidenced by the aquarium's grand re-opening luncheon, while the versatility of the space provides options for unique entertainment, such as acrobatic acts. And, with the ability to divide the ballroom into smaller areas, intimate events like a ceremony don't feel overwhelmed.

"We love knowing that each event host sees the aquarium as an incredible, incomparable experience."

—Bernie Marcus

Photograph by Patrick Williams

Photograph by Patrick Williams

Photograph by Patrick Williams

"We can really entertain our guests in style, but also we can educate people about what to buy and how to eat sustainably."

—Chef Wolfgang Puck

Above: With its ability to host up to 1,200 people, the Oceans Ballroom is the perfect place to give everyone an amazing view of the Ocean Voyager habitat during dinner.

Facing page: With chef Wolfgang Puck and executive chef Greg Brickman at the helm, the aquarium views aren't the only stimulating element. Whether they provide watermelon squares, mini burgers, or delectable crème puffs, their inspiration never stops.

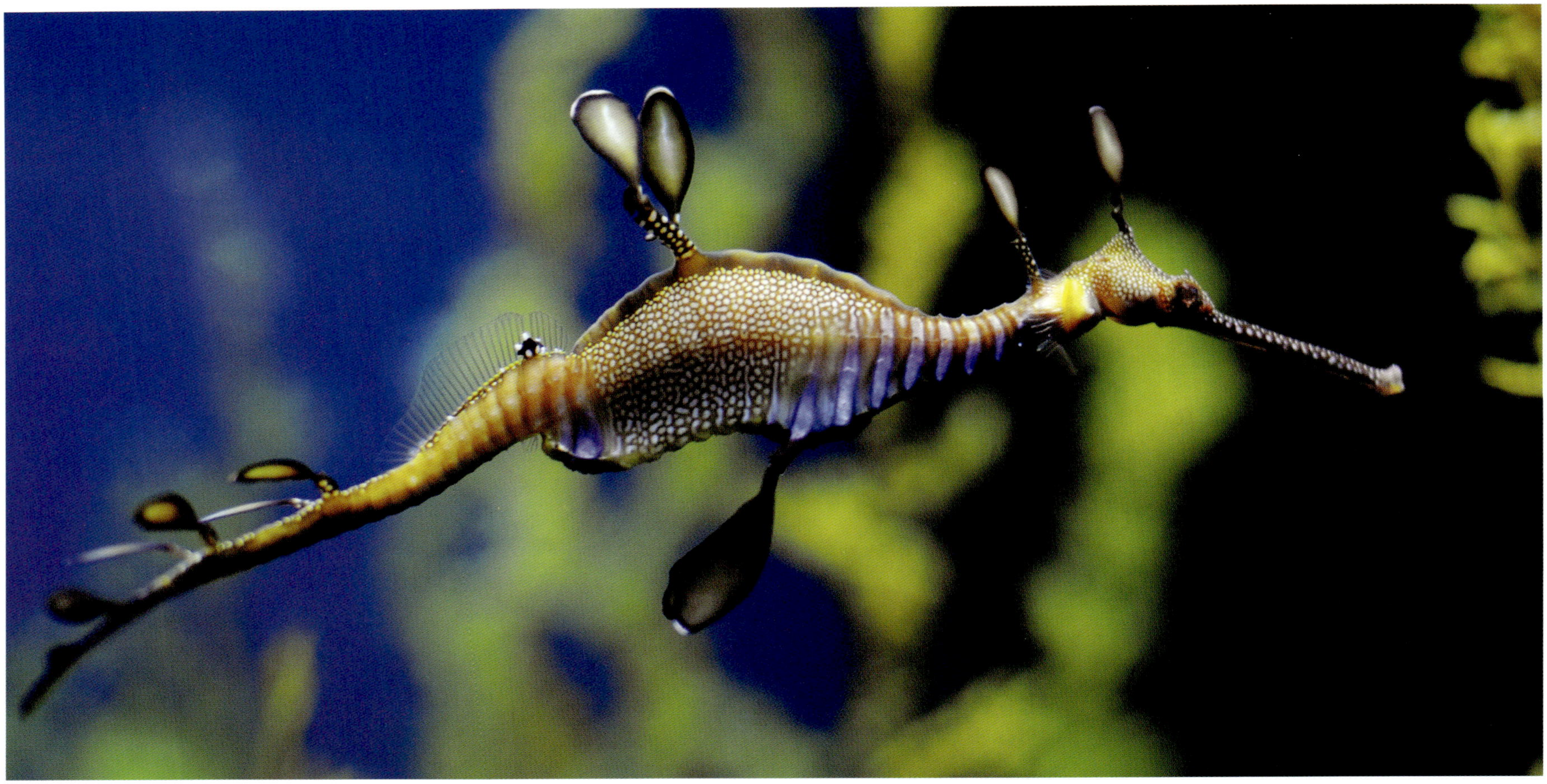

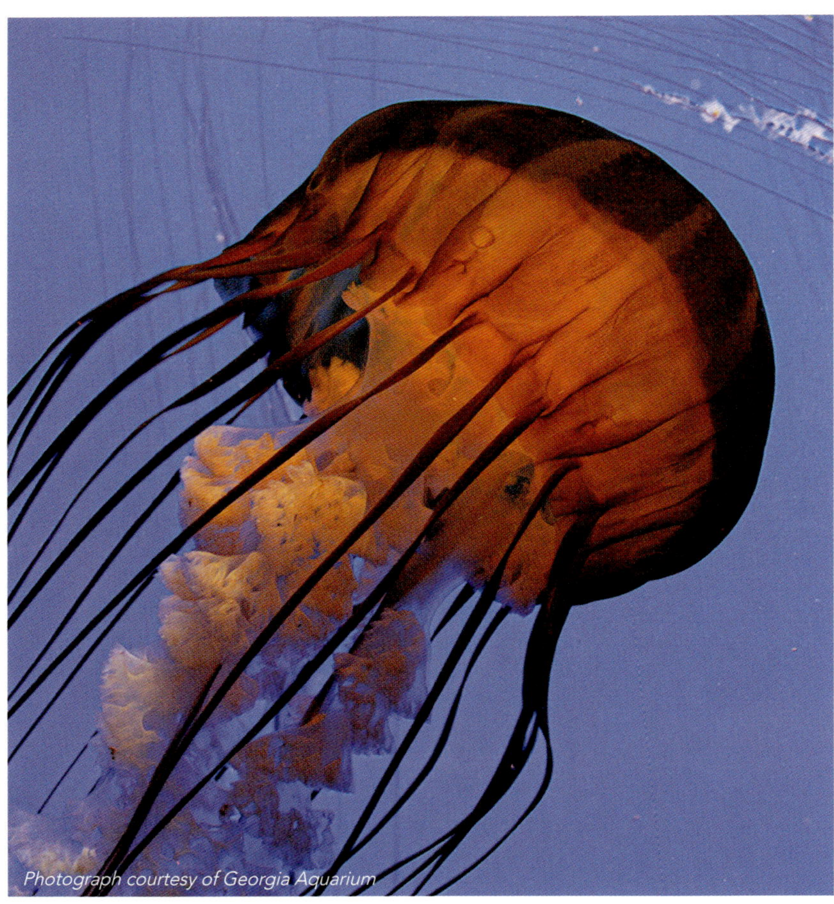

Photograph courtesy of Georgia Aquarium

Photograph courtesy of Georgia Aquarium

Numerous galleries exist throughout the aquarium and can be utilized during an event. Within the Georgia-Pacific Cold Water Quest Gallery, curious African penguins, majestic beluga whales, and beautifully camouflaged weedy sea dragons live among other cold water ocean animals. In the Tropical Diver Gallery, presented by AirTran, viewers can watch a smack of Pacific sea nettles, and guests can get up close and personal with a toothy sand tiger shark in the Ocean Voyager Gallery, built by The Home Depot.

"Seeing an animal up close and personal gives you a greater appreciation for their mystery and splendor."

—Natasha Cary

Photograph courtesy of Georgia Aquarium

Photograph courtesy of Georgia Aquarium

Photograph courtesy of Georgia Aquarium

Photograph courtesy of Georgia Aquarium

Photograph courtesy of Georgia Aquarium

> "An ever-changing mural of aquatic animal life adds a bit of flavor and excitement to every event."
>
> —Natasha Cary

For a more intimate reception of up to 200 guests, the Ocean Voyager Gallery offers a swimmingly good time. Ocean Voyager tunnel provides an underwater view of the whale sharks and manta rays and makes a great setting for a scenic cocktail hour.

views

When planning an event, don't underestimate the venue's appeal to draw a crowd. Hosting a private event in a unique setting, one that is a premier attraction, for example, can generate buzz that drives attendance.

WORLD OF COCA-COLA

As one of the most successful brands in the world, The Coca-Cola Company has infused its rich history of innovation into a revolutionary attraction for everyone to enjoy. Originally located at Underground Atlanta for 17 years, the World of Coca-Cola hosted more than 13 million visitors who marveled at the collection of Coca-Cola artifacts and stories from around the world.

In May 2007, a new state-of-the-art experience opened in the heart of Atlanta at Pemberton Place, a 20-acre site located across from Centennial Olympic Park that is quickly becoming a top destination for both Atlantans and visitors from around the globe. The new World of Coca-Cola is twice its former size and houses more than 1,200 never-before-seen artifacts that depict the brand's history. Showcasing more than 90,000 square feet of space, the World of Coca-Cola offers interactive exhibits, three theaters, an art gallery, a tasting room, and a fully functioning bottling line.

As a dynamic event space, the World of Coca-Cola is leading the way for a large, innovative venue that has the flexibility and design to accommodate events ranging from intimate groups of 10 to 10,000 guests. By incorporating numerous private entrances for use during events, the World of Coca-Cola has created a nontraditional venue—dismiss the ballroom concept and embrace an adaptable space with a multitude of uses—that reflects the past, present, and future of The Coca-Cola Company.

As an entertaining attraction by day and stunning venue at night, the World of Coca-Cola offers the best of both worlds: one-of-a-kind surroundings and a first-rate staff that can make even the impossible happen. Through intricate planning and a dedicated attitude, we assure the setup and execution of events will bring a smile not only to the host but to their guests as well.

Photograph by Rick Payne Photography

Photograph by Michael Pugh Photography

Photograph by Rick Payne Photography

Photograph by Rick Payne Photography

Photograph by Rick Payne Photography

The first encounter within the building leads guests into a linear experience that begins in the Lobby featuring its handcrafted Coca-Cola folk-art bottles from around the world. After traversing the Loft to see additional artifacts, guests arrive in the Happiness Factory, the state-of-the-art stadium-seating theater. This unique venue has been home to award shows, dynamic presentations, team-building movie nights, live cooking shows, and product launches. As the experience concludes, the screen magically lifts to unveil an illuminated tunnel that connects to the Hub, the atrium of the building.

Photograph by Rick Payne Photography

With 8,000 square feet on two levels, the Hub has played host to concerts, elegant dinners for heads of state, and one-of-a-kind celebrations. The beauty of the architecture with its glass wall and towering height provides a stunning space that doesn't necessitate additional décor. The starburst ceiling design and intelligent lighting ensure everything is ready for personalization. As the center of exploration, the Hub bestows leisurely access to the interactive exhibits with ambassadors available to answer guests' questions. Whether guests have an interest in art, technology, or history, everyone will find something to connect with throughout the exhibits.

Photograph by J.D. Tyre Photography

"We are all in the happiness business, connecting the hearts and minds of our guests and creating smiles born out of an experience that lifts us to new heights."

—Karen Brunke

Photograph by Jim Roof

Photograph by Rick Payne Photography

Photograph by Rick Payne Photography

"A refreshing event experience for both the host and guests means stopping at nothing to exceed their expectations."

—Rachel Hood

Above and facing page top and bottom right: Only one place in the world exists where over 60 beverages of the Company can be enjoyed in one room—the refreshing space of Taste It! Easily accommodating up to 250 guests for a reception, the space encourages conversation as guests enjoy the different flavors from around the world. Taste It! provides the perfect platform for an engaging networking reception while allowing the event planner to customize the space with an all-inclusive audio-visual package.

Facing page bottom left: An important aspect to the venue is its LEED Gold certification from the U.S. Green Building Council and its incorporation of the latest advances in environmentally friendly technology and design. Going further than just the design of the building, we encourage event professionals to find ways to bring sustainability to life. One celebration featured chandeliers crafted from repurposed 20-ounce plastic Coca-Cola bottles; the resulting ambience was playful yet intimate.

Photograph by Karen Brunke

Photograph by Rick Payne Photography

Photograph by Rick Payne Photography

Right: Pemberton Place, named after the pharmacist who invented Coca-Cola in 1886, is home to 160,000 square feet of green space that overlooks downtown Atlanta. Able to accommodate both open-air and tented events for up to 10,000 guests, the green space offers the unique characteristics of a privately owned park. The World of Coca-Cola is not limited to public-park city restrictions and may completely close off the area for a truly exclusive experience.

Facing page: With former guests including notable celebrities and dignitaries, the Bottlecap Suite is a more intimate space with two-story ceilings, glass walls, and a private entrance. And who doesn't love the famous Coca-Cola Polar Bear? Originally designed by Jim Henson, this loveable character is available to entertain and bring out the kid in all of us. Ryan Seacrest shares a moment with the Polar Bear before hosting the Ronald McDonald House Charity Gala.

Photograph by Rick Payne Photography

views

People are always amazed at our ability to quickly transform from a daytime attraction into an unbelievable evening event space. Flexibility, attention to detail, broad service offerings, and the desire to continually surprise and impress are the characteristics of an ideal venue.

THE RITZ-CARLTON, ATLANTA

TOD MORROW | KURT SCHWAN | ROBIN KREITNER

Like a beacon of luxury, The Ritz-Carlton, Atlanta is poised in the heart of the city where a mélange of entertainment and urban flair alludes to the chic soul of Georgia. With such rich history and style at its doorstep, the hotel has continuously embraced that essence since its opening in 1985 as one of the five original Ritz-Carlton hotels. Thanks to the ladies and gentlemen on staff who have perfected the art of entertaining, they offer Southern hospitality with an elegance beyond measure.

To celebrate the hotel's 25th anniversary in the epicenter of Atlanta, a transformation in the entrance foyer, lobby, and event spaces created dramatic new interiors that offer a fresh, vibrant ambience with a respectful thread to the past. From a sideboard refinished in a gilded platinum tone to shrouds caressing the magnificent crystal chandeliers, many traditional elements were transposed to a contemporary sophistication. The updated opulence in the foyer, lobby, and lobby bar is paired nicely with the softer yet luxurious ambience in the ballroom.

What remains unchanged is the driving force to not only accommodate but also go above and beyond the preferences and desires expressed by event hosts and guests. To achieve this lofty goal, the close-knit team relies on strong communication and ensures each event host is comfortable throughout the entire process. The family-like atmosphere among all of the ladies and gentlemen at the hotel brings about a passion for perfection that sets The Ritz-Carlton, Atlanta apart.

Ghost chairs adorned with Swarovski crystals surround the fabulous tablescape that offers a glimpse of the excellent attention to detail that we offer. Guided by The Ritz-Carlton's philosophies, our driving goal centers on impeccable service.

Photograph by Ron Starr Photography

Photograph by Paula M. Gould

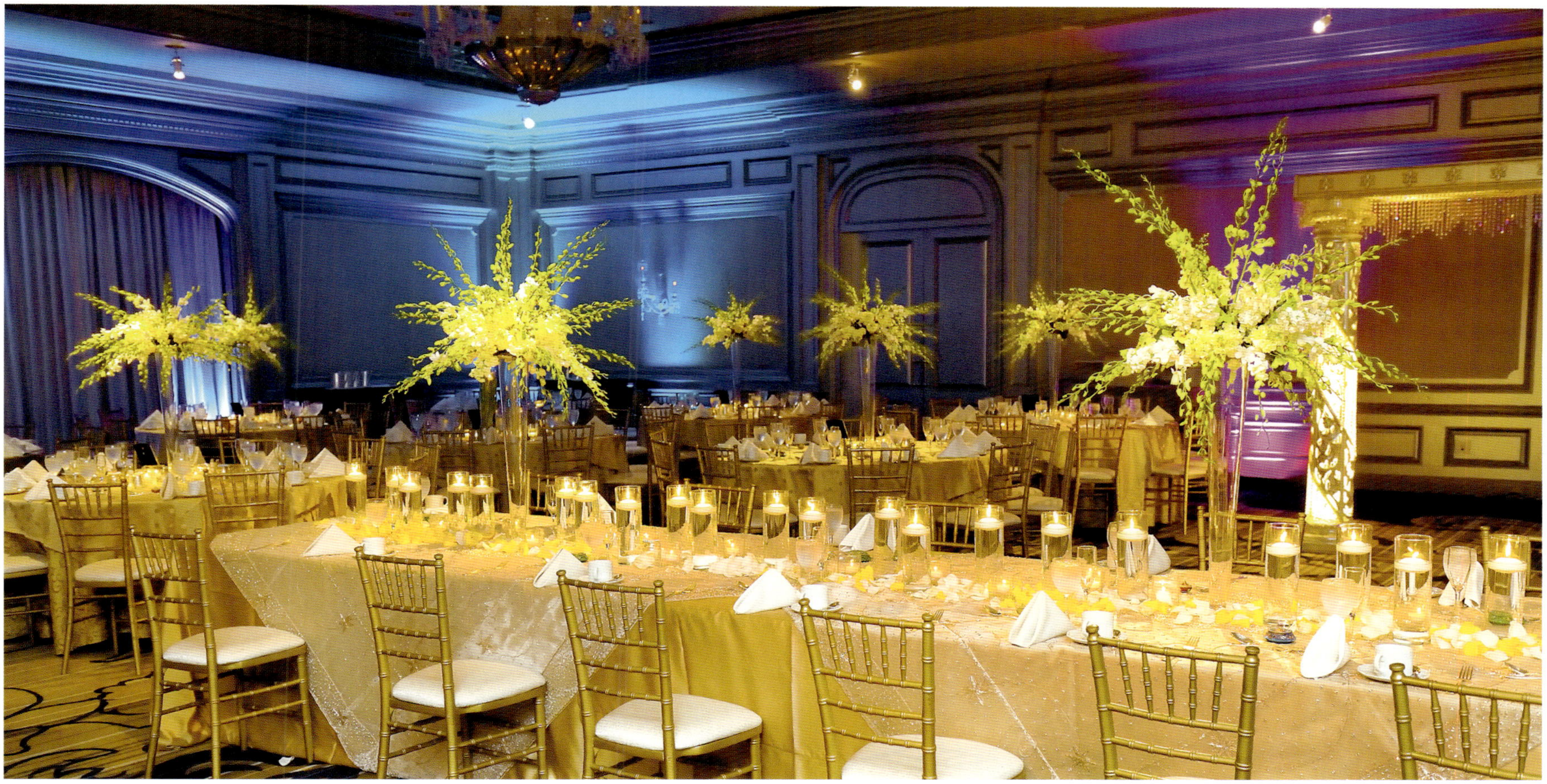

Photograph by Zamana Photography

Designed with flexibility in mind, the ballroom perfectly caresses events in a wide range of styles and colors. Whether the vision involves red tones with a combination of family-style estate tables and banquet rounds or a desire to merge an Indian background with modern flair, we can transform the ballroom into a spectacular oasis.

Photograph by John Campbell Photography

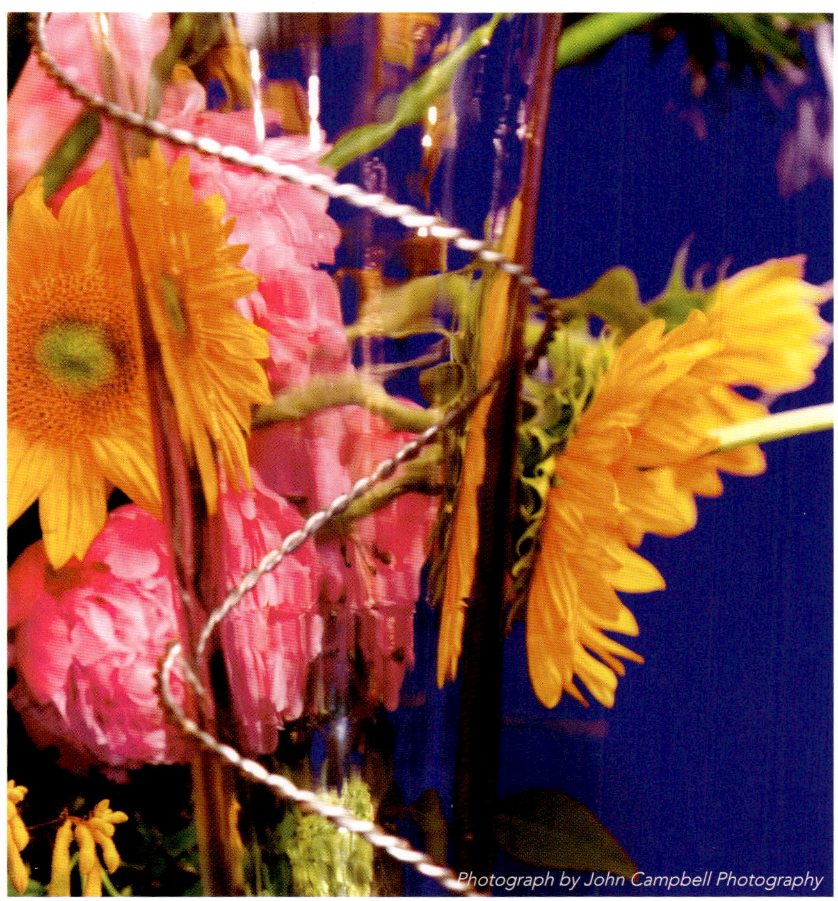

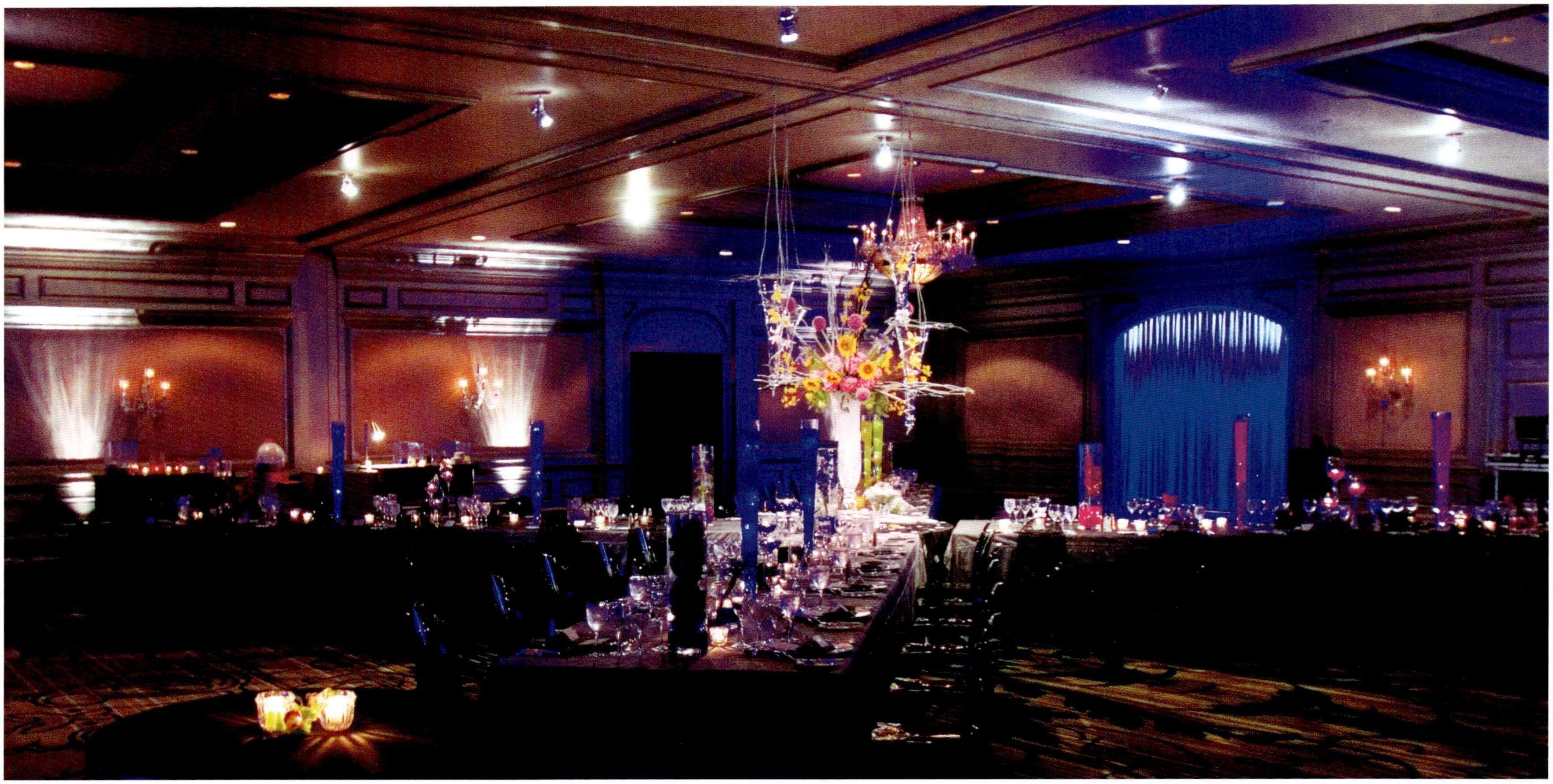

Photograph by John Campbell Photography

Photograph by John Campbell Photography

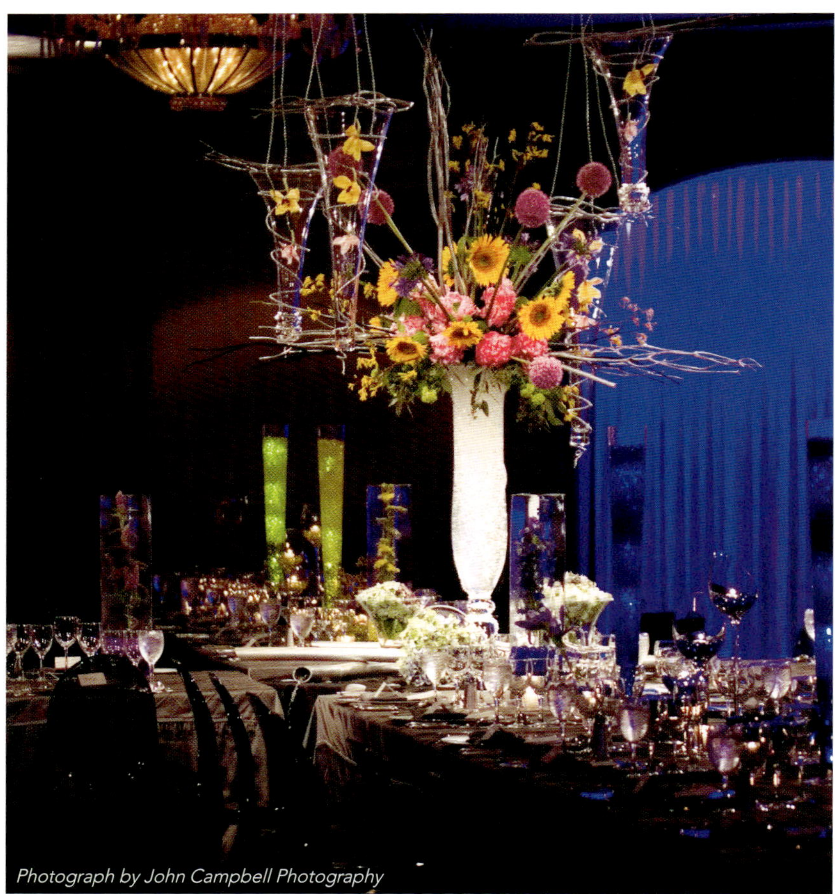

Above and left: Even though the ballroom can accommodate hundreds of people, we can arrange the room so that a smaller group of 50 will still feel comfortable. One way to do this is through the x-shaped table design. Hanging centerpieces from the ceiling, incorporating movement through bubbles in the vases, and placing an emphasis on lighting added a high-energy vibe to the room.

Facing page: We love that many of our event hosts are emotionally connected to their event. One mother and daughter were moved to tears when they first saw the tablescape design with its tall candelabras and interspersed flowers.

"A fabulous event starts with a vision and continues with the experience and enthusiasm necessary to make it happen."

—Robin Kreitner

Photograph by White Rose Photography

Photograph by White Rose Photography

Photograph by Ron Starr Photography

Photograph by Ron Starr Photography

"Personal traditions and cultural backgrounds bring a unique energy to the planning process."

—Paul Tramonte

Guests can mingle in The Ritz-Carlton's lobby bar, Lumen, which features gorgeous crystal chandeliers, exceptional details, and stunning artwork. To create extra sparkle in the evening, the chandeliers change color and hidden lights cast a vibrant glow on the windows.

Photograph by Ron Starr Photography

views

Lighting is such an important part of the overall feel of the room. Even with twinkling chandeliers, it is necessary to consider the lighting and work with a professional to coordinate uplighting, gobos, LEDs, natural light, and candles to ensure they reflect the desired mood.

THE RITZ-CARLTON, BUCKHEAD

JON MCGAVIN | KURT SCHWAN | HOPE NUDELMAN

Similar to a string of pearls, The Ritz-Carlton, Buckhead exudes a timeless elegance that quietly transcends ephemeral styles. While the hotel's physical characteristics add numerous pearls to its proverbial strand, the hotel is centered on its ladies and gentlemen who go beyond mere service to extend unexpected but much-welcomed luxury.

Set in the renowned Buckhead neighborhood—which is hailed as a jewel in the city and has been the social center of Atlanta for nearly 25 years—The Ritz-Carlton, Buckhead has held quite the array of major events. Even Nat King Cole's younger brother, Freddy, used to frequent the piano in the lobby lounge. On par with its impressive surroundings and rich history, the interior offers elegant colors, a grand fireplace, and an impressive collection of art in the lobby and pre-function areas. Well-appointed ballrooms and the warm gallery offer traditional, versatile spaces to accentuate any special occasion.

Yet the most important elements of an event at The Ritz-Carlton, Buckhead are the ladies and gentlemen on the staff. More than half of them have served with The Ritz-Carlton for more than five years, which has allowed them to fully embrace the gold-standard culture. Daily discussions and regular role-playing sessions further ensure the philosophies are more than just lip service; deeply embedded, the standards spring from a personal accountability to take care of everything so guests feel a sense of well-being.

Whether the event leans more toward a contemporary or traditional style, more vibrant or understated, our grand ballroom's gracious ambience and beautiful colors coordinate well. The height of the room also lends itself to tall centerpieces, while the ceiling's detailed millwork accommodates smaller arrangements.

Photograph by Drew Newman

Photograph by Ric Mershon Photographers

Above: The placement and color of monochromatic lighting in the Ritz-Carlton ballroom gave us the ability to create the stunning vision that the host wanted. Sheer white fabric along the walls and above the huppah, as well as a wide aisle runner, added softness to the brilliant hues.

Facing page: Whatever the vision, the ballrooms provide a solid foundation upon which we can create amazing designs. For a nod to both contemporary and traditional, variations of estate and round tables with a plethora of lighting styles beautifully accentuate the two-toned color scheme.

Previous pages: The addition of fabric and décor can significantly transform a room into an entirely new feel. Coordinating with the salmon-colored walls, we installed dramatic draperies around the perimeter for pizzazz. Mirrors behind the fabric visually enlarge the room and still maintain an intimate feel.

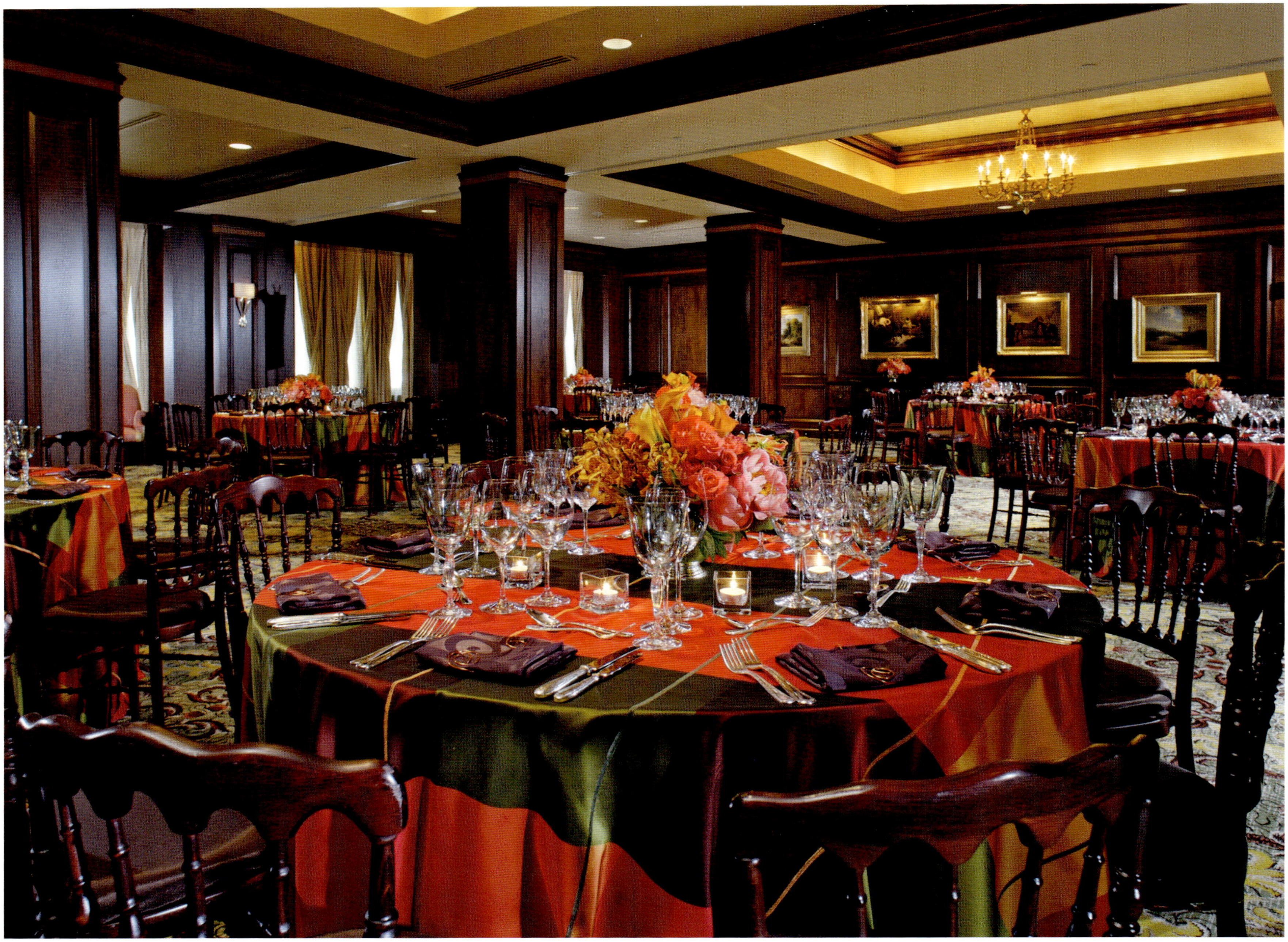

Photograph by Mark Wieland Photography

Photograph © Daemon Baizan, DAEMONpictures.com

Photograph © Daemon Baizan, DAEMONpictures.com

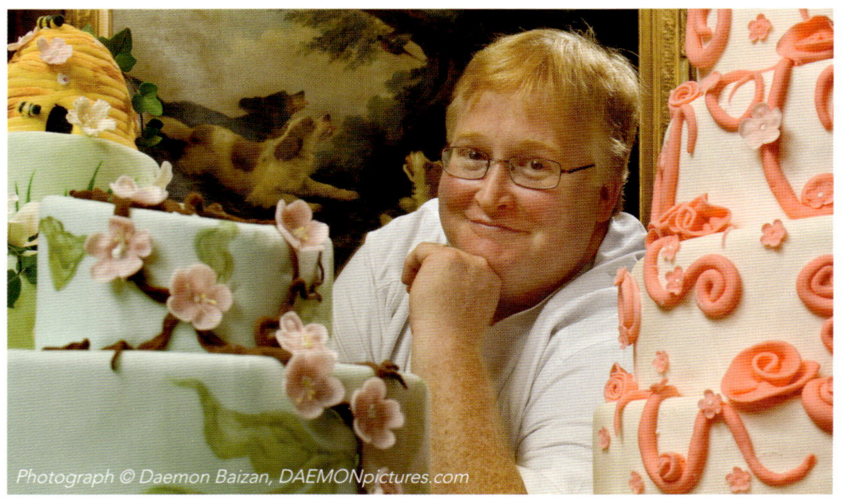

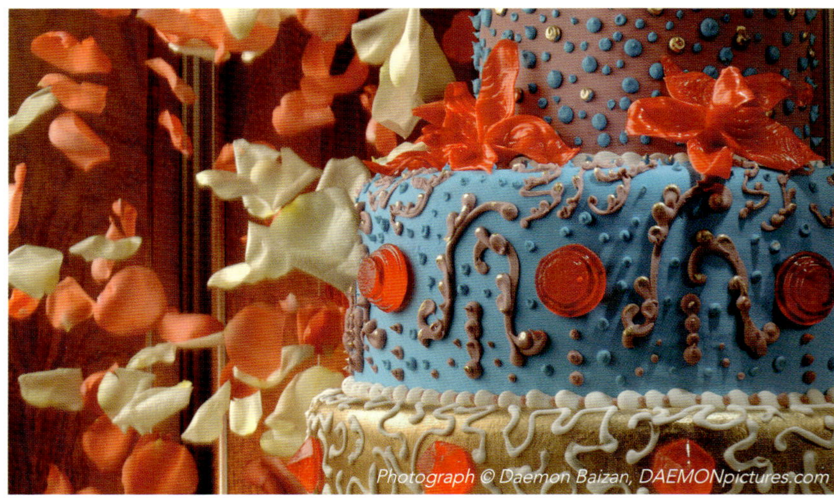

"The sexiest venue is still dependent on people to bring it to life."

—Jon McGavin

Right and facing page top: Our gallery and dining room offer an elegant, rich feel on a different level than the ballrooms. With more of an art-gallery-meets-country-club ambience, the gallery features some of our most prized artwork on the dark mahogany walls. In our dining room, the show kitchen allows guests to watch the master chefs create their own works of art.

Facing page bottom: Executive pastry chef James Satterwhite came from humble beginnings on a farm to hone his craft. Now he fashions our delectable desserts and carries each event's vision through to the smallest details in his culinary discipline.

views

A successful event involves three parameters: attendees were able to connect with those around them, guests leave with a sense of awe, and the host's goals were achieved. This is no easy feat but is achieved by ensuring every one of the moving pieces is perfectly synchronized.

Atlanta Botanical Garden

Set in the heart of an urban landscape, the Atlanta Botanical Garden presents a perfect convergence of stunning natural beauty and sophisticated indoor venues suitable for a variety of occasions. Continuing the founders' vision, the delightful acreage provides an enjoyable experience for the hundreds of thousands of visitors annually.

From a 60-foot aquatic plant pond filled with lilies and lotuses to an exquisite Japanese garden created even before the Atlanta Botanical Garden was chartered, each area of the luscious landscape allows visitors to linger in the matchless sights, smells, and sounds of the natural world. Guests can meander through a sweet-scented rose garden, admire the Trustees' Garden from underneath one of its classical pavilions, revel in the local beauty of the Southern Seasons Garden, or take in the unique sites of the Southern Rock Garden. The indoor spaces, including multiple halls, classrooms, and workshops, meld with these natural landscapes to allow the ultimate in flexibility during celebrations, corporate events, retreats, and symposiums.

With the preservation of the natural world a key mission, the Atlanta Botanical Garden not only provides an eco-friendly setting but also strives to assist in the conservation and research of native plants, global collections, amphibians, and hard-to-propagate species. Each event held here ensures these programs—and the gardens themselves—preserve the dreams and goals of the civic-minded Atlantans who created the garden nearly 40 years ago.

Considered the heart of the garden, the Howell Fountain and the Great Lawn with the Fuqua Conservatory in the background offer a beautiful urban oasis in the heart of Midtown Atlanta. The lawn is home to numerous events each year, from Concerts in the Garden to the Garden of Eden Ball, one of the most magnificent social events in Atlanta.

Photograph by Drew Newman

Photograph by Danny Lentz

"The ever-changing color and landscape present an outdoor, living museum."

—Mary Pat Matheson

Photograph by Matt Adcock-del Sol

Photograph by Matt Adcock-del Sol

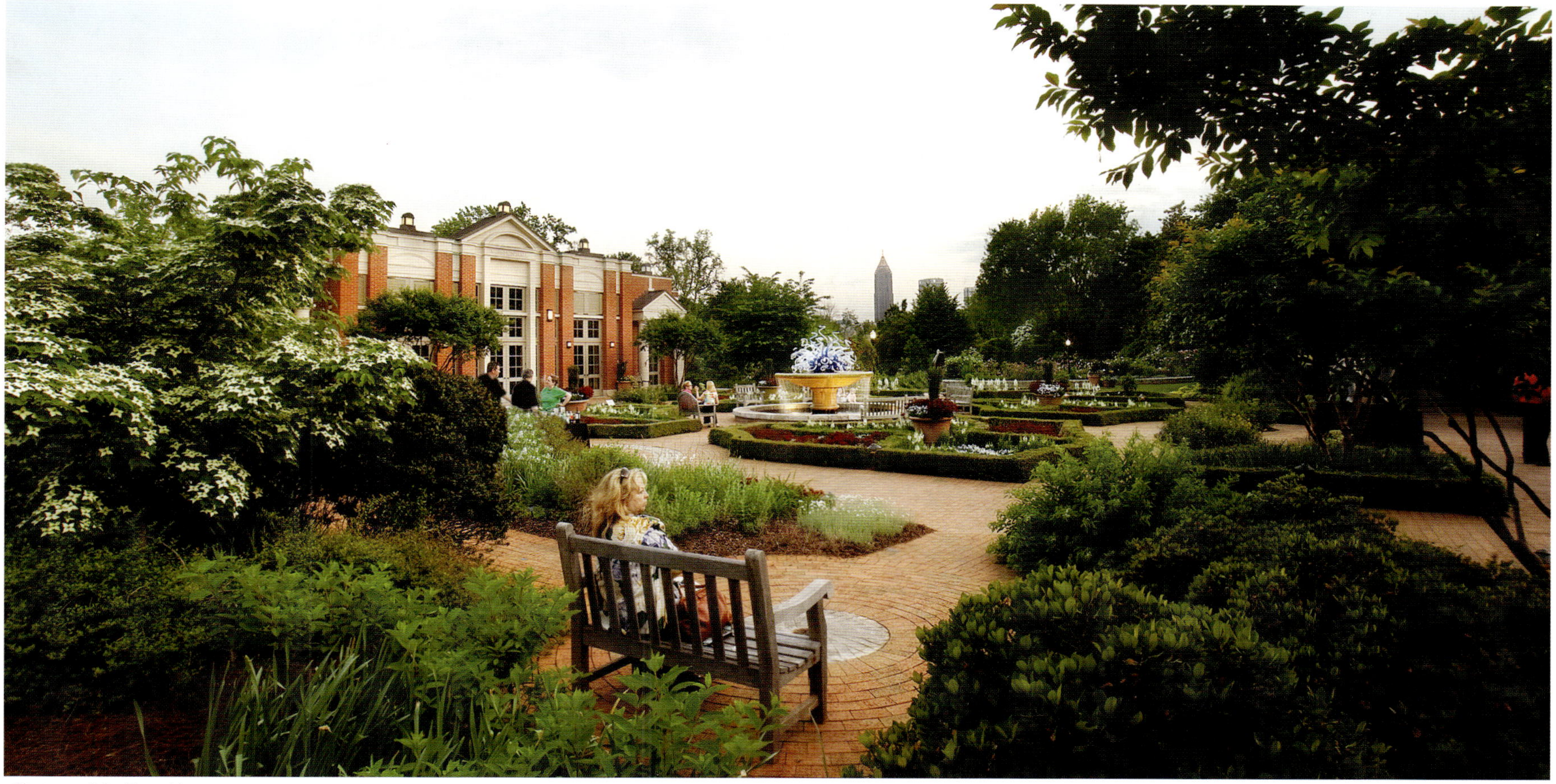

Photograph by Drew Newman

Above: The classical Mershon Hall opens to the Levy Parterre—French for maze or pathways—as an idyllic setting. The open space flows seamlessly between indoors and out, from the bamboo floors through the double Palladian doors into the meandering pathways lined with beautiful roses and stunning boxwood-edged beds.

Right: The Levy Parterre is arranged symmetrically around an Italian limestone fountain featuring artist Dale Chihuly's dazzling blue and white glass sculpture.

Facing page: In the Fuqua Orchid Center, events are held among the more than 10,000 rare and endangered species of orchids. The variety of the orchids' mesmerizing scents spill onto the connected Robinson Gazebo that gazes onto the gorgeous Atlanta skyline. In another part of the garden, the generous space of the Levy Parterre offers a unique canvas waiting for the imagination's inimitable touches.

Photograph by Matt Adcock-del Sol

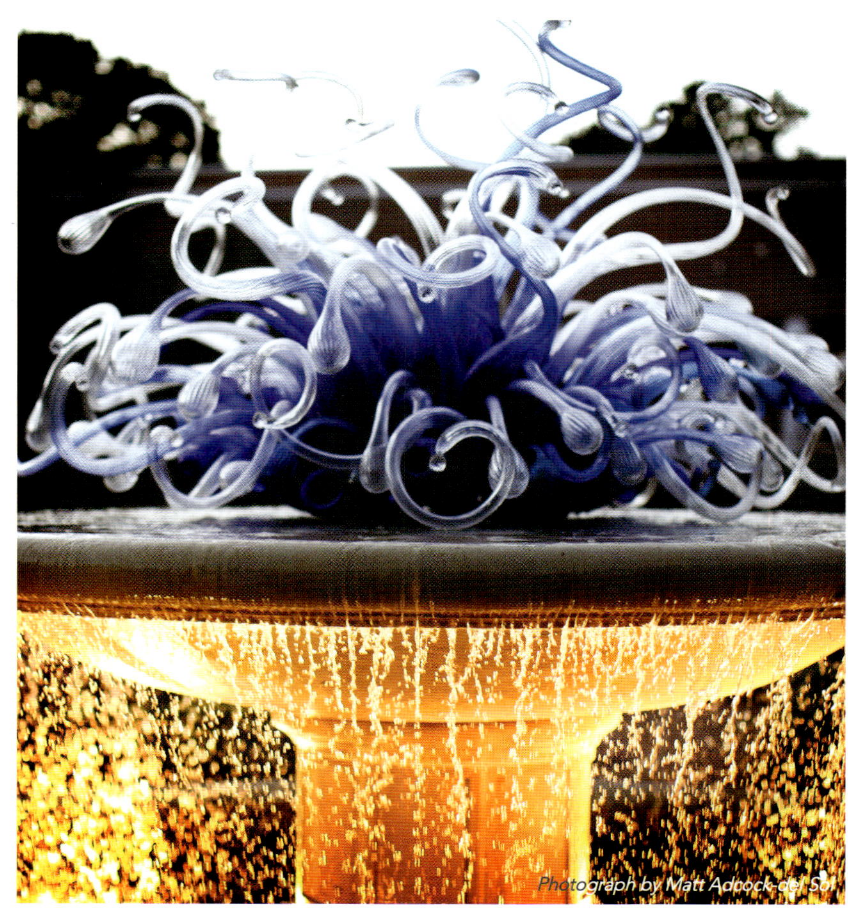

Photograph by Drew Newman

Photograph by Jim Fitts

Photograph by Matt Adcock-del Sol

"The excitement of hosting a garden event stems from the blank canvas that is only bound by the imagination."

—Kimberly Gild

Right: Day Hall's high-ceilinged ballroom with its organic palette and floor-to-ceiling windows opens to the west into Cox Courtyard and to the east onto the partially covered Lanier Terrace.

Facing page top: From the soothing double waterfall to the Hardin Visitor Center's transparent structure built to the U.S. Green Building Council's specifications, guests are greeted with every imaginable beauty.

Facing page bottom left: The week-long transformation for the 25th annual Garden of Eden Ball included constructing the enormous tented space, dance floor, and numerous bars, and decorating with a luxurious "Breakfast at Tiffany's" theme.

Facing page bottom right: The lawn metamorphosed after dark. The Midtown lights illuminate the urban landscape and the moonlight dances on ornate columns that flank the setting.

Photograph by Drew Newman

views

Even with its inherently eco-friendly qualities, the Atlanta Botanical Garden continues to expand in environmentally friendly ways. The 600-foot-long, 40-foot-high Canopy Walk through Storza Woods was designed with minimal impact to the trees and the forest floor. The Edible Garden provides educational programming, including classes on cooking with fresh, healthy produce.

Novare Events

MYRNA ANTAR

The Atlanta area offers an immense array of venues, from elegant and historic to modern and dramatic. But who has the time to visit every location to determine what will provide the best background for the event?

To ease the venue selection process, Myrna Antar with Novare Events gladly steps in. With a degree in business management and more than two decades working in event management in Atlanta, Myrna knows the city inside and out. This knowledge and her ability to envision an empty space as a stunning event allows her to pair each event host with just the right Novare Events venue. Not only that, but her passion for spectacular events makes for an exciting, joyous experience.

Begun in 2002, Novare Events was established as the only caterer-independent event facility management company in Atlanta. Today, Novare boasts a stunning collection of venues that offer a wide variety of styles and functional attributes. From European-inspired spaces like The Biltmore Hotel ballrooms and Summerour Studio to buildings with a modern industrial feel like The Foundry at Puritan Mill to the clean, contemporary lines of the ballroom at TWELVE Atlantic Station, Novare Events has developed an uncanny ability to help event hosts find just what they're looking for.

Exuding its original 1920s Georgian splendor, the Imperial Ballroom at The Biltmore features high, original handcrafted plaster relief ceilings, fully restored sparkling crystal chandeliers, and large Palladian windows.

Photograph by Sean Randall Photography

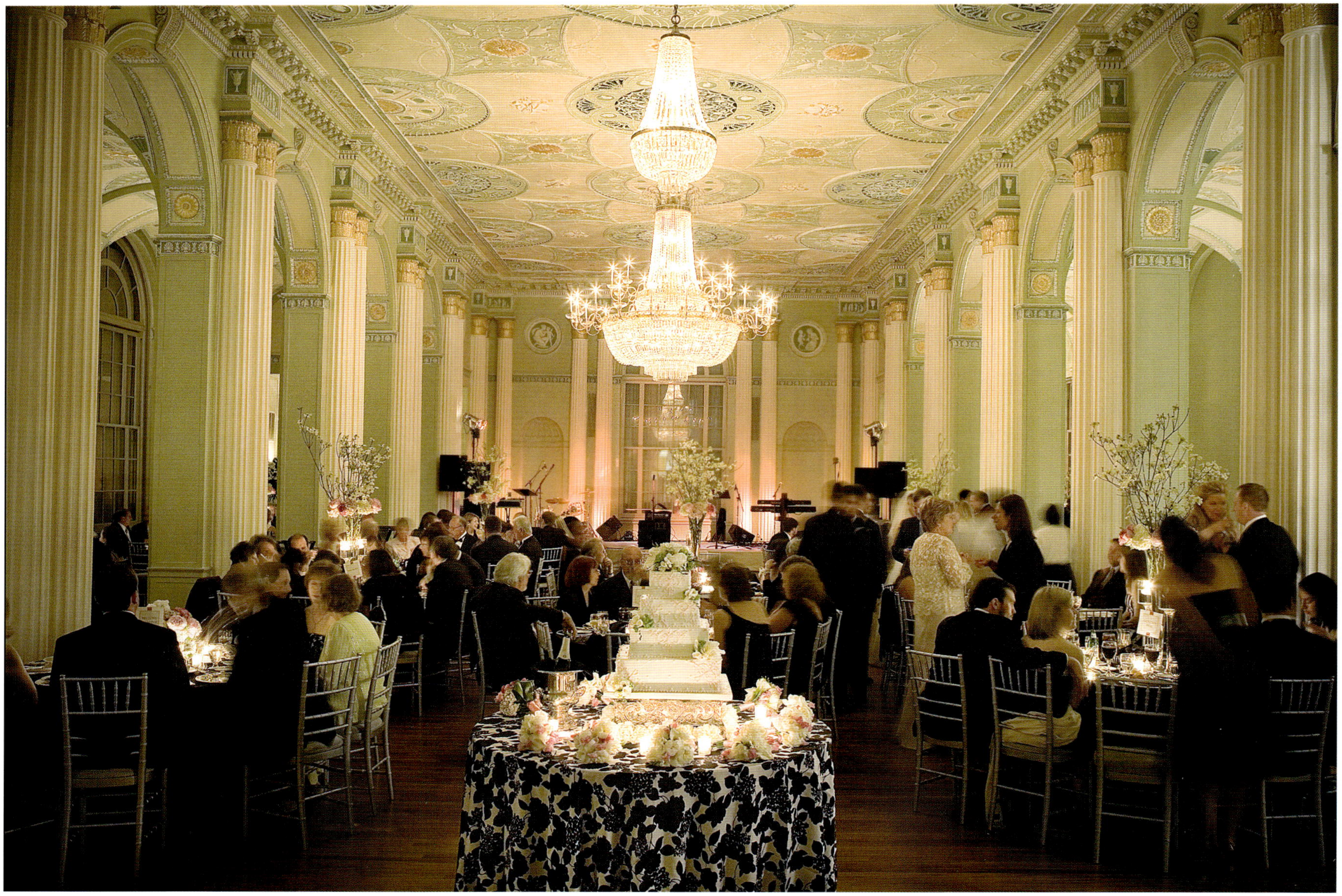

Photograph by Drew Newman

Photograph by Eric Wittmayer Photography

Photograph by Eric Wittmayer Photography

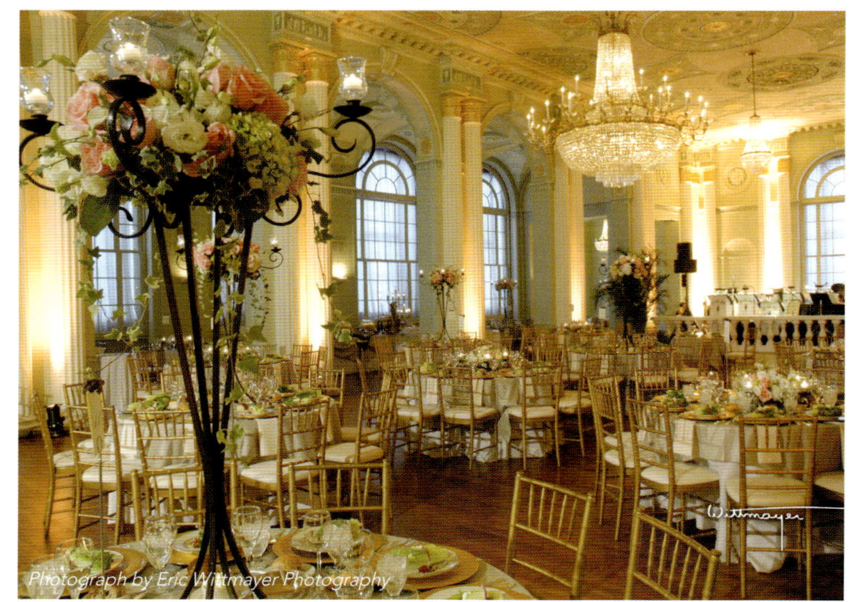

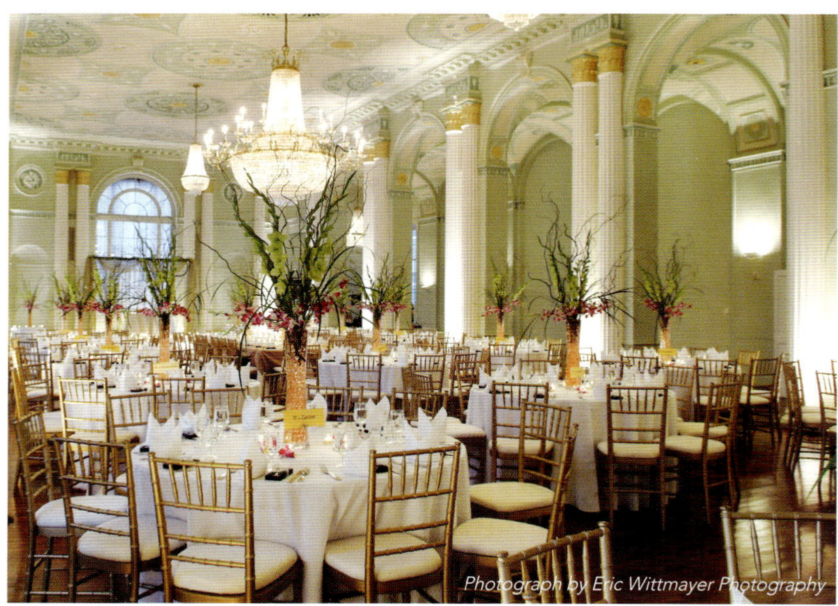

Photograph by PWP Studio

Above: Once the headquarters for The Puritan Soap Company, The Foundry at Puritan Mill is 12,000 square feet of classic, utilitarian, brick-and-beam loft-style space. Soft, natural light from the north-facing windows and painted façade signs add immense charm. The innate historical elements with modern perks and amenities ideally blend old and new.

Facing page: Located in bustling Midtown Atlanta, The Biltmore Hotel provides a regal, dramatic backdrop ideal for a range of events. On the National Register of Historic Places, the hotel represents a rescued piece of history. The Georgian Ballroom offers a spectacular space that commemorates Atlanta's rich heritage.

Photograph by Luke Hock

"Choosing a venue is like choosing a wedding dress—as soon as you try it on, you know it's the one."

—Myrna Antar

In direct relation to its home as the main studio for Summerour & Associates, Summerour Studio is an impressively refurbished warehouse that overlooks Atlanta's robust Atlantic Station. From the sloped tiled roof to the graveled courtyard, Summerour is a one-of-a-kind Tuscan-style villa in the heart of a modern Southern metropolis. All types of events—from corporate meetings and social gatherings to nonprofit galas and family celebrations—take on a unique flavor at Summerour Studio.

Photograph by Eric Wittmayer Photography

views

Always walk through your event from beginning to end as if you were a guest. Make sure a synergy exists among every element and that every person involved shares your vision, otherwise the event may seem fragmented to attendees.

Turner Field

Merging old-time charm with contemporary quality is no easy feat. But special events director Sabrina Jenkins says that's the beauty of working at the home of the longest continuously operating franchise in Major League Baseball—the Atlanta Braves. Even though Turner Field has only been open since 1997, the history of the Atlanta location goes back to the '60s and the Braves franchise can be traced back to 1871.

This rich history was preserved in Turner Field, both in the atmosphere of the ballpark and in the Braves Museum and Hall of Fame. With displays including the 1995 World Series trophy and Hank Aaron's 715th record-breaking bat and ball, the museum is part of a unique set of locales within the park. From the Grand Entry Plaza with capacity for up to 3,000 people to the intimate SunTrust Club located steps away from home plate, the variety and luxury in space is unrivaled.

Paired with the historical essence of the franchise, the cuisine is anything but traditional. The Canadian chef delivers everything from tempting tapas to delectable desserts, and five-course dinners to family-style meals—all exceptionally chic both in presentation and in quality. Perhaps because of the many unique aspects of the field, the overall effect is a superior blend of historical ambience and modern amenities.

Turner Field boasts 16 unique sites. One of the largest areas, the Grand Entry Plaza, is centrally located under the giant screen with close proximity to the Braves Museum and Hall of Fame, Cartoon Network area, and Scout's Alley. As an example of the plaza's versatility, we have hosted company picnics, social receptions, nonprofit galas, and active events with rock climbing walls.

Photograph by Atlanta Braves

Photograph by Atlanta Braves

"Transform the conventional into the phenomenal by selecting a venue that provides a change of pace from the norm."

—Sabrina Jenkins

Photograph by Atlanta Braves

Photograph by Atlanta Braves

Above: Miniature desserts crafted in unique designs are one of our most popular requests. Pleasing for the eye and the palate, the desserts also appease the calorie-conscious guest because of the petite size.

Right: We occasionally host programs that include a multitude of stand-alone segments. In one evening, a corporation hosted 250 guests for an on-field dinner, batting practice in the outfield, and dazzling entertainment that included a marching band, a Stomp performance, and BMX bikers.

Facing page: From a festival utilizing a full stage on the Grand Entry Plaza to a private reception amid more than 600 artifacts in the Braves Museum and Hall of Fame, each is encapsulated in a beautiful and distinct setting.

Photograph by Atlanta Braves

Photograph by Atlanta Braves

Right: In an amazing excavation behind home plate, the belowground SunTrust Club and its outside seating area were created as an all-inclusive club during games and an intimate reception area for private events. Garnering recognition as the closest venue to home plate in any U.S. ballpark, the club opens onto the field next to the Braves dugout.

Facing page: On-field events offer a spectacular ambience, which we merge with the first-class feel that would be expected in a luxurious ballroom. Under a tent designed for nearly 250 people and a rock band, guests enjoyed both interactive food stations and a delectable plated dinner. Dessert and fireworks pleased multiple senses from the Grand Entry Plaza near the end of the evening.

views

When working in unique settings and dual-purpose spaces, knowing and respecting the venue is crucial for the success of the event. Experienced planners will understand the feasibility of the event within the space as well as maintain a professional relationship with the venue's staff so everyone remains satisfied throughout the planning process.

200 Peachtree

In the heart of downtown Atlanta lies historic Peachtree Street, the city's main north-south avenue. Since the street's first use in the 1800s, it has seen the city literally grow up around it, with many grand buildings highlighting its magnificence. Now receiving a new name and an impressive facelift, 200 Peachtree brings an exceptional option to the city's venue repertoire while maintaining the historical roots.

The original building was designed by Philip Shutze, Atlanta's foremost neoclassical architect, and opened in 1927 as the retail store Davison-Paxon, an affiliate of Macy's. First referred to as a temple of commerce, it was the largest retail department store south of Philadelphia and represented the largest investment in retail business enterprise in the U.S. at that time. Now, 82 years later, 180 Real Estate Development Group, led by Robert Patterson, has revived the building as the grandest venue in downtown Atlanta.

In what was Davisons' elegant main lobby, the Grand Atrium has been restored to showcase a beautiful limestone floor with marble inlays, majestic Corinthian columns, and dramatic 30-foot ceilings. Even the historic 14-foot chandeliers, which once graced the flagship Macy's in New York City before becoming a treasure in the Atlanta store, have been reinstalled. With well over 18,000 square feet and the capacity to hold more than 800 for a seated dinner, the versatility of the building combined with the grandeur of its restoration provide an unmatched venue for all occasions.

Restored to its original glory, the Grand Atrium is surrounded by a mezzanine-level balcony for an elegant event space. Other event areas include the Gallery with more than 20,000 square feet, the Carnegie Foyer with exposed brick walls for an urban feel, and a conference center with five meeting rooms that can be separated or joined in various ways.

Rendering courtesy of 200 Peachtree

Photograph courtesy of Atlanta History Center

Photograph courtesy of Atlanta History Center

Photograph courtesy of Atlanta History Center

"There is no better feeling than resurrecting a building full of history for people to enjoy far into the future."

—Robert Patterson

In retaining the original façade, 200 Peachtree boasts magnificent Palladian windows topped by colorful stained-glass accents. As it has been for over a century, Peachtree Street is a constant bustle of activity. To accommodate guests amidst this downtown location, valet service and an adjacent parking garage ensure easy access to the building.

views

Only a few things in life are truly important—history is one of them. Understanding the past and preserving the best from days gone by are key to moving in the right direction in the future. Through renovating 200 Peachtree, a piece of the past will be preserved by evoking the same civic pride that was first felt when the Davison's department store opened in the '20s.

Bohemian Hotel Savannah Riverfront

In 1733, British maritime settlers first landed on the banks of the Savannah River, where charming towns sprung up featuring cobblestone streets full of commerce and activity. Today, Savannah is home to the nation's largest urban historic district, which encompasses nearly two square miles. Overlooking the river, the Bohemian Hotel sits like a jewel along the historic 18th-century cobblestone River Street.

The hotel's design is inspired by the diverse history of the river. British campaign furniture, oyster shell fixtures, driftwood, and river rock adorn the spaces and maintain the link to the area's beginnings, yet sophisticated, modern style is anything but overlooked. The Bohemian boasts original works of art by internationally renowned artists in each guestroom and throughout the public spaces. Most notably, the importance of the guest experience is demonstrated by the hotel's attention to quality detail and intuitive service that is synonymous with The Kessler Collection—a portfolio of boutique hotels owned by entrepreneur and visionary Richard C. Kessler.

Designed with an intimate ambience in mind, the Bohemian features a boardroom, private dining room in Rocks Modern Grill, and Rocks on the Roof, a vibrant rooftop bar and lounge with spectacular views of the river, historic district, and South Carolina's low country. Rocks on the River features American comfort food infused with a touch of the South, and the staff offers the attention that each guest deserves—all to ensure the Bohemian experience is worthy of its stunning interiors, perfect location, and rich history.

Rocks on the Roof offers unparalleled views of passing ships and a sparkling ambience for guests.

Photograph by Raymond Martinot

Photograph by Raymond Martinot

Photograph by Raymond Martinot

"The artistic inclusion of natural elements like wood, stone, fire, and shells provides for even the most luxurious of events a grounded, connected feel."

—Mark Kessler

The authentic brick façade is a stunning entrance to the hotel that embodies style, a nod to the past with modern sophistication. Inside, fiery red accents add a touch of passion to the elegant atmosphere and the floor-to-ceiling windows take full advantage of the gorgeous surroundings.

Photograph by Raymond Martinot

views

An event's success can be measured on many levels, yet the guest interaction is paramount to the experience. Weave in everything from décor and flowers to food and venue to ensure guests enjoy themselves and feel comfortable mingling with others.

Four Seasons Hotel Atlanta

Isadore (Issy) Sharp had a different vision for a hotel—one that encompassed hosting down-to-earth people yet treating them as if they were dukes and duchesses. Not only did he want guests to be well taken care of, but he also wanted them to feel a warmth and friendliness from each person they encountered. Translating his vision into reality, he opened the first Four Seasons Hotel in 1961 in Canada.

Remarkably similar to the epitome of Southern hospitality, Four Seasons' warm, respectful approach to each guest has carried through the years and across countries to a vibrant vein of the South—Atlanta. Located in Midtown where culture and art abound, Four Seasons Hotel Atlanta combines Old World elegance with the intimacy of a boutique resort.

To achieve the flawless standard that Issy so highly valued, the staff applies an intuitive approach to achieve the dreams and desires of each event host. With turnkey, personalized service, the host is not passed along from department to department but rather builds a relationship with one contact through the entire planning process. This allows the staff at Four Seasons to ensure they are always four steps ahead, whether it involves foresight to fly a mother and grandmother in from Nigeria to teach the culinary staff in preparation for a traditional African wedding, or simply the experience to prevent problems before they occur. Regardless of the method, what remains is an unrivaled depth of reliability and trust.

From large events with hundreds of people to more intimate celebrations, the spacious Four Seasons ballroom offers exceptional beauty featuring chandeliers that reflect a warm glow off of a wall of mirrors on one side and large picture windows on the other.

Photograph by Ric Mershon Photographers

Photograph by Ric Mershon Photographers

Photograph by Jeff Zaruba

"Anyone can build a beautiful building, but the true hallmark of an extraordinary venue is the staff."

—Elissa Wallis

Right: Overlooking the dramatic downtown skyline, the 50th floor offers the city's only venue with this kind of view.

Facing page: From the lobby with its magnificent staircase and Baccarat crystal chandelier to the foyer of the grand ballroom, Four Seasons offers flexibility to bring a vision to life and an elegant palette to make a personalized statement.

Photograph by Peter Vitale

views

Don't be afraid to ask for something you think might not be feasible, especially if it's very important to you. When working with such an ingenious group of people, you never know when that near-impossible idea can become reality.

Fox Theatre

Attending the theatre was once a grand event where guests dressed in the finest attire and enjoyed a cultural experience unlike any other. In the heart of Atlanta, the Fox Theatre stands as one of the few locations where hints of that era still exist.

The Fox Theatre maintains the grandness and opulence that once qualified an evening out on the town. Built in 1929 as the Yaarab Temple Shrine Mosque and later used as a venue for movies and other entertainment, the theatre was tragically being considered for destruction in the '70s. Atlanta Landmarks, Inc., a nonprofit organization of local citizens, stepped in and turned the Fox into a National Historic Landmark. The organization embarked on an extensive project to restore the venue to its original grandeur.

Amidst such a historical, luxurious ambience, Jennifer Farmer and her team at Fox Theatre treasure their opportunities to work each event. Jim Lane, the onsite coordinator with more than 20 years of experience at the Fox, is one example of the passion that the team exudes. He is not only the first person at the theatre during an event's setup and the last person to leave, but he's also the can-do guy who will give his shoes to a groomsman who misplaced his own or bustle a wedding gown. This enthusiastic attitude converges with the spectacular building to create breathtaking events.

The Fox Theatre was influenced by the magnificence of the pharaohs and Middle Eastern palaces since it was designed shortly after the discovery of King Tut's tomb. Appropriately named the Egyptian Ballroom, the largest event space features massive columns that climb to the 30-foot ceiling. With a built-in stage, wonderful acoustics, and state-of-the-art technology, the ballroom offers versatility for events with up to 800 people.

Photograph by Sandra and Greg Scott, Picture This! Photography

Photograph by Sara Foltz

Photograph courtesy of Fox Theatre

Photograph by Yukari Umekawa

"A beautiful building with a deep history allows guests to feel a grand sense of occasion."

—Jennifer Farmer

Right: With a location on Peachtree Street, the Fox Theatre's grand arcade entrance with its beautiful marquee is the perfect place to welcome guests inside.

Facing page: Every inch of the building is unparalleled in its design and décor. In the main theatre, a glance upward reveals a show in itself. Simulating a sky complete with stars and floating clouds, the ceiling overlooks the famous Möller pipe organ. Custom made in 1929, the instrument still holds the title of the second largest theater organ in the world. Guests entering the ballrooms step back in time to the opulent splendor of the Egyptian pharaohs or the mystique of a Moorish palace. Both the Egyptian Ballroom and Grand Salon of the Fox Theatre are lavishly decorated with sweeping columns and ornamentation, creating the perfect setting for any event.

Photograph by Our Labor of Love Photography

views

Event hosts often ask if hiring an event planner is beneficial. A properly seasoned and licensed planner can provide an array of services and help event hosts attain a peace of mind.

Magic Moments at Flint Hill

KENDALL COLLIER | TERESA DAY

Introducing a new concept in event facilities to Atlanta, Magic Moments Catering opened its first venue, Flint Hill, in 1987. With an emphasis on weddings, Flint Hill offers a gracious home setting and garden dedicated exclusively to special events.

A sense of elegant, comfortable entertaining first brought Kendall Collier and Teresa Day together as friends in 1971, along with shared passions in cooking, gardening, antiquing, and designing. Upon first discovering Flint Hill, Kendall's entrepreneurial spirit sensed an opportunity as she linked the antebellum home to an event space; so began Magic Moments.

Built in 1835, Flint Hill embraces the essence of genuine Southern hospitality. After renovating the house and adding a ballroom encased with French doors, Kendall and Teresa turned their attention to the landscaping. Teresa envisioned a series of garden rooms mimicking those inside to create an easy flow between the two spaces. Today, the mature gardens form a natural shield around the property, which allows Flint Hill to retain its enduring moment in time.

An immediate success, Flint Hill provided the business model to grow Magic Moments, which now owns and operates four event venues in greater Atlanta. Through the years, Kendall and Teresa have built a well-trained team empowered to make decisions. Believing in never-ending improvement, the team stays focused on the concept that "company is coming," keeping everyone alert and on their collective toes.

A gracious entrance with its wide brick walkway and grand, two-story veranda, which mirrors the central hall inside, welcomes guests into the meticulously maintained, residential setting.

Photograph by Matt Yung

Photograph by Terrilyn Bayne

Photograph by Christine Gallagher

Photograph by John Day

Photograph by John Day

"A beautiful garden can hold many secrets."

—Teresa Day

Right: The green and white bridal garden with its pineapple fountain offers a private retreat for guests to discover.

Facing page top left: Just as one room leads to another in the house, alluring passageways do the same in the garden.

Facing page top right: We love to incorporate new ideas, such as the ceremony-in-the-round.

Facing page bottom left: For a group of 60 Japanese businessmen intrigued with the Old South, we created an intimate setting by transforming the ballroom into a plant-filled conservatory in keeping with the era of the home.

Facing page bottom right: French doors lining the ballroom overlook the garden during a romantic, seated dinner.

Photograph by Jessica Horwitz

views

Creating the desired ambience becomes a guidepost for keeping a designer focused. Décor used to enhance an existing feature provides added value for the client. But if an event element does not advance the theme, it dilutes the integrity of the concept.

Magic Moments at Little Gardens
KENDALL COLLIER | TERESA DAY

When the opportunity to purchase Little Gardens presented itself to Kendall Collier and Teresa Day in 2008, they knew it would fit perfectly as a Magic Moments property. Set atop a three-acre estate with a rolling front lawn, Little Gardens was built in the 1930s and, through time, became entrenched in the community.

First serving as a private residence, the property was named after the owner's childhood farmhouse with its many small gardens. Later as a fine dining establishment, many an anxious lad requested the "sweetheart table" in front of the balcony to surprise his one true love with a ring. It is only appropriate that Little Gardens now operates exclusively as a full-service special event facility designed with brides in mind.

As guests turn onto the winding driveway leading up to Little Gardens, they are delighted by the secluded setting the gardens provide. Not another neighbor is visible from the backyard by the koi pond. Amid blooming antique roses, hydrangeas, daylilies, jonquils, cherry trees, crepe myrtles, and gardenia bushes, it is no surprise that Little Gardens attracts both brides and butterflies.

Through a wall of glass doors, the ballroom overlooks this stunning garden and provides a captivating view, even for winter events. Graced with undeniable charm, Little Gardens is a venue for all seasons. The team's constant focus on maintaining the estate setting and improving the facility ensures that it meets Magic Moments' exacting standards—and perhaps even exceeds them.

Inspired by its original purpose as a private home, Little Gardens guards this legacy for others to experience with small touches such as rocking chairs on the porch and a colorful, English-style garden.

Photograph by Jessica Horwitz

Photograph by Jessica Horwitz

Photograph by Jessica Horwitz

Photograph by Jessica Horwitz

Photograph by Jessica Horwitz

Right and facing page top right: The opportunity to discover unexpected elements, like the koi pond and waterfall, encourages guests to wander the garden paths.

Facing page top and bottom left: A neutral color scheme allows the host the opportunity to personalize the home. To keep the interior inviting and guest-friendly, we place key pieces of furniture to suggest a room's purpose without crowding the space or turning it into a museum.

Facing page bottom right: To accommodate a large number of guests, we have a commercial-sized bar. Its low profile maintains the residential atmosphere.

Photograph by Jessica Horwitz

views

Keep pushing forward until you hit a brick wall; then go back for the bulldozer. When it comes to implementing new ideas, this is our advice: If you know you can do it, then do it.

Magic Moments at Primrose Cottage

KENDALL COLLIER | TERESA DAY

Set back from the road and separated by a hand-turned fence, Primrose Cottage radiates an ambience that hangs in the air like the undeniable fragrance of magnolia. Throughout the property, branches of venerable oak trees weave a lacy canopy that sets it apart from its surroundings and offers a sanctuary to all who enter.

Built in 1839 by Roswell King, a planter, industrialist, and the city of Roswell's founder, the home is listed on the National Register of Historic Places. As the town's oldest permanent home, the historic nature has been preserved despite its transformation into an event facility with modern amenities. The home's innate grace and elegance are part of its continuing legacy that the entire community claims.

As an event facility, the three-level cottage features large, open rooms and wide hallways that allow for an easy flow not often found in historic homes. Attached to the main house on the terrace level, two ballrooms connect to form an L-shape with more than 4,000 square feet of space. Amazingly, these modern additions are not even visible from the front of the home.

Just outside, a 350-year-old white oak anchors the courtyard leading to the brick patio used for outdoor ceremonies. Overlooking the terraced woodland garden, this beguiling setting is indeed seductive. Further in the landscape, subtle lighting, charming fountains, vine-covered arbors, antique iron fencing, and ancient moss-laden stone walls and staircases draw guests deeper into this alluring, almost primordial garden.

With its horseshoe gravel driveway edging an expansive front lawn, Primrose Cottage is in keeping with the era of this prestigious, historic property.

Photograph by Kevin McManus

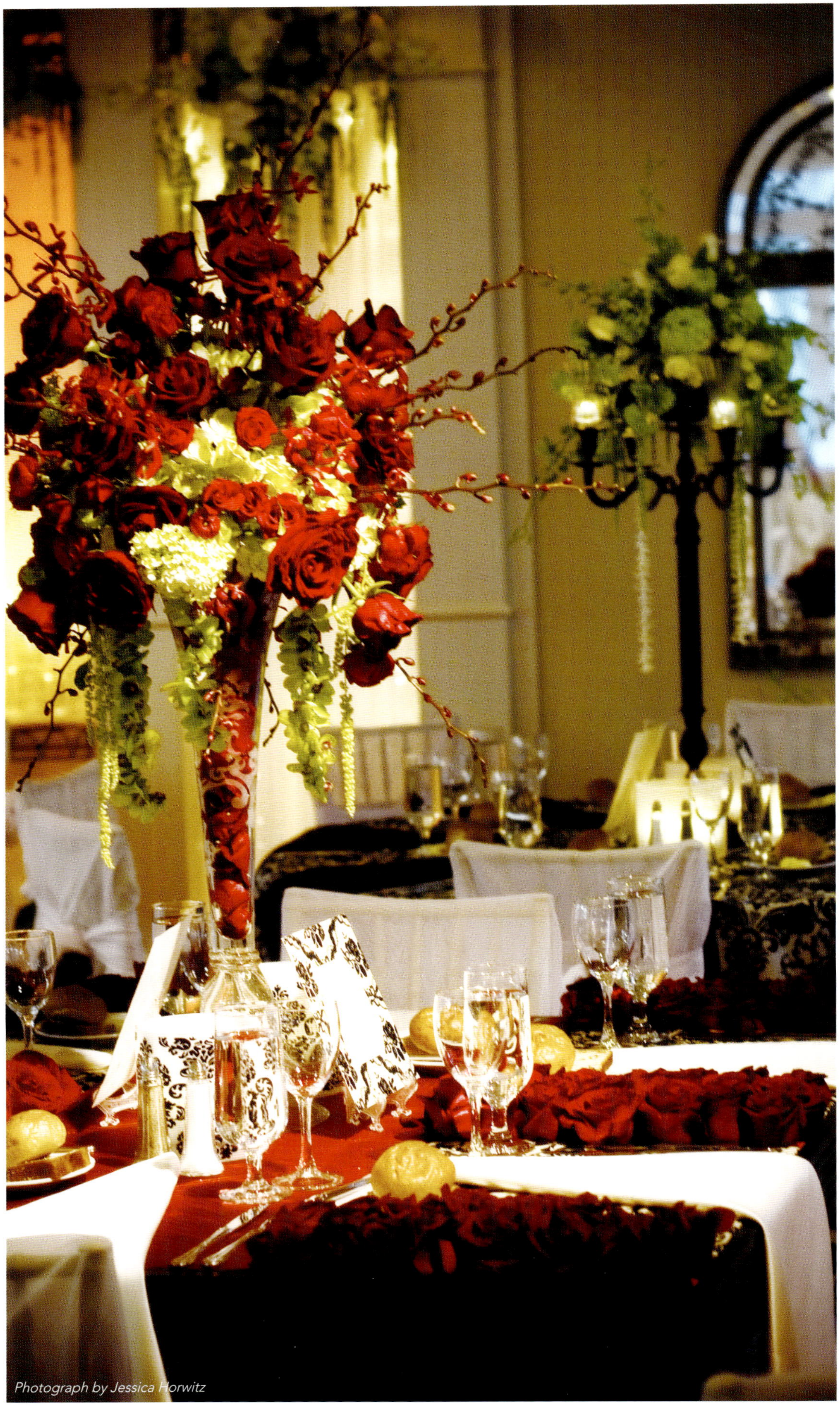
Photograph by Jessica Horwitz

Photograph by John Day

Photograph by Jessica Horwitz

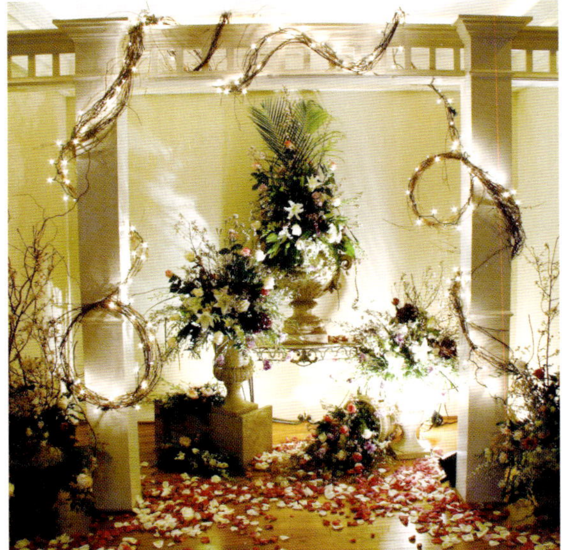

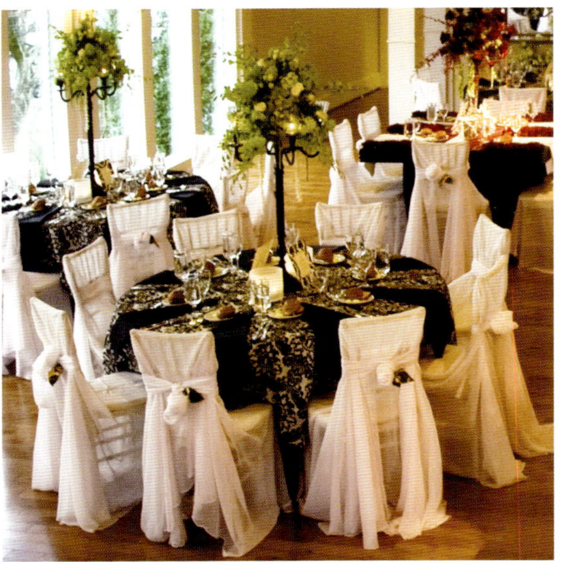

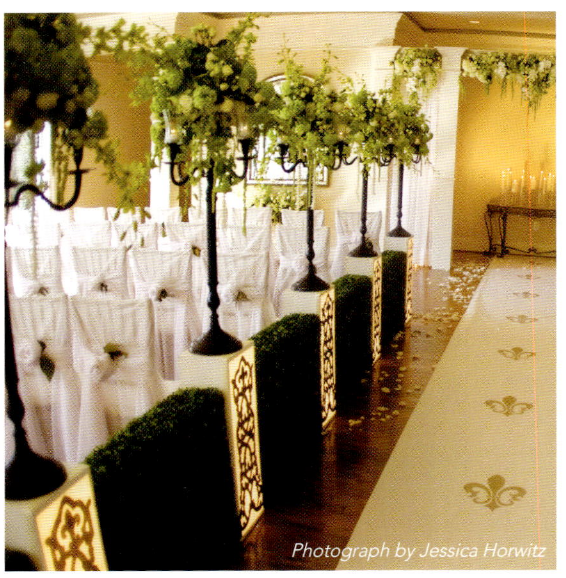

Photograph by Jessica Horwitz

"The most memorable events are the ones where guests lose all sense of time and place."

—Teresa Day

Right: Primrose maintains much of its original charm as evidenced in the rustic garden shed and the mood of the woodland landscape overlooking the stacked stone terraces leading to a spring-fed creek.

Facing page: Whether guests are mingling in the ballroom, the house, or the gardens, there exists an alluring ambience. Paired with customized décor and award-winning catering, the atmosphere is at once timeless, up-to-date, and full of personal touches and surprises.

views

We encourage our brides to display items that could personalize the interior. These might include family photos, parents or grandparents' wedding paraphernalia, or private collections from dolls to baseball cards.

Magic Moments at The Atrium

KENDALL COLLIER | TERESA DAY

Known in its early days as "Atlanta's favorite summer resort," the city of Norcross continues to embrace its Southern heritage. With styles ranging from antebellum homes and narrow brick buildings to Victorian residences and a restored train depot, the historic downtown area offers a nostalgic glimpse into the past.

Set amidst this vibrant, quaint community is an unexpected treasure—a modern version of an ancient Greek temple hidden within a lush secret garden. At The Atrium, Magic Moments' Kendall Collier and Teresa Day have transformed a neoclassical building into a surprising special event facility with an impressive two-story ballroom and balcony. Floor-to-ceiling windows allow guests to experience all of the action, whether inside or out. For a more intimate area, the second-story balcony provides a chic, club feel with a view below. Along with the hundreds of twinkle lights, it is this connected quality that guests find so appealing at The Atrium.

Outside, a walled garden encompasses an Italian marble gazebo, a romantic three-tier fountain, and upper and lower private courtyards. Even when the weather does not cooperate, all of Magic Moments' venues offer both inside and outdoor spaces, making them venues for all seasons.

Because Magic Moments' properties are used solely for special events, each strives to enhance the event experience for every guest by offering award-winning food, flowers, and fun in unforgettable settings.

Rooted in a secret garden, The Atrium is nestled in the heart of town. The glass panels visually dissolve the barrier between inside and out to create an engaging blend of the two spaces.

Photograph by Jessica Horwitz

Photograph by John Day

Photograph by John Day

Photograph by John Day

Photograph by John Day

"To transform a space on a limited budget, nothing beats professional lighting."

—Kendall Collier

Right: Full Circle Lighting and Production added patterns of light showcasing the built-in dance floor to quickly alter the mood with magical results.

Facing page top: Numerous outdoor elements provide an amazing backdrop that can be enhanced to fit the host's style.

Facing page bottom: Whether indoors or out, with interactive stations or a seated dinner, the right setting can create an unforgettable dining experience.

Photograph by Jessica Horwitz

views

It is amazing how many new ideas come directly from our brides. After all, some of them have spent years planning, researching, mulling it over, and dreaming. "Handle with care" is our mantra.

Mansion on Forsyth Park

A memorable event should make guests feel as if they've been whisked away to another place or time. The Mansion on Forsyth Park does just that. The unique juxtaposition of a Victorian-Romanesque façade with stunning high-design interiors makes guests feel transported to another era.

Located in the heart of Savannah's legendary historic district, the Mansion represents a new era of style in this Southern city. From the moment guests enter the lobby, they experience chic elegance blended with classic European touches such as Versace rugs and 200-year-old Verona marble columns. The hotel's attentive staff ensures that every detail is perfected for events in the Viennese Ballroom, the Marble Garden Courtyard overlooking the pool, or the acclaimed 700 Drayton Restaurant.

The Mansion on Forsyth Park's cuisine is as artful as its stunning surroundings. Chef Michael Semancik of 700 Drayton and 700 Kitchen cooking school's Chef Darin Sehnert, who has appeared on Food Network and HGTV, create eclectic dishes that blend fresh, local ingredients with international preparations. From the unique on-site cooking school to the numerous lounges and 700 Drayton Restaurant, the Mansion leaves no taste bud uninspired. Forsyth Park, made famous in "Midnight in the Garden of Good and Evil," is just across the street, allowing guests to explore the timeless intrigue and excitement that is synonymous with Savannah.

The Viennese Ballroom is adorned with gold-leafed pillars, custom-designed wool carpet, gilded-thread draperies, 15-foot ceilings, European cut-crystal chandeliers, and an Imperial Grand Bösendorfer piano.

Photograph by John Bateman

Photograph by John Bateman

Photograph by John Bateman

Photograph by John Bateman

"The deliberate and mindful juxtaposition of antique pieces and modern design elements ensures a forward-looking ambience grounded by a healthy appreciation of the past."

—Mark Kessler

Within the Mansion's setting, a variety of spaces for both indoor and fresh-air events allows guests to choose the perfect location. Each area exudes its own unique ambience and maintains a continuity of opulence, in part through the hotel's collection of more than 400 pieces of original artwork.

Photograph courtesy of Mansion on Forsyth Park

views

While children are taught from an early age about fairy tales, they often become disillusioned at some point in their lives. When it comes to special events, we encourage the event host to bring that fairy tale back to life for guests.

Opera Atlanta

MICHELLE DAUBLE

From the first glance at Opera, visions of flappers, jazz music, and theatrical performances come to mind—and well they should. First built in the 1920s, Opera served as a performance theater for the Atlanta Woman's Club. Since its founding, the venue has undergone a myriad of changes—the most recent a multimillion dollar renovation in 2007. While the building's purpose has varied over the years, its theatrical roots have always remained at the forefront.

Set in the heart of Midtown, Opera exudes an intriguing historical ambience with hints of modern technology and style. Old World elegance with contemporary sophistication provides an exceptional setting in the three spaces at Opera. The spacious but cozy Opera House offers multiple connected levels. Mingling can occur in the Venetian Room under its skylights or out on the adjoining patio. A stunning city view complete with three 10-foot stone water features and cascading maples in Cabana provides the ultimate urban oasis.

The historical yet modern aura doesn't stop with the building. Director of Events Michelle Dauble, who boasts more than 10 years of experience in the private event industry, heads up the outstanding team that combines contemporary ideas with a quality of service reminiscent of a bygone era. On the culinary side, Executive Chef Jeffrey McGar, who apprenticed for several years under American Culinary Federation Certified Master Chefs, has established his own history with Opera's win of the 2009 Allie Award for Best Buffet/Reception Menu. His forward-thinking methodology provides custom menus for each event featuring restaurant-quality cuisine and world-fusion tastes. Opera's method of excellence is woven not only throughout each culinary work, but also through the professionally trained culinary staff, who exude passion in every step.

With three levels in the Opera House, guests can mingle throughout the rich décor and vibrant colors of the main room with its high ceilings and stunning architectural details, then move on to the second-floor balcony and third-floor mezzanine with a private bar, luxurious opera boxes, and stunning views of the entire room. The proscenium arch, red velvet curtains, and gold foil theater faces emanate the historical ambience of the original building.

Photograph by Ben Rose Photography

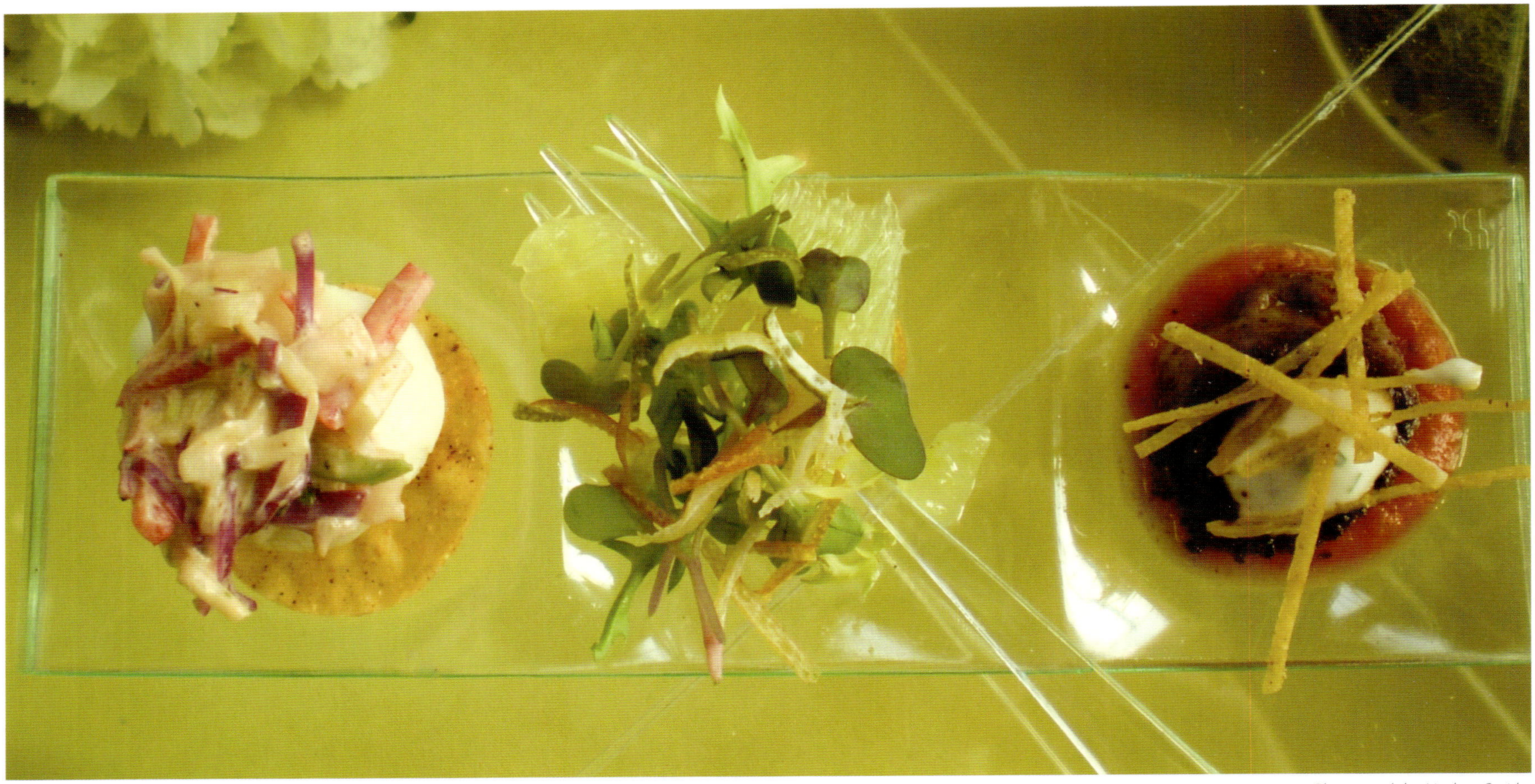

Photograph by Lindsay Smith

Photograph by Lindsay Smith

Photograph by Jeffrey McGar

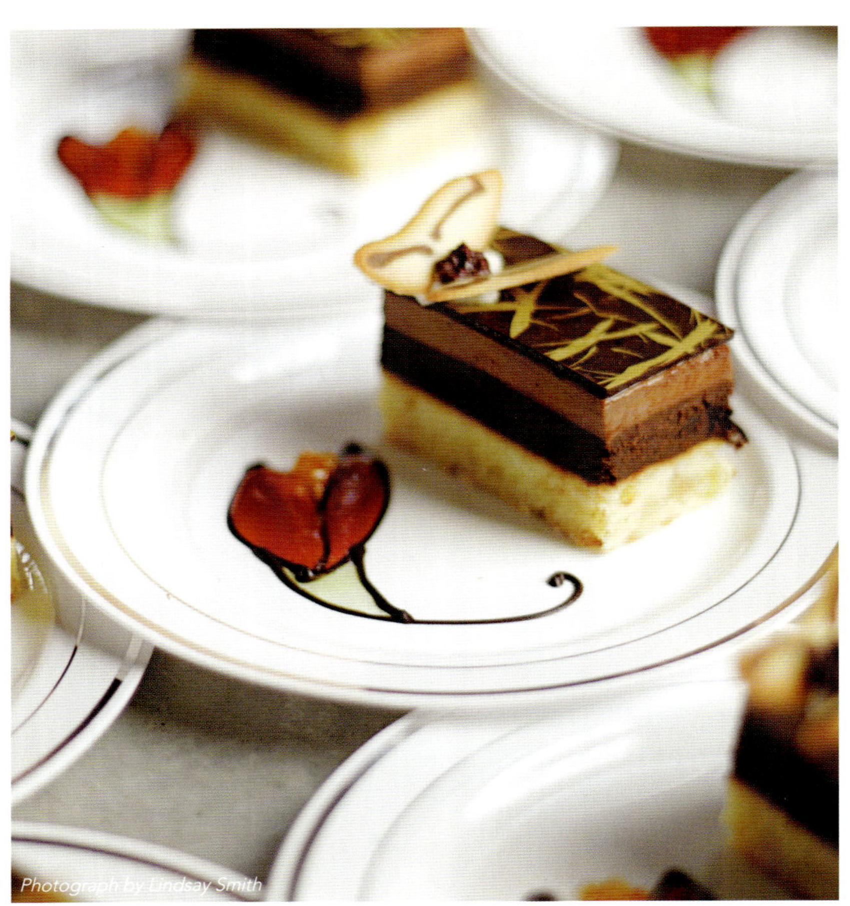

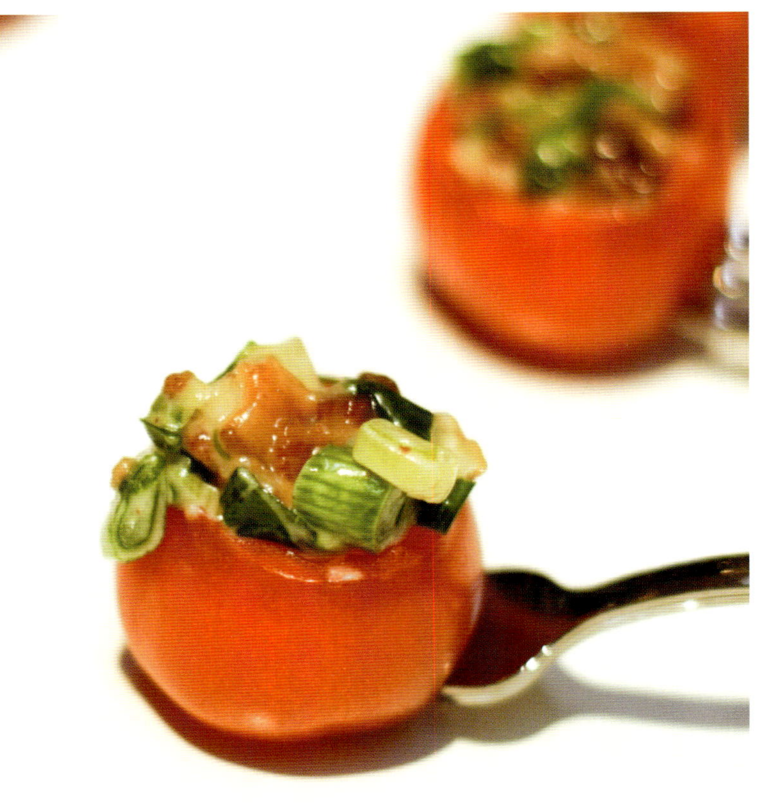

"Opera's historical flair and contemporary amenities allow every guest, whether young or old, to feel comfortable and engaged—this is the sign of a remarkable event."

—Michelle Dauble

Right: Cabana offers an amazing outdoor retreat with private cabanas and views of Midtown. Hosts often highlight the relaxing ambience to provide a contrast to the more lively Opera House.

Facing page: While each event's cuisine is unique, the tantalizing taste is always paramount. For an association meeting of event industry professionals, Chef Jeffrey McGar created a surf and turf dish with a scallop ceviche, a citrus salad, and an ancho-lime beef tenderloin. A delectable chocolate napoleon was featured for dessert. As one of the hors d'oeuvre selections, Chef McGar offered a BLT mini tomato, complete with smooth buttermilk ranch.

Photograph by Ben Rose Photography

views

A large part of the success for any celebration is in the passion of the people involved. Whether it's the caterer, the venue staff, or the florist, meet with those who will actually work the event to ensure they are passionate and dedicated.

Creating an

Ambience

Robert Long Flora Design

Robert Long

Describe beauty. Is it subtle or dramatic? Refined or raw? Restrained or wild? There really is no definition; and much is left to subjective interpretation. But sometimes an artist or designer can create something with undeniably high aesthetic value—which is exactly what Robert Long has done for nearly 20 years. He has mastered the art of creating beauty and finding the fine balance between opposing elements; nothing is too mild and nothing is too bold.

With Robert Long Flora Design, Robert really does achieve the impossible. He blends historical perspective, literary references, and art movements into an unexpected medium—and does so with unanimous praise. By embracing the arts as his ultimate inspiration, every arrangement incorporates elements of a great painting, literary work, or historical allusion. Located in Atlanta and working across the country, Robert gains inspiration through travel, study, and often times, the most unpredictable places. Fields of Scottish heather may inform a design, while a passage by Tolstoy could influence a Russian-themed dinner. Something as small as the shape of a tree or as grand as Louis XIV's lavishly appointed Palace of Versailles can spark an idea in Robert and launch the design of an event. From Kensington Palace to pop art images, any idea can be incorporated into a special occasion. Nothing is off limits.

It's possible to create drama without being ostentatious. By toning down one aspect of a design, I showed restraint and established an understated elegance for the occasion. I kept the colors soft and organic to infuse the event with a light, relaxed feel.

Photograph by Priscilla Wannamaker

Photograph by Priscilla Wannamaker

Photograph by Priscilla Wannamaker

Photograph by Priscilla Wannamaker

Above: Centerpieces vary as widely as flower varieties do; and I often use the bride's favorite flower as an inspiration to create distinct arrangements.

Facing page: We used muted lighting and uplit the ceiling to downplay the presence of bold colors and dramatic accessories. The exotic gem lapis lazuli was our inspiration for the brilliant colors of the evening's gala.

"By taking a fresh approach to classic events, designers stimulate the imagination."

—Robert Long

"Always show restraint, even when it's over-the-top."

—Robert Long

Above: For an event centered around the Old South, my team and I were able to fuse the best of old and new to create our signature version of Southern Nouvelle. We used earth tones to reflect tradition while boxed gardenia trees gave a look forward.

Facing page: Whites and creams look beautiful with almost any color, and I like to take advantage of the crisp, clean look it affords a space. Whether it's set against lavender, green, or silver, white hues take on a completely different look.

Photograph by Marcus Krause

Photograph by Marcus Krause

Photograph by Marcus Krause

Photograph by Jim Fitts

Wray
e Hurrell 1934
Myrna Loy
by Clarence Sinclair Bull 1932
Marlene Dietr
Veronica Lake
by George Hurrell 19
Photograph by Jim Fitts

Photograph by Jim Fitts

Above: Art history and literature took center stage at a white-tie museum reception. Separated into rooms, groups of guests got to view artwork based on the mythology surrounding the life of Aphrodite. Blue tones alluded to the watery birth of the goddess.

Facing page top: The pop art version of "Pygmalion" made for eye-catching imagery and great conversation.

Facing page bottom: We revealed the 20th-century's version of Aphrodite with soft, vintage black-and-white images of Hollywood's goddesses.

"It always goes back to history."

—Robert Long

Photograph by Marcus Krause

I used a mixture of surfaces and shapes to stimulate the eye. From shiny reflective glass and sleek oval stones, to round, layered foliage and thin, extended arrangements, each texture evokes a strong response. Our goal was to capture the essence of "De-Lovely," the film chronicling the life of lyricist and composer Cole Porter.

Photograph by Marcus Krause

Photograph by Marcus Krause

Photograph by Marcus Krause

Photograph by Philip Shone

Photograph by Philip Shone

Photograph by Philip Shone

Photograph by Philip Shone

Passion always comes across in my work. By taking the personality and taste of the host or hostess and blending my enthusiasm into the design, I create rooms with just the right amount of drama.

views

When I design, I pay attention to four fundamentals: hue, height, harmony, and history. They're critical to orchestrating a room and making the aesthetic a success. Even for the smallest dinners, this rule of thumb works beautifully and can be adapted for any specific taste. By bringing in a historical aspect, the event takes on personality and depth that wouldn't be present otherwise.

Active Production and Design, Inc.

MATTHEW R. CLOUSER | STEVEN M. ZAUG | JOHN E. FOX

A white room leaves ample freedom for adding stunning visual design, but rarely does a lighting designer work with a blank canvas. In most events, fabulous décor and scrumptious displays of food already exist. So Active Production and Design team members bring the existing elements to life by enhancing the décor, food, and theme and by blending the lighting elements into the background.

For nearly two decades, founder Matt Clouser has instilled a stunning sense of creativity and an award-winning style into his experienced audiovisual design team—who he trusts unequivocally to do the job correctly. In part, the team members' success stems from their ability to fulfill nearly every production need with Active's enormous quantity of production equipment. Active prides itself on being an industry resource and can be counted on to accommodate every request and answer every question.

From large events in a 100,000-square-foot space in Las Vegas to an intimate reception at a residence, Active Production and Design has seen and done it all. The team members' extensive and varied backgrounds allow a perfect harmony of talent and creative thinking when working with the art of lighting and event production. Even when Active Production and Design's audiovisual role is complete, the team never hesitates to help complete the overall event setup because of their teamwork mentality and dedication to the event.

At an annual fundraising gala, we used a variety of blue hues and a moving wave pattern of gobo lights to coordinate with the Bell'acqua theme under the enormous tent. The custom chandeliers and the luster of the centerpieces were highlighted to continue the elegant underwater ambience that fused well with the magnificent garden setting.

"

Photograph by Clydette R. Morton, Active Production and Design

Photograph by Clydette R. Morton, Active Production and Design

Photograph by Clydette R. Morton, Active Production and Design

Above and left: Annual fundraiser galas provide a unique opportunity to work in the same venue but create something completely different each year. With the deep blue color wash permeating the entire space at the Bell'acqua event, white lights add a touch of brightness to highlight certain elements, such as the centerpieces. Featuring a more lively shade of pink that harmonized with the rest of the décor, the Flight of Fancy-themed gala portrayed a whimsical, springtime feel. The butterfly gobos on the tent ceiling added the proverbial icing on the top of the cake.

Facing page: Challenges exist in nearly every design, but we love a challenge. At an industry conference reception with a Passionata theme, communication was critical because of the immense number of volunteers for the event and no single point person. At a corporate awards show featuring acrobatic entertainers, a small window of rehearsal time made preparation and the use of intelligent lighting key.

"Somewhere between being a
musician and a lighting coordinator,
I fell in love with the creative, artsy
aspect of lighting design."

—Matthew R. Clouser

Photograph by Mark Baker Creative

Photograph by Matt Clouser, Active Production and Design

Photograph by Tim Wilkerson Photography

Photograph by Clydette R. Morton, Active Production and Design

Photograph by Clydette R. Morton, Active Production and Design

Photograph by Tim Wilkerson Photography

Above: Warm hues with a hint of purple combined with the lighting design on the floor accentuate the otherwise formal space but still allude to elegance. The pin spotting of the cake focuses all attention on the most desired element.

Facing page: Whether beam effects with gobo lights dance on a checkered dance floor, pin spots meld with the clean lines for an "inside the art" feel, or wavy blues and purples take guests deep under water, the visual aspect can be changed and massaged until just the right ambience is captured.

"Lighting can breathe life into the décor and floral elements."

—Matthew R. Clouser

"The lighting of an event is a beautiful dance with all of the other elements in the program."

—Jason Shadix

Above: The historic Train Shed that served as a covered city parking lot during the day was transformed into an elegant soirée. We diverted the focus to the architectural elements of the shed and the beautiful décor with multicultural lighting. Italian string bulbs on the ceiling, Japanese lanterns above lounge areas, and the bright pink on the drapery infused color without overwhelming the area.

Facing page: While some events dictate more conventional lighting—such as the Under the Sea-themed event at which we focused on color saturation to maintain the feel for the entire program—other programs need versatility and flexibility. At a highbrow soirée, a warm orange palette during cocktails was transformed into a lively afterparty. During dinner, a request for over-the-top design was achieved by enhancing the floral and décor with directional lighting and changing the mood of the event with LED lights that slowly changed colors behind the fabric and floral canopy.

Photograph by Philip Shone

Photograph by Philip Shone

Photograph by Ray Swords Photography

Photograph by Northlight Photography

Photograph by Priscilla Wannamaker

Photograph by Color and Magic

Photograph by Bob Vardaman Designs

Right: The details make the high-end events luxurious. At a reception, gobo lighting on the floor creates a focal point that prompts guests to notice the magnificent floral arrangement, which otherwise might have simply blended in with the traditional white wedding scheme.

Facing page: Dramatic scenery is the order of the day. From a sky on stretched fabric created with conventional and intelligent lighting to over 500 Japanese paper lanterns with virtually no infrastructure from which to hang, a single spotlight and circular projection screen that focuses attention on the performer to a unique monochromatic theme in each of the venue's rooms, the use of color and lighting can make or break an event's emphasis.

Photograph by Tim Wilkerson Photography

Each event needs a vision. Once that vision is established, determine how to express it to those partnering in the event design and allow the professionals to run with the dream. We love the creative element that allows us to craft something completely custom and out of this world.

TONY BREWER & COMPANY

TONY BREWER

The concept of teamwork takes on an entirely new meaning at Tony Brewer & Company. Even though Tony Brewer is the founder, he firmly believes that the rest of his team is just as important as he is.

With an innate knack for design and creativity—partially from his mother's example as a wonderful hostess—Tony planned his first wedding at age 14 for a family friend. Soon thereafter, he left his Mississippi home and the family's construction business and moved to Atlanta, where he jumped headfirst into event planning and design.

After nearly 30 years in the industry, Tony has built a storehouse of knowledge and experience that ensures each event is so well-planned and organized that it can virtually run itself. Paired with his extreme attention to detail—to the point at which he coordinates with landscapers to make sure sprinklers don't go off during an event—Tony's theatrical touch makes for unprecedented ideas. Most importantly, he's surrounded himself with exceptional, seasoned people who turn ordinary events into truly extraordinary ones. From his core team, Shawn Alexander, Janet Dockery, Jenna Hrabovsky, Randall Sheffield, and Eleanor Simmons, to countless hourly employees, each team member adds the finishing details on Tony's brilliant, big-picture visions.

Events benefiting nonprofits are a much-welcomed opportunity to make a difference in the community. At the Piedmont Ball—the only white-tie ball in the city—the sophisticated décor was inspired by the theme, "An Age of Elegance." Careful use of lavish fabrics, thousands of roses, highly polished silver, and custom china all came together to commemorate the Centennial Celebration of Piedmont Hospital.

Photograph by Picture This! Photography

"The orientation of each object in the room affects the energy of the entire event."

—Tony Brewer

Right: Custom linens backed by a 10-foot-tall hedge wall set the stage for a spring ambience. My inspiration came from the celadon vase, which—along with the delicate branches—added a structural element to give dimension to the table.

Facing page: Simple changes in the color or texture of a floral arrangement can make a drastic difference in the ambience. Abundant greenery gives off a garden feel, an all-white motif speaks of vintage Hollywood, and a bit of soft color adds a romantic air to the atmosphere.

Photograph by Michael Ray White

"Today, with so many resources from around the world at our fingertips, nothing beats the pleasure of seeing it all come together to create a feast for the senses."

—Tony Brewer

"Without flowers, an event feels empty and cold. Arrangements make the party."

—Darryl Wiseman

Photograph by The Decisive Moment

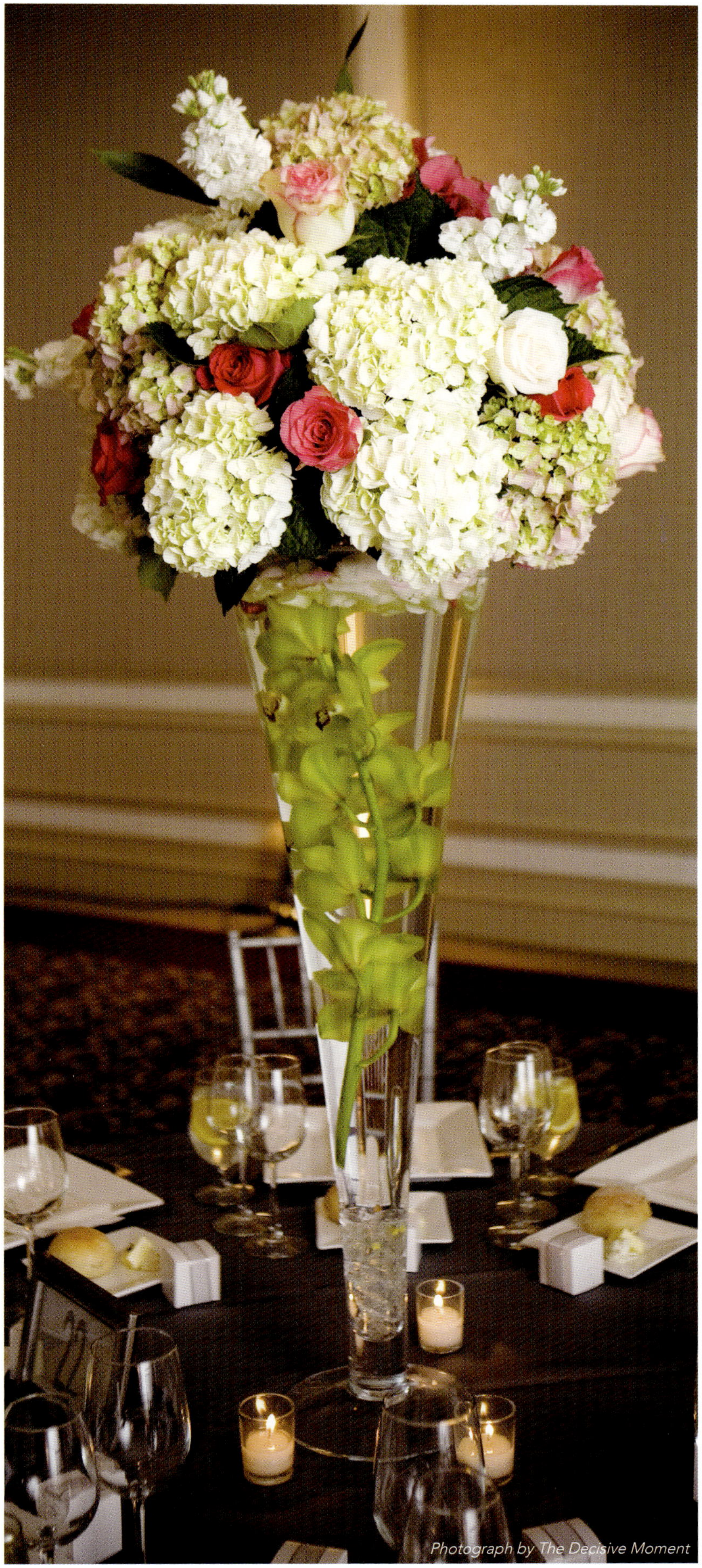

Photograph by The Decisive Moment

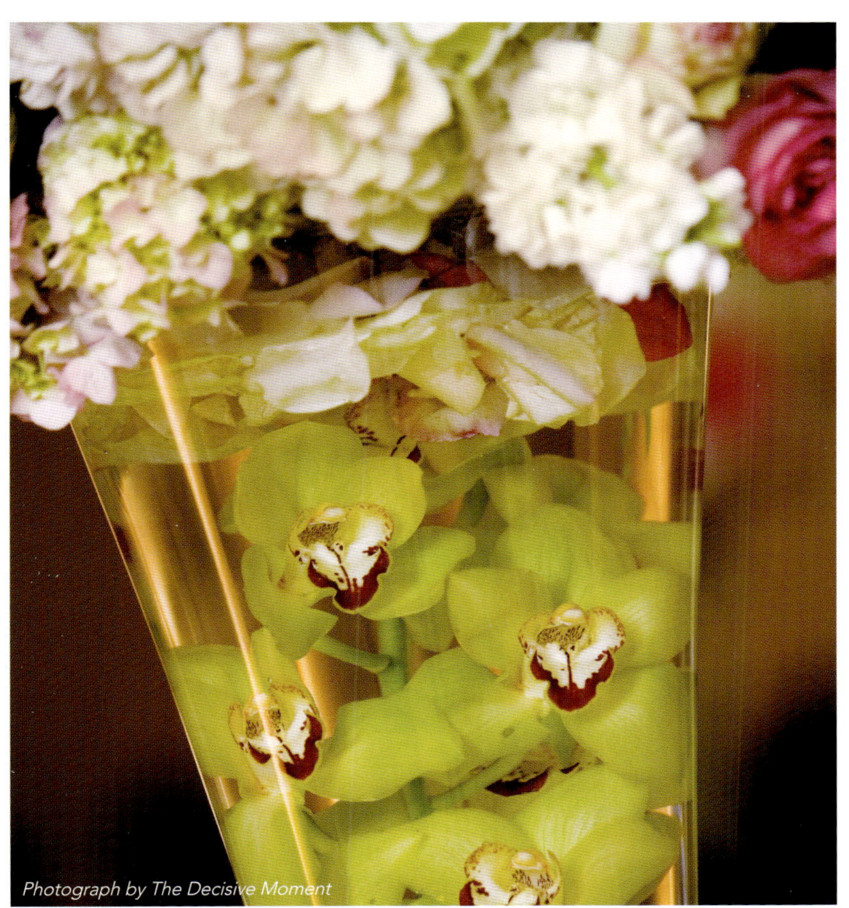

Photograph by Philip Shone

"When everyone involved in the planning process shares a high level of comfort and camaraderie, it carries over to the event and gives the evening a fun, calm energy."

—Darryl Wiseman

Right: I emphasize the fact that we don't just design events—we make conversation pieces. By blending antique candelabras with an elegant mix of flowers, we created a warm, Old World look that conveyed true elegance and gave the space a complete look. We placed silver julep cups on the tables as well, adding visual interest with varying heights.

Facing page: When a bride wanted a glamorous, Hollywood reception, that's exactly what we gave her. The décor portrayed a feminine, imaginative feel with vivid colors and graceful details. The couple left the event in an elaborate carriage—true fairy-tale fashion.

Photograph by Rene Brock Photography

views

Certain aspects of an event are worth spending a little extra money and shouldn't be kept on a tight budget. High quality linens will go far in creating a luxurious event; guests will have the opportunity to see them up close and feel the rich textures. Candles are also imperative to craft the ambience you're looking for—don't hesitate to invest in them.

EVENT DESIGN GROUP
MYRNA ANTAR | DEB STEEGE

At the helm of Event Design Group's collective of professionals are executive director Myrna Antar—who has nearly two decades of experience in event management—and managing director Deb Steege—whose schooling in theatrical set design and her penchant for multidimensional events have led to numerous awards. With leaders like these and a just-as-impressive team, it's no wonder their work has made its way around the globe.

With an exceptional array of event design and décor since 1992, Event Design Group nearly does it all—from overall planning and design to the nitty-gritty creation and management of events. And whether it's a simple but important dinner for two or large-scale convention entertainment, the group's professionals inject their passion and fresh perspectives; the end results are innovative events featuring contemporary flair.

Creativity drives each member of the Event Design Group team. Staying constantly aware of their surroundings, their inspiration comes from a range of places, objects, and experiences. They can be inspired by a paint-peeled barn, an antique picture frame, or a distant childhood memory. Their radar is always running. The professionals at Event Design Group are adept at translating these everyday experiences and objects into fodder for future designs.

A summer event prompted senior designer Christopher Macksey to create an indoor summer garden that oozed romance. Peonies and lilacs' soft colors and textures provided the perfect focal point at the top of an acanthus leaf candelabra.

Photograph by Ric Mershon Photographers

Photograph by Eric Wittmayer

Photograph courtesy of Event Design Group

Above: Through the use of soft colors, fabrics, and lighting, the room takes on an ethereal look to coordinate with the theme, which features the big band era of the 1940s.

Facing page: Team member Louis Bourne was asked to create an intimate dinner setting for 80 guests in a space designed to hold 500. We sectioned off a pre-function area with different styled drapery and lighting and broke up the space using both rounds and aged wooden farmhouse tables. A Tuscan theme transcended the entire area to maintain a consistent feel.

"You don't have to be complicated to be fabulous."

—Deb Steege

Photograph by Ric Mershon Photographers

Photograph courtesy of Event Design Group

Photograph courtesy of Event Design Group

Photograph courtesy of Event Design Group

Right: A long, narrow space needed drama, so we created custom wall elements that included painted images set in a three-dimensional frame. Real, fresh-cut flowers and branches jut out from the center for a theatrical effect.

Facing page: Many elements go into the perfect floral centerpieces, including the style and color of the flowers as well as their accessories. Lush flowers and candlelight can make a huge impact yet create a more intimate atmosphere. Inspirations from the seasons—with cool purples for winter and bright hues for summer—can make four different arrangements at one event have a synergetic effect. Even the vases can enhance the atmosphere, as with tall, glass containers that allow clear sight lines to the stage.

Photograph courtesy of Event Design Group

views

If it's difficult to choose one specific style or color for an event, don't force yourself to make a decision. Bring in a trusted professional who can help you weave together your ideas and incorporate the varying styles in a pleasing way.

EventScapes

J. WILBUR SMITH

Integrity and comfort are two of the most important words for J. Wilbur Smith at EventScapes. Woven throughout each of his projects, whether simple, extraordinary, or somewhere in between, these ideals are essential in creating fabulous events that address the event hosts as well as the guests.

From the first moment planning begins, J. Wilbur focuses on honesty, which encompasses relaying accurate information, being realistic about his ability to meet expectations, as well as truly learning about the hosts and their event goals. From thorough questions to perusing magazines for ideas to browsing EventScapes' large showroom, event hosts are given every opportunity to express their likes and dislikes, their hopes and dreams for the event. All of this culminates in J. Wilbur's hands-on approach; his involvement extends from the original creative process all the way to production and then overseeing the event setup. By following an event from beginning to end, he carries the design ideas from paper to actuality and instills a confidence that puts even the most nervous host at ease.

J. Wilbur and his team take every step necessary to guarantee the ultimate comfort of the guests. With people drawn to celebrations that are impressive but more importantly allow guests to simply be together, sacrificing comfort is not an option. Accomplished through his dedicated team—some who have worked more than a decade with EventScapes—celebrations designed by J. Wilbur maximize the aspects involved to forge a process and an event that exceed expectations.

A bar mitzvah at The Ritz-Carlton, Buckhead provided the challenge of capturing an upscale celebration while maintaining a whimsical aspect. Helene & Company brought in inspiration from summer in the Hamptons and the guest of honor's love of surfing, so we incorporated an underwater ambience—complete with seashells on the table and starfish suspended above the centerpieces—and added sophisticated accents with the floral arrangements and stemmed goblets.

Photograph by Ric Mershon Photographers

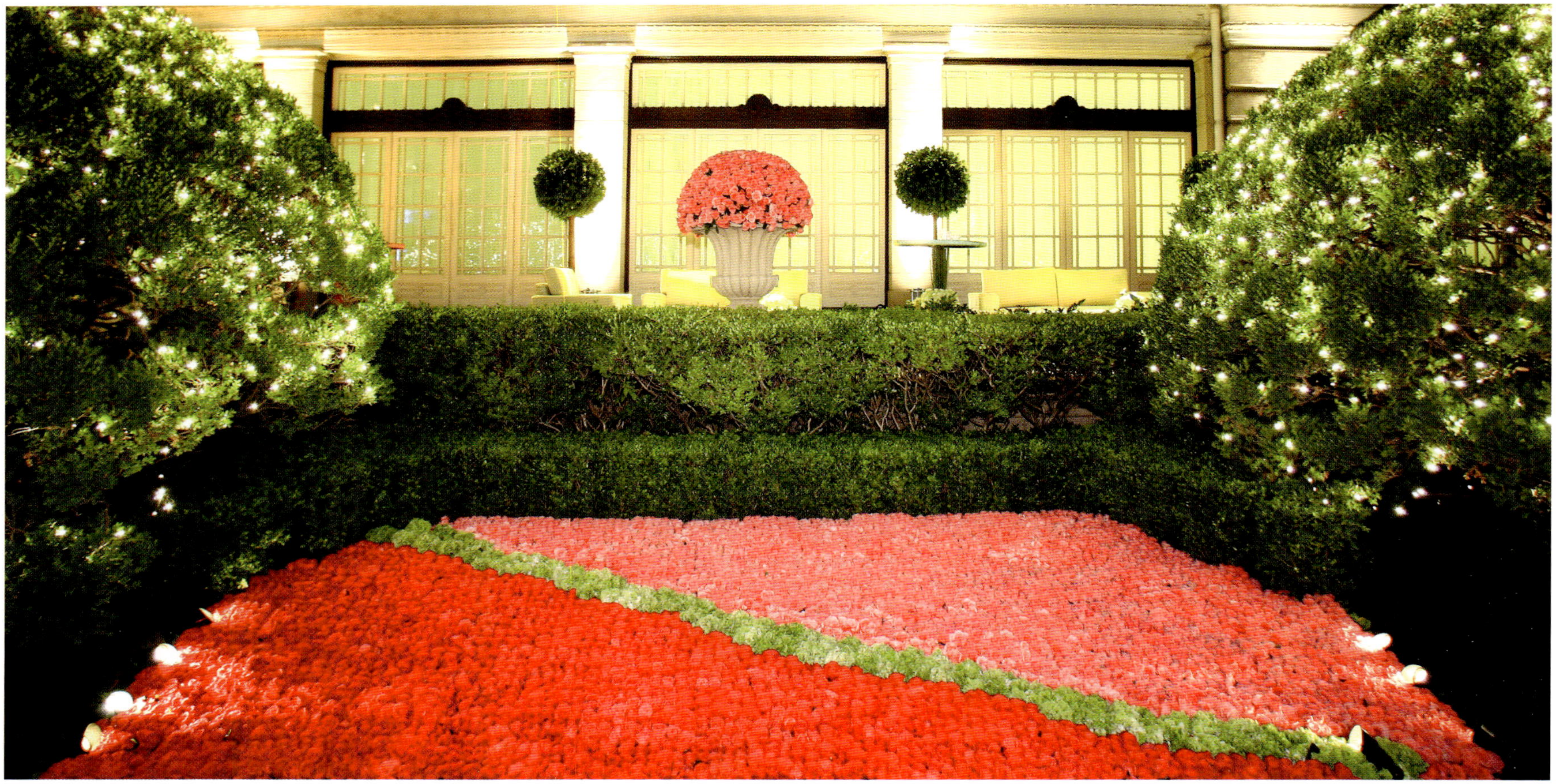

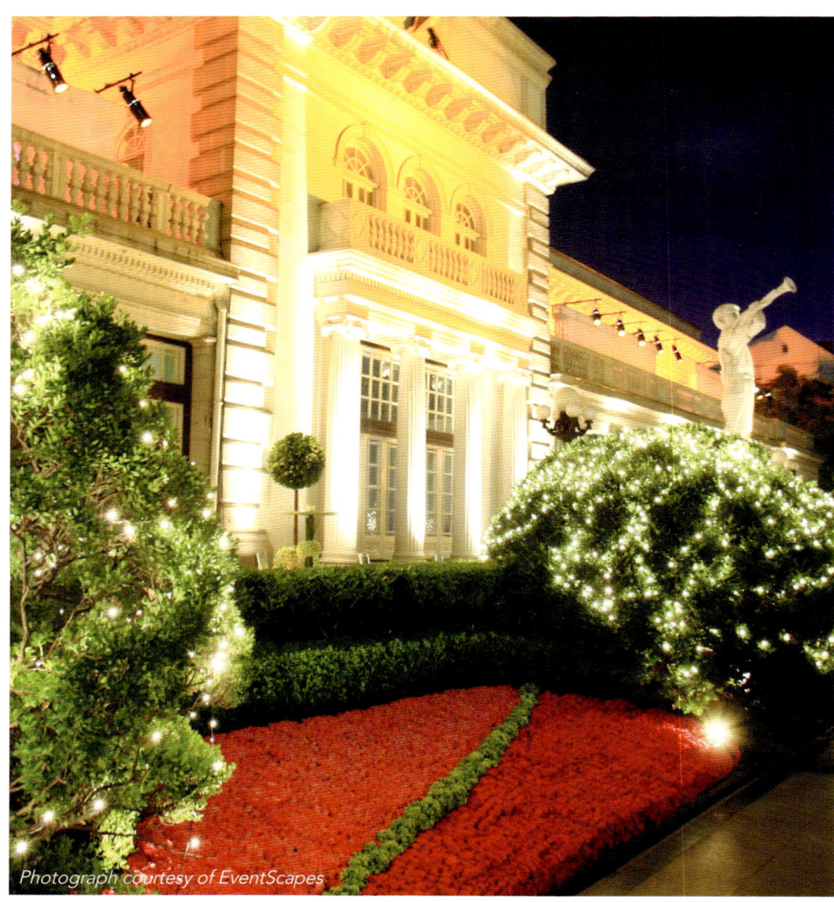

Photograph courtesy of EventScapes

Photograph courtesy of EventScapes

At the Children's Palace in Shanghai, I focused on designing an elegant, welcoming evening that showed off the city's beauty. Four gardens surrounding the palace needed a new life for the event, so we replaced the existing flora with 5,000 roses in each garden and a lush stripe of green hydrangeas. Along the walkway, we reproduced a few of the existing urns to maintain the integrity of the location and filled each of those with hundreds of roses. The terrace level contained custom highboy tables covered with horsetail and accented with balls of roses. Handmade boxwood hedge topiaries added additional height. Warm lighting throughout the gardens and highlighting the beautiful exterior captured the essence of the mood.

"Celebrations inject meaning into life and reflect the lives of those involved."

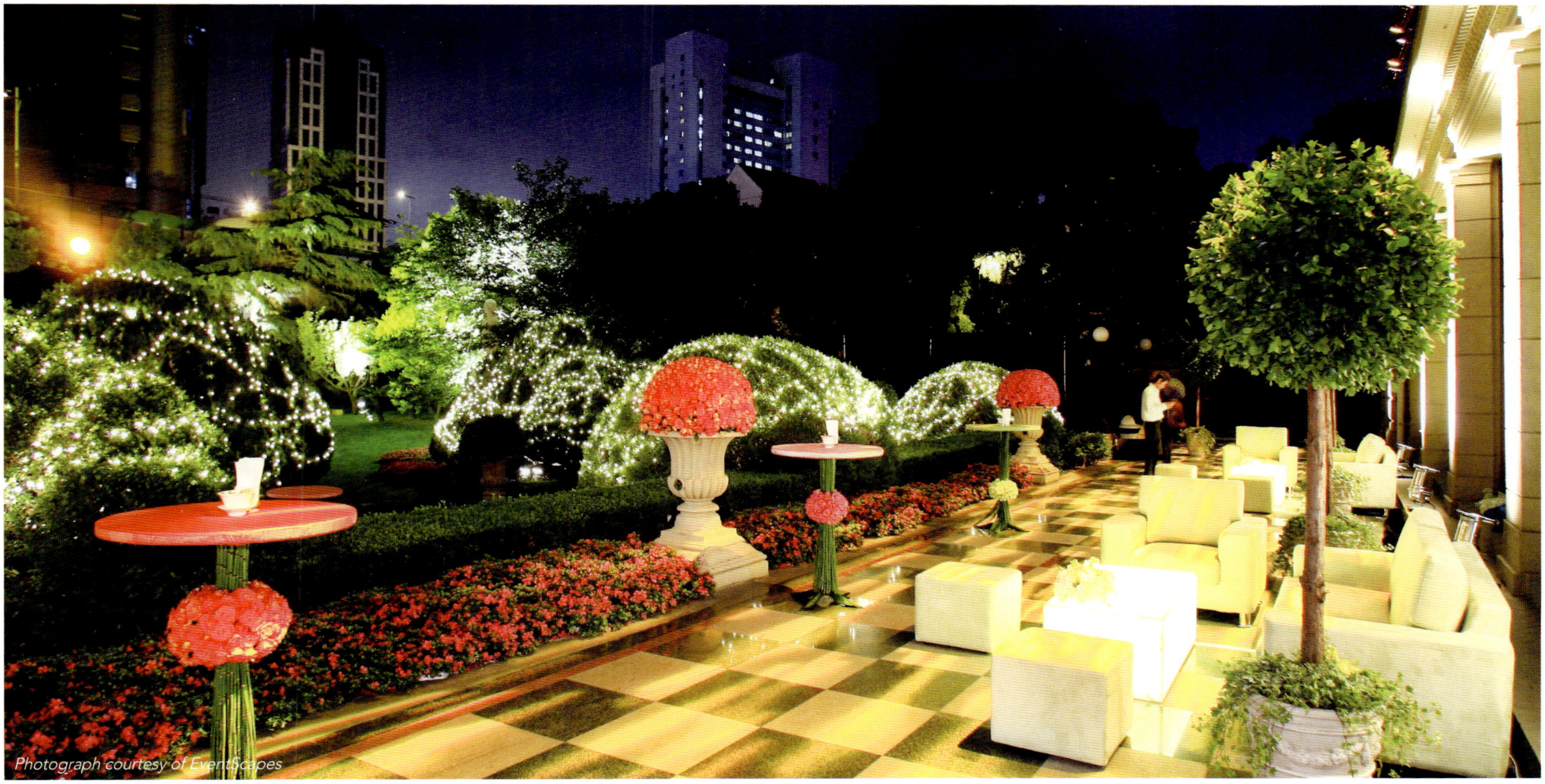

—J. Wilbur Smith

Pirates Cove
Port Royal

"Instead of a themed event, use color to inject energy and establish the overall desired ambience."

—J. Wilbur Smith

Right: To accommodate the bride's desire for a natural ambience and the parents' preference for upscale elegance, we worked with Helene & Company to highlight refined nature through sandblasted manzanita branches, modern floral pomanders, and hand-strung crystals.

Facing page top: A larger-than-life flower, created with floral pomanders surrounded by mirrored organza-covered petals, engenders the fantasy ambience instilled by Helene & Company. We draped hot pink crinkle taffeta linens over the highboy tables and topped them with custom mosaics. The custom bar-height estate tables are enhanced with water droplet ribbon and metallic fuchsia trim.

Facing page bottom: Guests entered the Caribbean-inspired event, orchestrated by WM Events, via a plank walkway that was flanked with dock pilings, lush foliage, and the option to journey to Port Royal or the daunting Pirates Cove. Inside, we transformed the ballroom with a three-layer handmade chandelier of locally grown bamboo, six fire pots, foliage, torn burlap, and more than 1,000 lights. Pirate ship crawling ropes extend the look an additional 30 feet in each direction.

Photograph by Denis Reggie Photographers

views

For any event professional, learning what the host dislikes is just as important as determining what they like. When discussing ideas and details for an event, be sure to express both the things you'd imagine seeing at your event and the items you have no desire to use. This saves time in the planning process and helps facilitate an outstanding event.

A Legendary Event

TONY CONWAY

Inspiration for design can come from countless places, as evidenced by A Legendary Event's creative director Steve Welsh and the entire creative team. Steve, who has a background in construction along with extensive experience working with interior designers and architects, uses his knowledge to find unique designs in unusual places—such as a book about color, floral design, or the treating of antique woods. Steve also draws on his extensive travel to incorporate atypical containers, pottery, baskets, glass, and memorabilia to create his signature design and floral looks.

Beginning with president and owner Tony Conway, who first started A Legendary Event with a catering division and expanded to floral and event design in 2006, the entire team works from a place of inspiration. The team also stays up-to-date with current fashion, seamlessly incorporating the season's newest colors, fabrics, and textures into their event designs. Whether the overall look is ruffled or sleek-lined, trendy elements appear at every turn.

Centered on first taking care of the event host and then wowing the guests, A Legendary Event's team appraises the host's wishes, reviews the space from every angle, and then brainstorms to take the design a step beyond the imaginable. Ultimately, the goal is to work within a budget to maintain the event's vision through unexpected excitement.

Working within a budget and an '80s prom theme, we designed a simple but elegant centerpiece with baby's breath and a clear celebration vase. The dance of color from the specialty lighting adds dimension and drama to the drapery treatment and overall room ambience.

Photograph by Ross DeLoach

Left: Our "Feast in the Forest" table celebrates the lush abundance of the forest's bounty—dark Champagne grapes, blackberries, currants, and pomegranates. As if from years of wild growth, the table is embedded with gnarled branches, curly willows, moss, lichen, and river rocks set adrift by the rainy season.

Facing page top and bottom left: Originally we created our sustainable table in response to a drought. We paved the entire table surface with wheat grass and added a series of vignettes using hearty succulents, cacti, and unique ground cover such as hens and chicks, flapjack succulents, and creeping sedum. A quirky combination of kosher rock salt, split peas, and personalized name place cards were visible through each hand-cut recycled glass section that topped each place setting. Each guest received a potted plant from the tablescape as a gift, and we donated the rest to Captain Planet Foundation for future use or fundraising purposes.

Facing page bottom right: Beautiful orchids embellish a contemporary table setting.

Photograph by Greg Mooney

Photograph by Greg Mooney

Photograph by Laura Stone

Photograph by Dawn Brewer

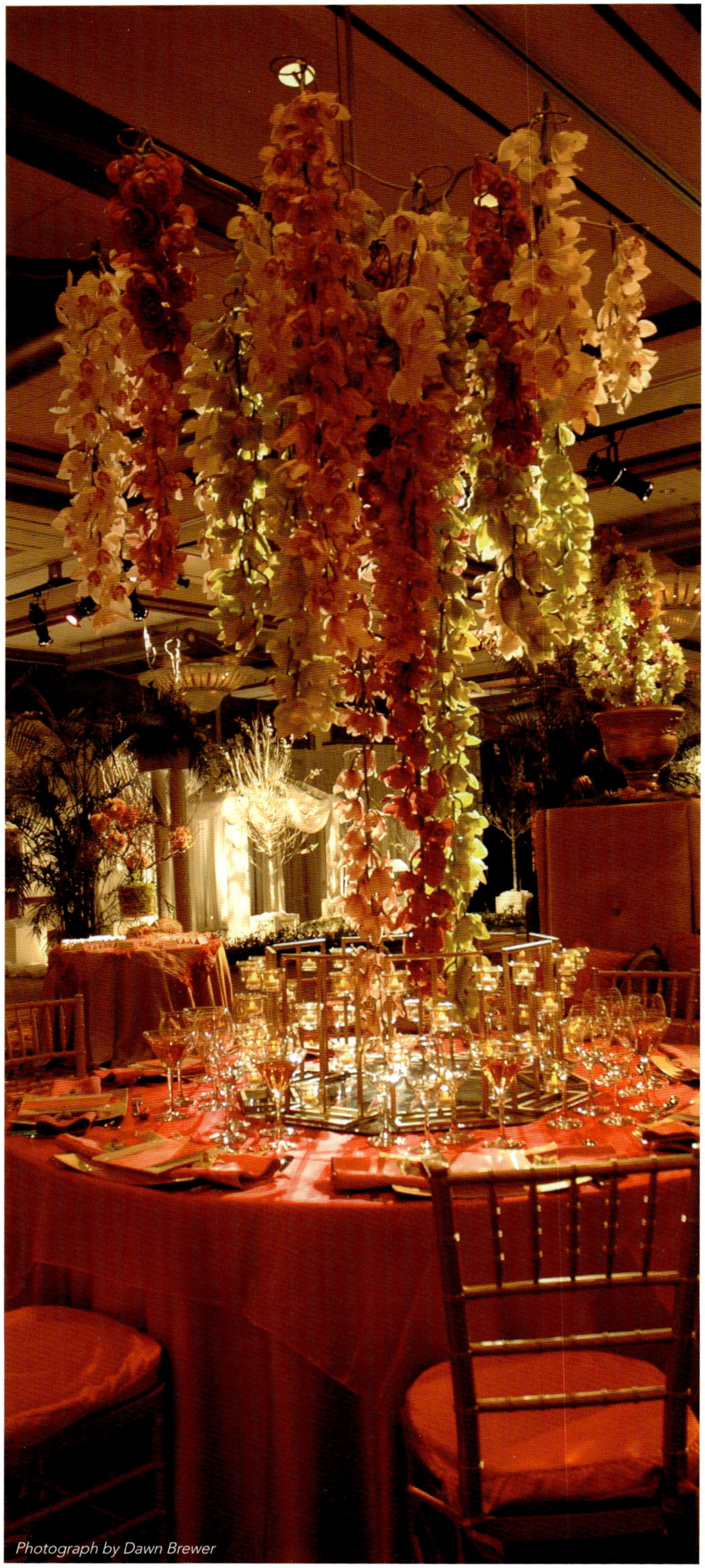
Photograph by Dawn Brewer

Photograph by John Day

Photograph by Jim Fitts

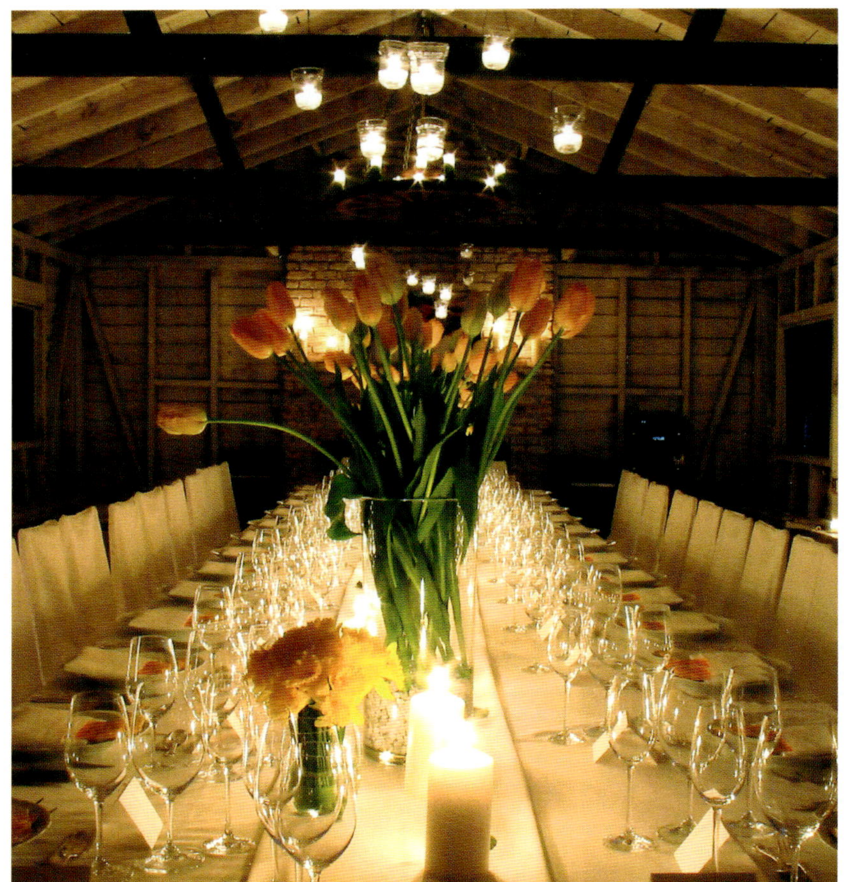

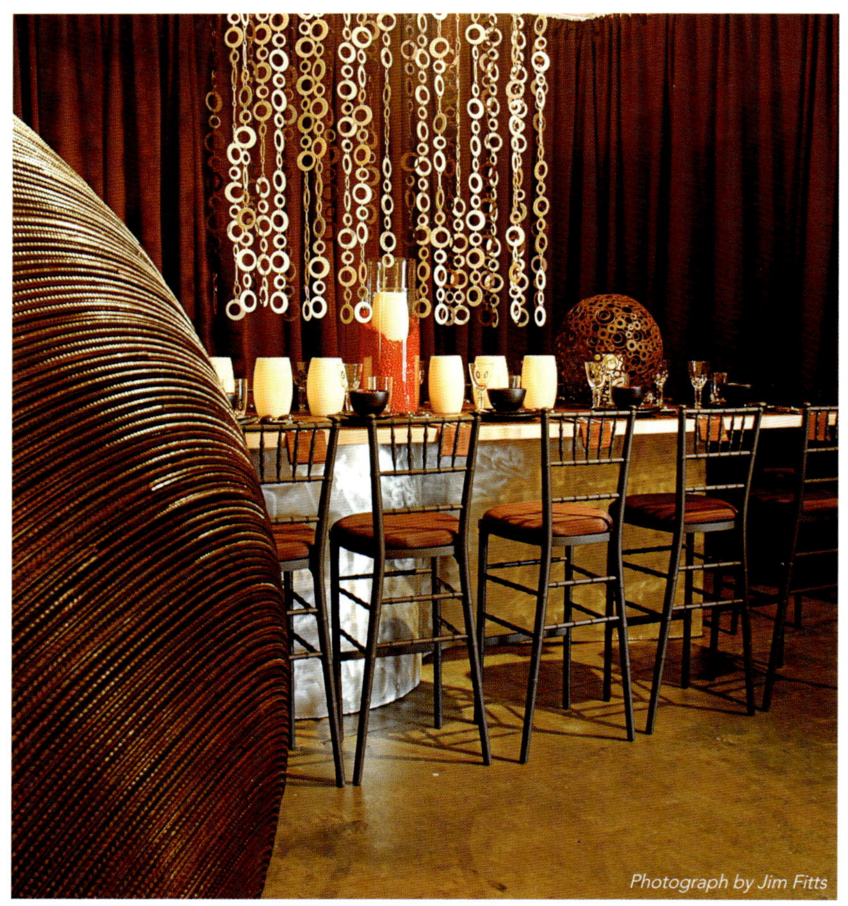

"The 'what if' scenario is immensely important in brainstorming sessions to create new and exciting ideas."

—Tony Conway

Right: The Bedouin-style drapery was one of the Egyptian-themed décor elements that we designed for the special event space at King Tut's exhibit at the Atlanta Civic Center. Two distinct spaces—the Luxor Lounge and Pharaoh's Palace—accommodated up to 400 people for events.

Facing page left: At a recent wedding, we created a chandelier of cymbidium orchids that rained down from the ceiling for a unique and dramatic centerpiece.

Facing page top right: For an intimate dinner in a private home, we placed more than 800 candles on and above the table as the only source of light in the room. The illuminated tulip centerpiece was the ideal focal point for such an elegant evening.

Facing page bottom right: Designed by our creative director, the chocolate table centered the space. Along with other elements, a mod chocolate chandelier and a massive chocolate decorative ball gave off a delightful scent of warming chocolate as the evening progressed.

Photograph by Greg Mooney

views

The wow factor should occur at each step of the event, so that guests are constantly encountering an unexpected surprise throughout the evening. Just when they think the entertainment is complete, for example, introduce something new, like mini cotton candy treats during dancing.

The MAGNUM Companies, Ltd.

TODD FINCH

For Todd Finch, president of The MAGNUM Companies, Ltd., lighting production can be described as painting a picture with light, texture, and color. The amount and placement of light in a room can completely transform the mood and ambience. So too can pattern and color. Whether it's a warm red or a cold blue, an exciting orange or a relaxing purple, the hue can affect the human emotion and play on the sense of sight.

This philosophy was garnered through years working in various areas of MAGNUM, which was started by his parents in 1980. Todd, who took on the leading role at MAGNUM in 2006, continues in his parents' tradition by focusing on teamwork and a near obsession with the details.

Teamwork at MAGNUM starts within the organization, but doesn't end there. During event setup, team members highly value the other vendors and event staff because they all operate interdependently. One cannot be successful without the other. As for the details, Todd believes both the process of working through the details as well as the actual minutiae are equally and desperately important. He insists his team must accomplish the end result while ensuring the process along the way was performed with integrity and just a bit of fun. From its humble beginning to its award-winning present and through to the unhindered future, MAGNUM's unwavering principle and passionate outlook endure.

The Piedmont Driving Club facility was challenging because there was no pre-existing infrastructure. After designing a structural plan, we created a winter wonderland using periwinkle blue. Pin spots highlighted the dazzling features and added a glow to the room.

Photograph by Picture This! Photography

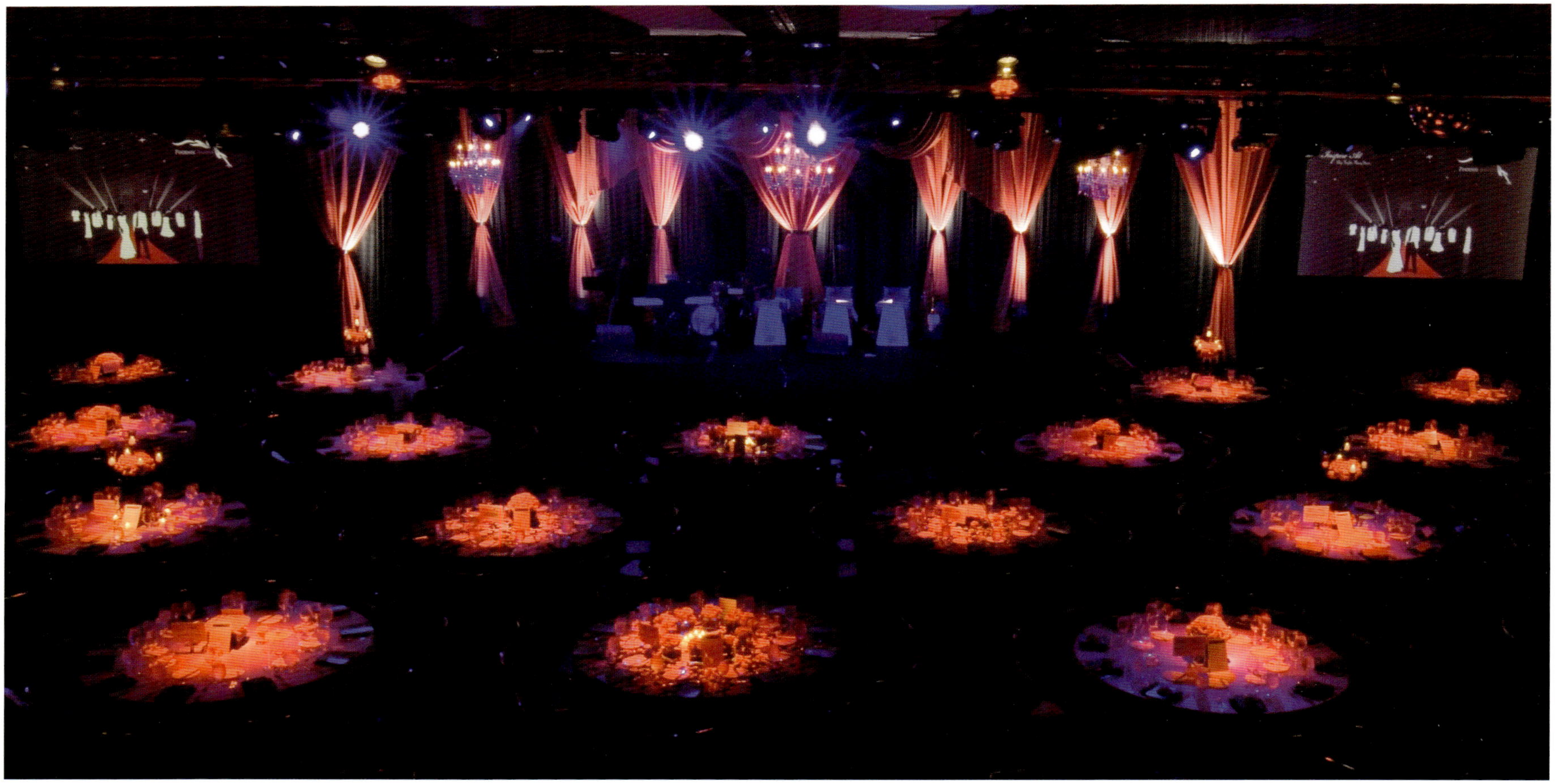

Photograph by Brandon Ward

Photograph by Brandon Ward

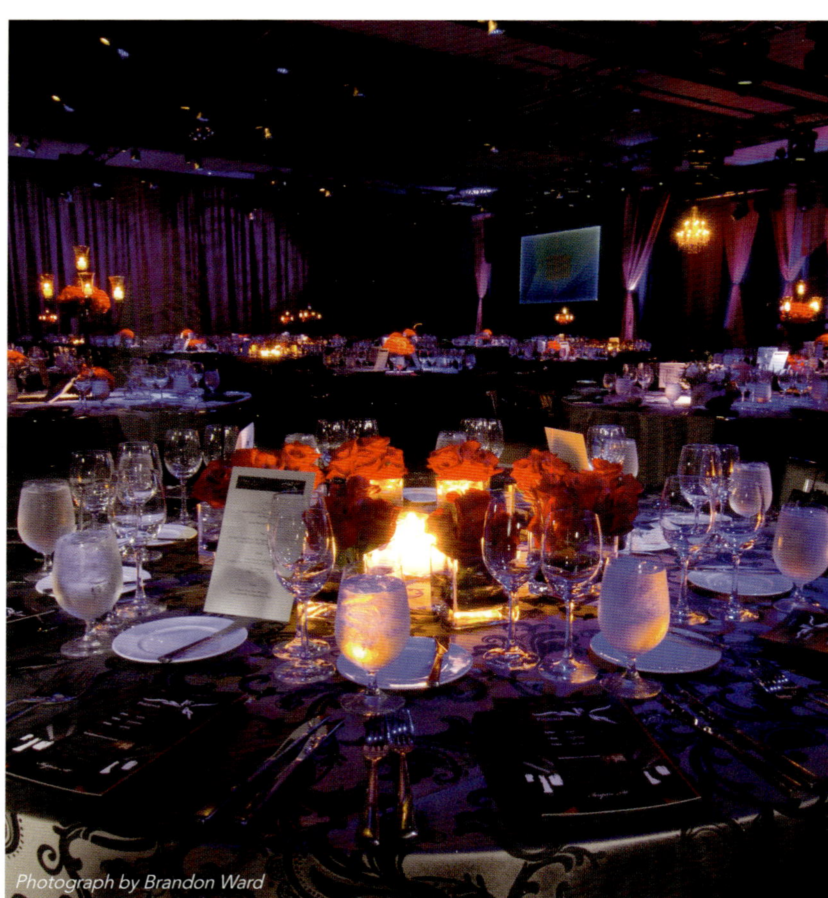

Above and left: An Academy Awards-style setting exuded an elegant and sophisticated glam. The dramatic surroundings were topped off with overhead LED lights that shone on the tables and changed colors throughout the evening.

Facing page: At a fundraiser for the High Museum of Art, we brought the event's invitation to life using light. After we transformed over 25,000 square feet, the purple and blue colors offered a vibrant, fun sophistication. We added additional technology by using screens so auction bidders could closely see the available items.

"Lighting production is like working a puzzle—the pieces and parts go together in a specific way. However, unlike the jigsaw puzzle, we get to dictate the picture on the box."

—Todd Finch

Photograph by Eric Wittmayer Photography

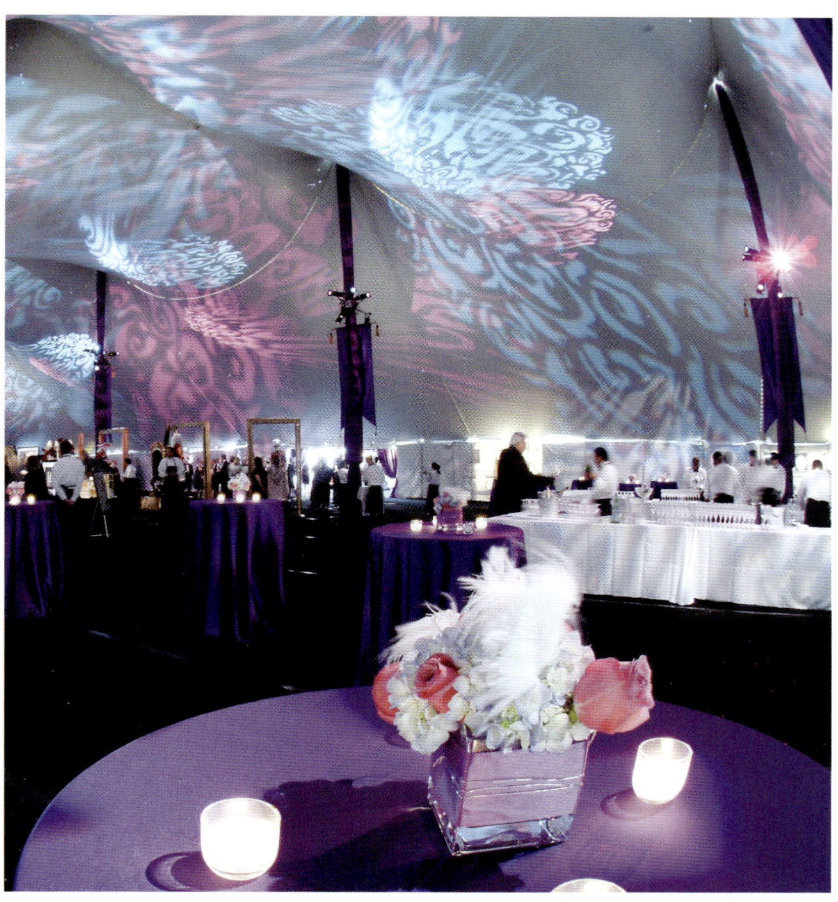

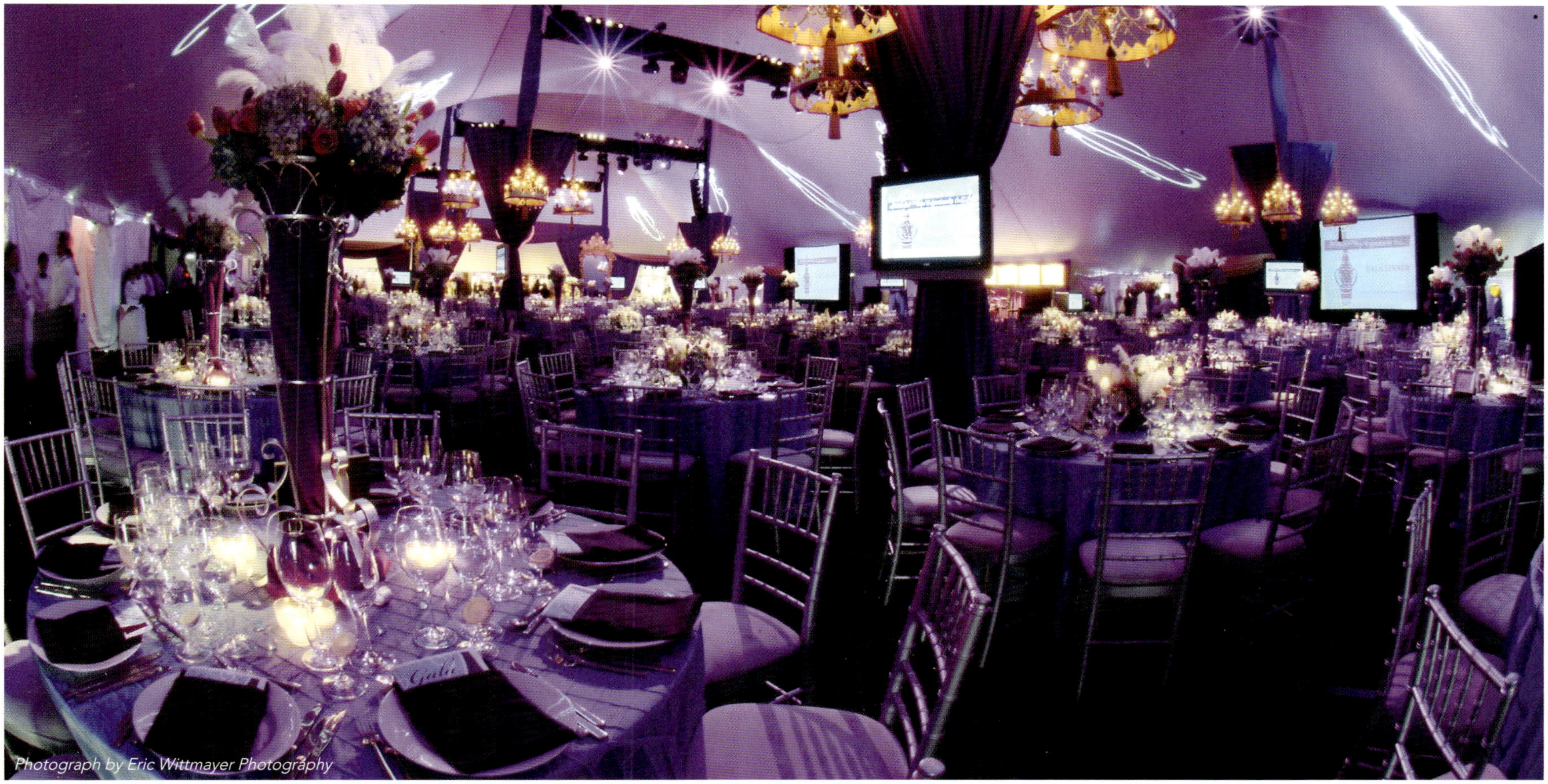

Photograph by Eric Wittmayer Photography

Photograph by James Harris

Photograph by James Harris

Photograph by James Harris

Photograph by James Harris

"Through the sense of sight, we affect human emotion using light, color, texture, and movement."

—Todd Finch

Right: An awards ceremony with an enchanted forest theme highlights the accuracy and emphasis of light. Within the dark space, we focused on a single item for a stunning effect. The simple use of light and dark can change guests' views of the space and their sensory reaction to the décor.

Facing page: At a rock concert in the Littlejohn Coliseum, we partnered with lighting designer Jason Huffer to transform an enormous space into a moving, living atmosphere. The visual aspect complemented the music and added a secondary sensory experience to the sound.

Photograph by Paul Beezley

views

A great design, a successful event, a happy host—each of these is the product of looking deeply into the details. This is where the answer lies.

Tents Unlimited

DAN NOLAN

Seizing the opportunity to employ cutting-edge technology to execute creative ideas is the everyday norm for Tents Unlimited, a subsidiary of The Nolan Companies.

First begun in 1934 with a focus on repairing venetian blinds and working with canvas, The Nolan Companies opened Chattanooga Tent Company to embrace the opportunity to manufacture canvas tents for the U.S. military during World War II. By 1992, The Nolan Companies encompassed three generations of the Nolan family and, through Tents Unlimited, had expanded to Atlanta in order to work with Olympic event planners for the 1996 Games. Always willing to incorporate new products, Tents Unlimited stayed in the forefront of the industry. The company was one of the first in the U.S. to use white vinyl tents and to introduce clearspan tents.

Dan Nolan, managing partner of Tents Unlimited, takes pride in the family business and in its longevity. His hard work—as evidenced by his experience in nearly every area of the company, including attending the washroom as a teenager—and his fascination with the day-to-day challenges have enabled him to build and maintain a dependable team with an extremely low turnover rate. Every team member, from the least experienced to the most experienced, started out the same way—as a tent installer. This training ensures that each person develops the ability to make on-the-job decisions and the flexibility to roll with the punches. The empowerment of the staff and the fact that Tents Unlimited manufactures its own tent material combine to provide outstanding service and high-quality custom creations.

Because the event's host didn't think in terms of limitations, she gave us the opportunity to do things a bit out of the ordinary. She wanted the tent to feel like an elegant room, so we introduced a custom ceiling treatment. The result was a soft, intimate quality. In this case, we worked on the creative process first, and then figured out how to accommodate the budget.

Photograph by Ross DeLoach, Northlight Photography

Photograph by Tents Unlimited

Clear tents offer a spectacular ambience through their unique ability to showcase the surrounding environment. Dramatically different atmospheres can be created in myriad styles. For the opening of the Louvre exhibit at the High Museum of Art in Atlanta, the small space and short installation timeframe provided a few challenges. In the end, the clear ceiling and walls allowed guests to be inside while maintaining a focus on the museum. At the grand opening of a Charlotte retailer, we enhanced the clear tent with custom flooring that was built to fit around existing landscaping. With a curved roof and clear walls, the tent at a new product launch for BMW met the company's exact specifications of clean lines with a classic, luxurious touch.

Photograph by Tents Unlimited

"A tent is like the artist's paper— its quality and style determine the direction for the design while allowing for flexibility."

—Dan Nolan

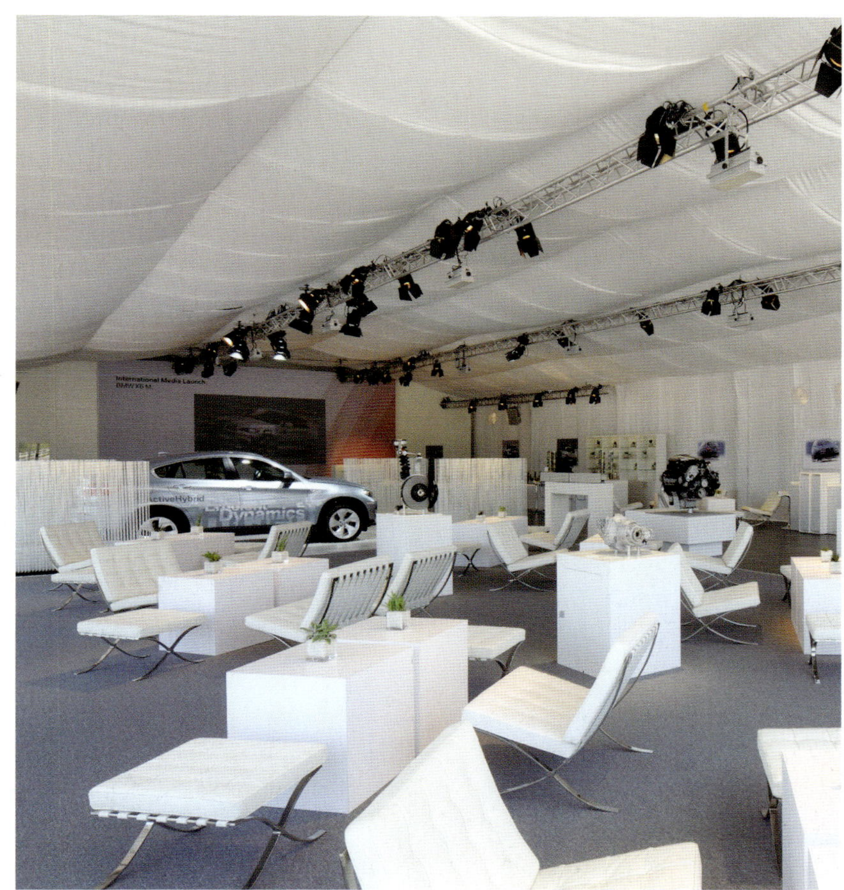

Photograph by Ross DeLoach, Northlight Photography

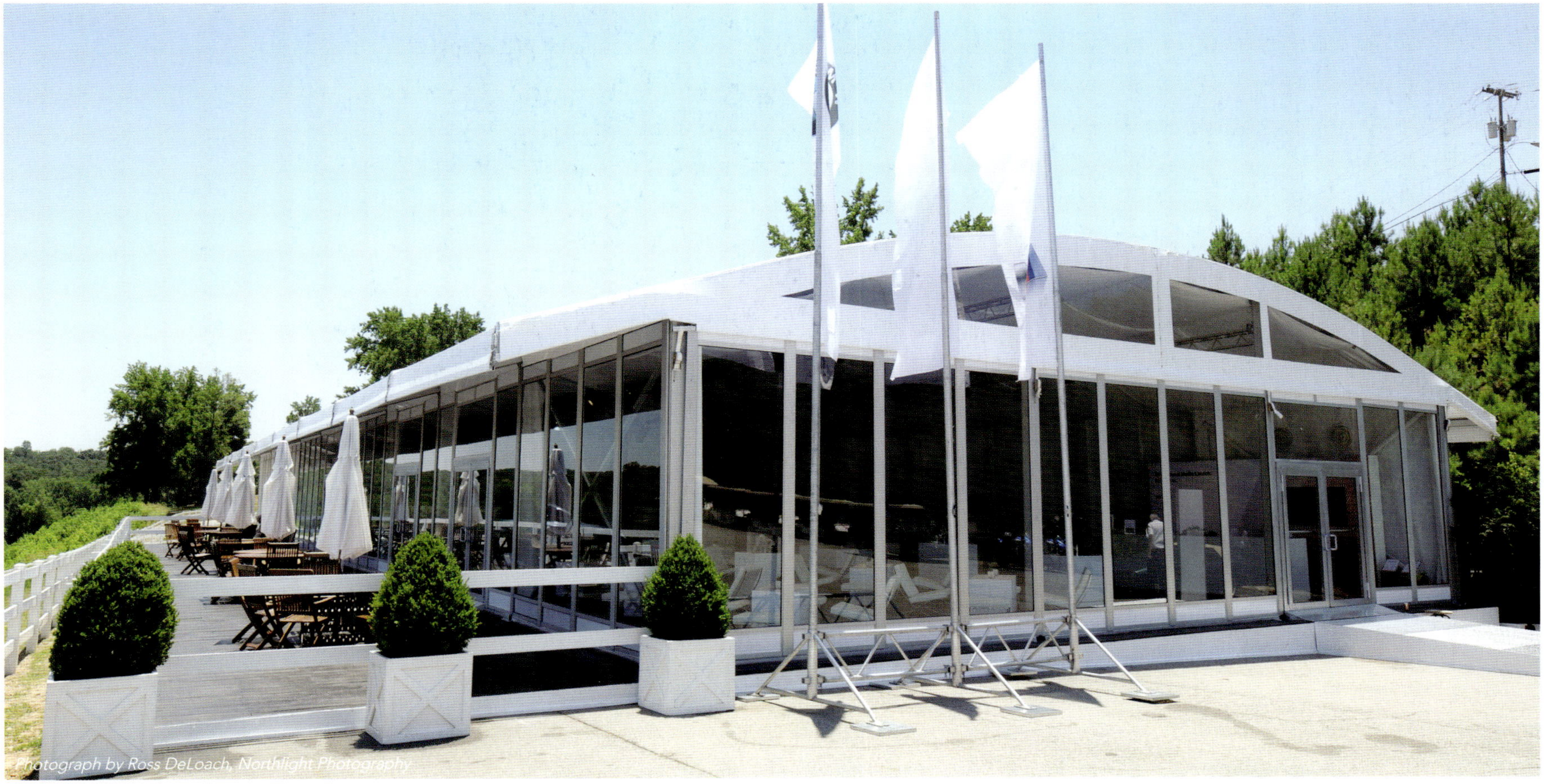

Photograph by Ross DeLoach, Northlight Photography

Photograph by Ross DeLoach Northlight Photography

"The moment we meet a new client holds a sense of wonderful first-date butterflies—an excitement about what's to follow."

—Dan Nolan

Photograph by Mery Donald

views

Don't hesitate to ask for a portfolio and references. Feel free to inquire about any project that may have started out as a disaster. The manner in which a company reacts to adversity reveals its true character.

Tulip

EVA BEHRENDT | HEATHER JONES

While unusual ideas may be a bit daunting for some, Eva Behrendt and Heather Jones embrace them. In fact, they insist uncommon elements are essential for an event to exude originality and excitement. Whether it's an entire landscape of natural materials created for an event at Zoo Atlanta or antique jewelry adorning tabletop vases, Eva and Heather always add a special touch.

Through Tulip, which opened in 2005 as a floral design studio, Eva and Heather have merged their dichotomous backgrounds and unique experiences to offer stunning designs. With flower shops dotting every corner of her German hometown, Eva was naturally inclined toward a deep appreciation for all things floral. Heather Jones, who coincidentally was born in America only four days apart from Eva, pursued a career in interior design but was drawn more specifically to events because of her love for entertainment. At a networking event, fate brought Heather and Eva together; Tulip was born.

While classic, traditional arrangements are certainly part of their repertoire, they also love to emphasize Eva's European roots or incorporate items found in a local park. Regardless of the type or style of the event, Eva and Heather inject their passion for nature's inherent beauty, a strong sense of color, shape, and design, and their lively personalities into each creation.

For a refreshing summer event, we incorporated cut tulips and fresh fruit for a convergence of delicious aromas. The natural elements blended well with vibrant hues of green, orange, and yellow, as well as with themed guest favors of cutting boards, fruit peelers, and apple corers. The design won first place in the Wedding Trends Tabletop Design competition.

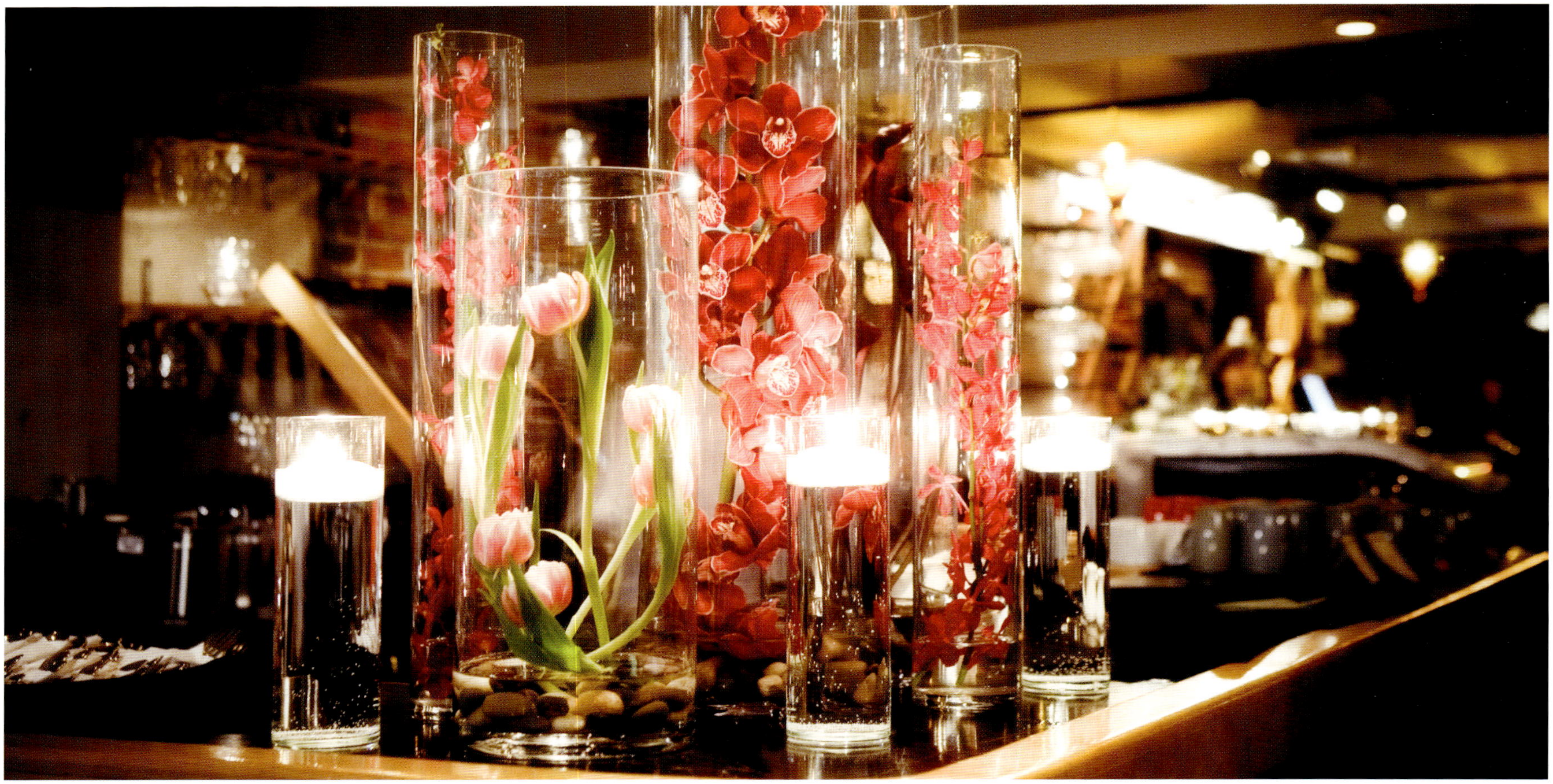

Photograph by Drew Newman Photography

Photograph by Drew Newman Photography

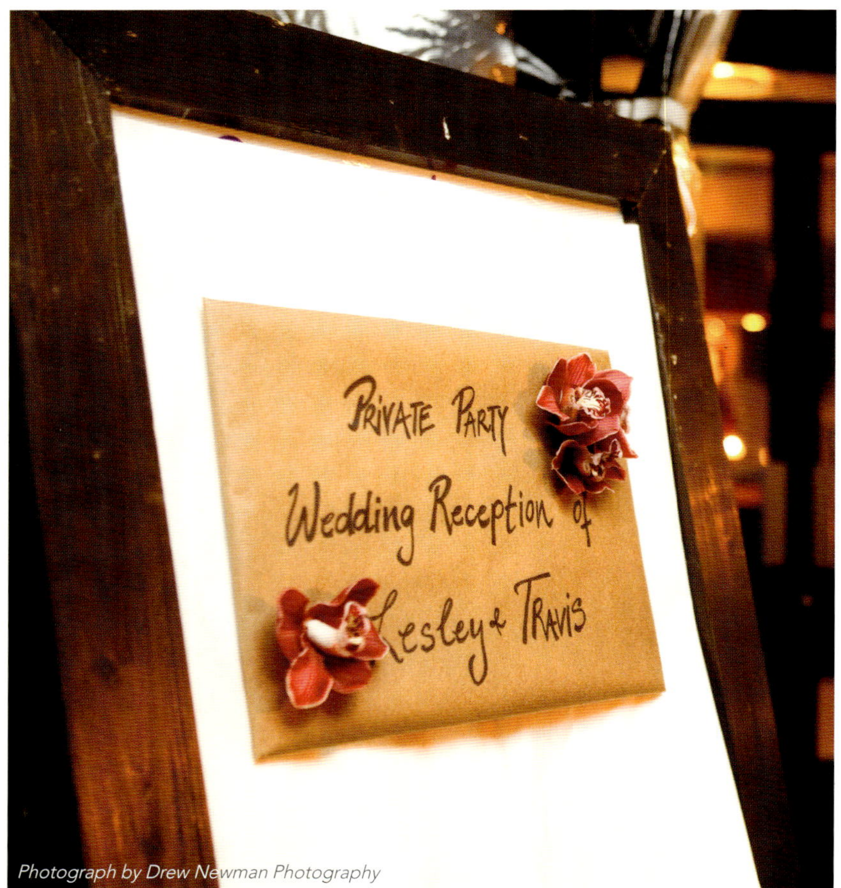

Above and left: We added a pop of rich but wonderful color with burgundy flowers. By submerging the tulip and orchid blooms in water and then arranging them with a few candles, we added a subtle element of surprise. A welcoming sign with a sample of the awaiting ambience directed guests into the couple's favorite restaurant.

Facing page: With only one week to create a fabulous bat mitzvah design, we jumped headfirst into a "Breakfast at Tiffany's" theme. Window displays of pearls and diamonds greeted guests entering the ballroom; an engraving station allowed them to sign silver platters. We constructed jewelry display cabinets and arranged stacked boxes to exude a sense of expectation. White calla lilies continued with the elegant feel.

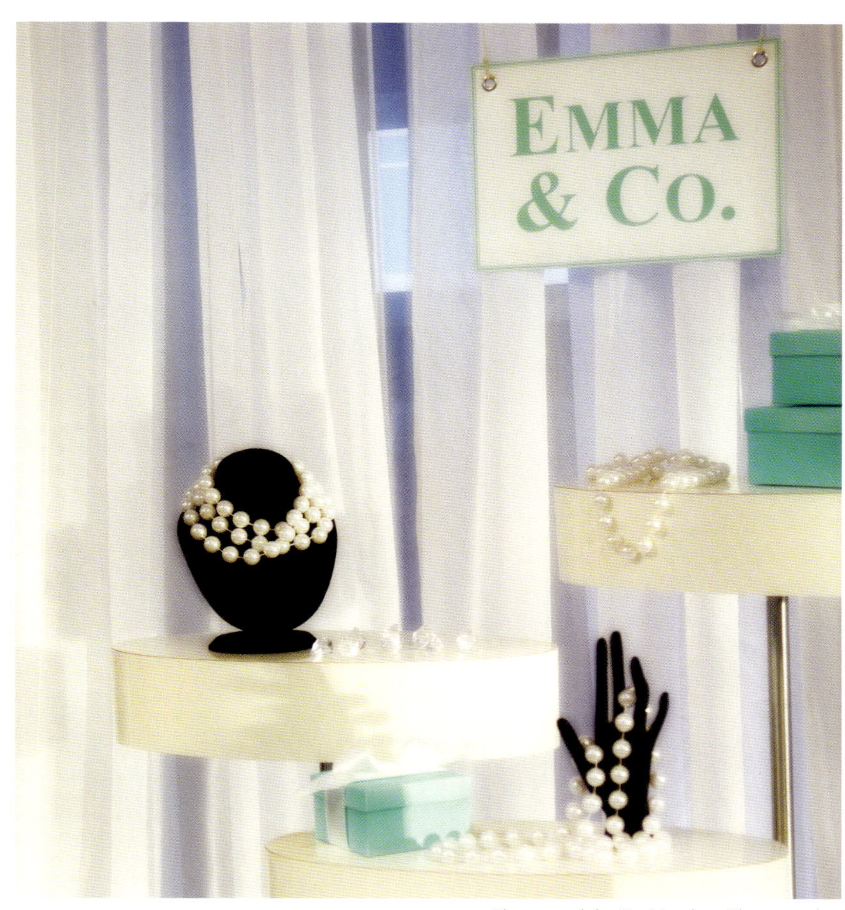

"Flowers basically create a design for themselves; their shape, natural setting, and range of hues offer clues to the best arrangements."

—Heather Jones

Photograph by Ric Mershon Photography

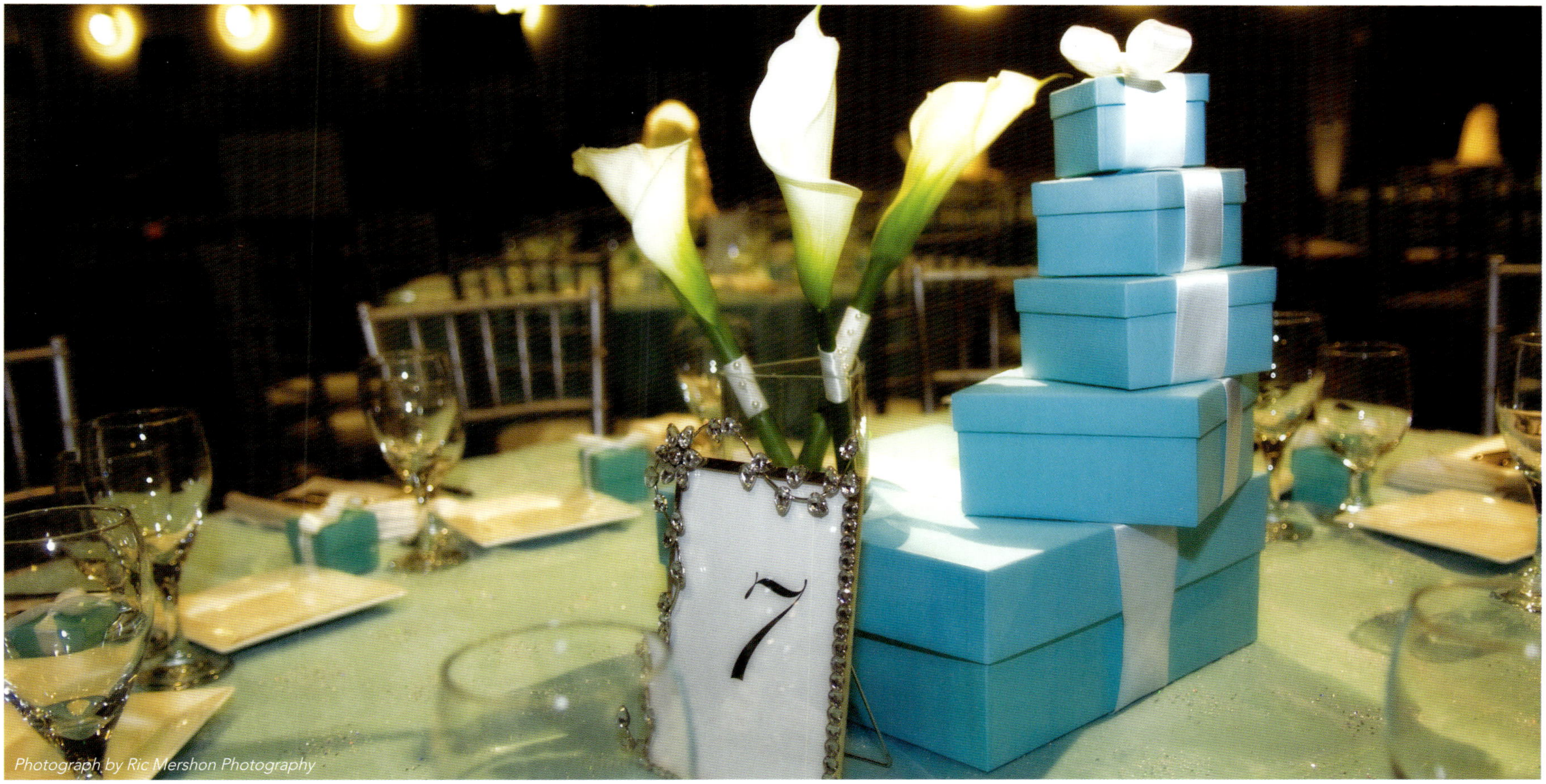

Photograph by Ric Mershon Photography

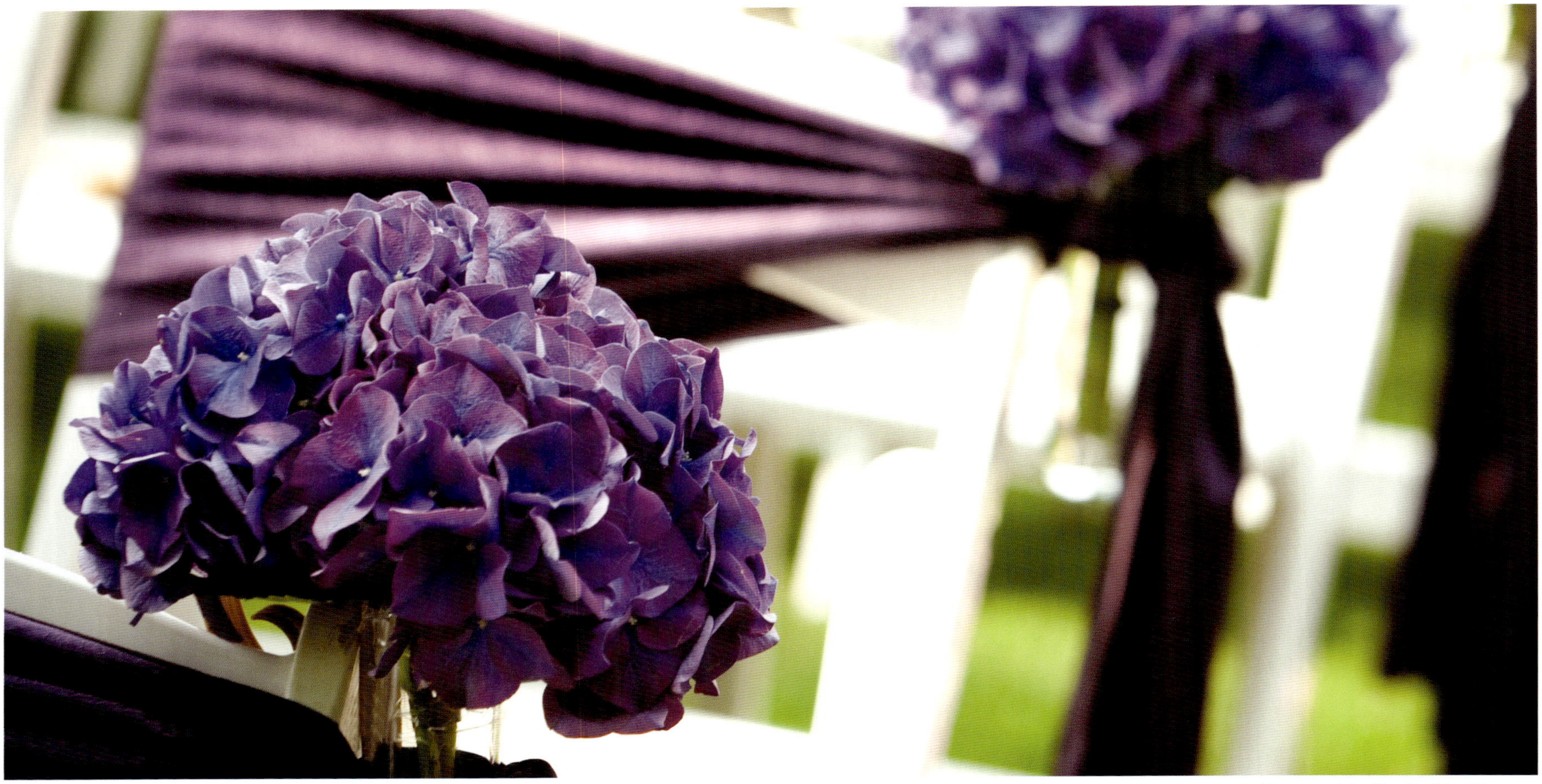

Photograph by The Decisive Moment

Photograph by The Decisive Moment

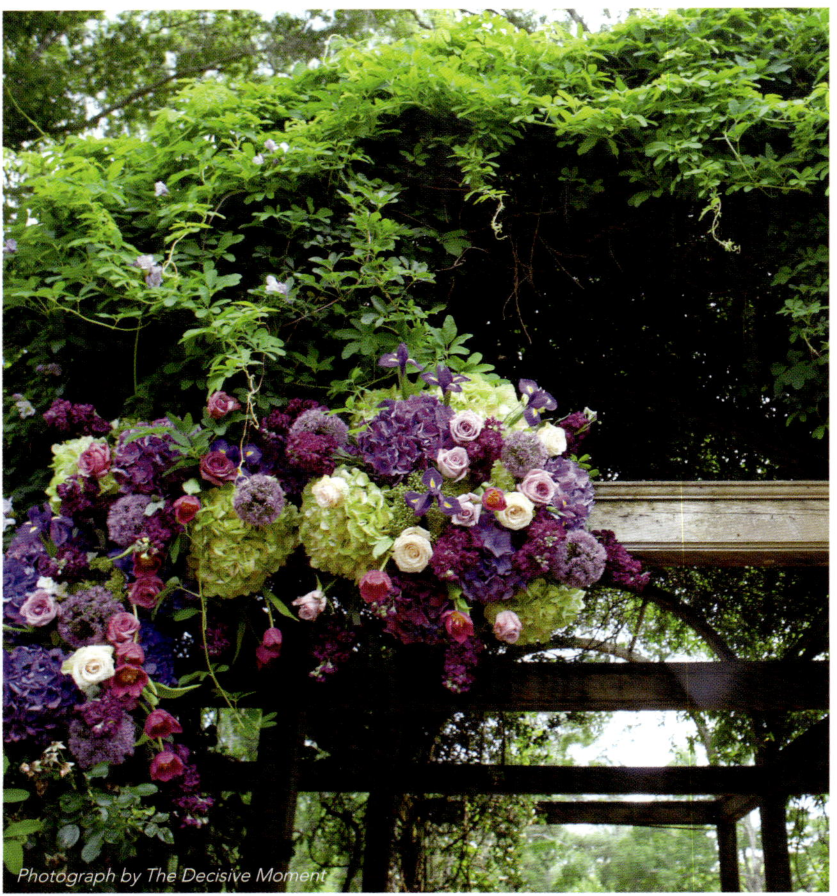

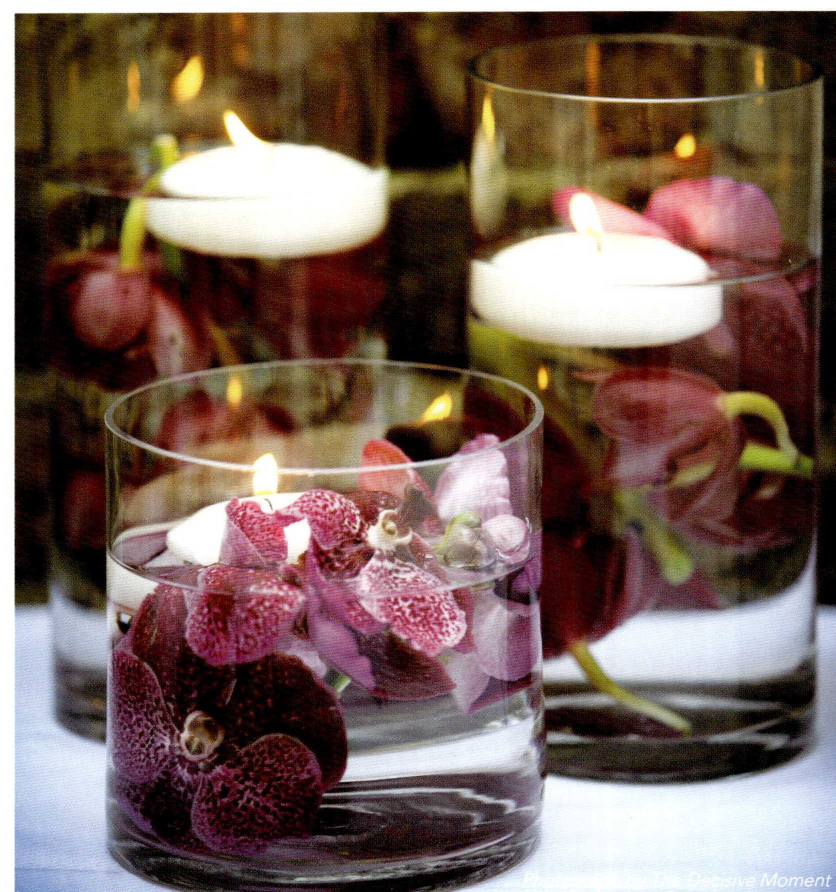

Photograph by The Decisive Moment

Photograph by The Decisive Moment

"Stunning flower arrangements
artistically transform a room into a
magical setting."

—Eva Behrendt

To celebrate a great love story, an outdoor event was held at the Barnsley Gardens Resort. Amidst lush gardens and the old ruins of a historic home, we added romantic blooms in passionate purples to create an inviting space. Our custom-designed metal votive tree, which offers a fantastic sense of style, enhanced the food table inside the remaining walls of the ruins.

views

Choose a designer who has a good reputation and then stick with that designer. Trust the designer to make your floral visions come to life; let that person work with his or her creativity during the design process.

 Arrangements
CATHERINE WALTHER

For Catherine Walther, an event is more than a gathering of people. It is more than beautiful flowers and stunning décor. At Arrangements, each event is built from numerous relationships that have evolved over time with people Catherine considers an extension of her family. These relationships bring meaning and joy to her work and ultimately, to her life.

It was this focus on relationships that prompted Catherine to enter the world of floral design and décor. Catherine's grandmother shared a love of flowers, which in turn influenced her from an early age. After entertaining for numerous years in Chicago for charity events, family, and friends, Catherine moved to Atlanta where a friend requested help with an event. From that point on, knowledge of Catherine's keen sense of style and her passion for events quickly spread throughout the Southeast.

Arrangements, with its studio set amidst more than two delightful acres in Atlanta, transforms dreams into magical reality with grace and expertise. From the grand floral creations to the more petite designs, which are all created by attentive staff who aren't distracted by the rigors of a retail shop, each arrangement can be complemented with luxurious linens, custom lighting, fabric draping, and other décor. Whether she's pulling the pollen out of lilies or transporting a 400-pound urn to an event, Catherine exudes a passion that is contagious to every relationship she enters.

The sparkling reflective properties of the candlelight and the mirrored tabletop over the linens create a sumptuous setting. We incorporated the soft matte texture of the flowers for a perfect element of design.

Photograph by Eric Wittmayer Photography LLC

Photograph by Beall & Thomas Photography

Photograph by Beall & Thomas Photography

Photograph by Eric Wittmayer Photography

Contrasting designs can be successfully accomplished. For example, a soft palette of roses and round tables can be paired with repetition and linear accents, such as square votives. Our orange orchids and dark brown tablecloths pop against the pale yellow and cream hue in a ballroom. Or, as with a celebration at the Blackberry Farm, the rustic barn atmosphere highlights the shabby chic silver accessories while a combination of earthy botanicals and grand florals work in harmony.

Photograph by Garrett Nudd Photography LLC

views

Gone are the days of one table size and the same décor at each table throughout the room. Add spice to the event through a variety of table sizes and slightly different décor.

Harvey Designs

Amy Harvey

Nature's art doesn't follow a specific design scheme. Flowers don't blossom according to a certain color palette; neither does a forest obey a height requirement. Instead, each element works together in a harmony that can only be discovered as the process unfolds.

For Amy Harvey of Harvey Designs, her floral and event designs react much in the same way. While she enjoys the unruffled structure of more traditional events, Amy thrives on working with unconventional ideas that allow her to delve into her cache of inspiration. From there, Amy's background in interior design and retail floral shop experience flourish. Merging her creative prowess, knowledge of design rules, and passion for throwing in a few unexpected elements, Amy creates personalized designs that are exceptionally executed.

To better deliver outstanding events, Amy has partnered with Doreen Karls, who provides more than two decades of experience—and a certification from the Association of Bridal Consultants—in event coordination. As one of the only event design firms in Savannah to boast an in-house certified wedding consultant, Harvey Designs accommodates a wide range of styles—from traditional garden events to funky, Art Deco-style celebrations—and an array of needs—from a few bouquets to complete event design and coordination. The common thread is Harvey Designs' unabashed willingness to embrace a design and passionately see it through to a successful event.

At the Mansion on Forsyth Park, the gold and slate blue ballroom was transformed into a profusion of fuchsia and black with a lot of bling. The color made quite a statement and I enhanced the tables with the combination of mirrored tops, candles, mercury glass, and hundreds of diamond-cut crystals.

To continue with the fuchsia and black color palette, I lined the courtyard's fountain ledge with an assortment of vases containing pearls, floating candles, and submerged orchids. At the entrance to the ballroom, I personalized the space with initials made out of dendrobium orchids to add a delicate, whimsical element to the starkness of the marble courtyard.

Photograph by Scarlett Lillian Photography

views

Be sure to keep all of the event professionals up-to-date with both the overall plan and the details of each aspect of the event. Creating a floral design based only on an idea and a description of the other design elements is very feasible. However, the ability to visually see some of the décor or talk to the other professionals creating the event can be tremendously helpful to ensure everything melds seamlessly on the day of the event.

Ice Sculpture Inc.

JIM DUGGAN

An ice sculpture in nature is ephemeral; the artist's handiwork will melt. But this doesn't bother Jim Duggan. He understands that the sculpture helps create an atmosphere for each event, one that he hopes will remain etched in guests' minds.

Ice was not always Jim's medium of choice. In fact, he attended culinary school to pursue a career in an equally short-lived but also rewarding medium. While working at the Atlanta Country Club as a line cook, he met an ice sculptor and got his first taste in the competitive, challenging industry. Years later, he left the culinary arts to deliver ice for a generous entrepreneur who agreed to let him practice carving ice after hours. Thus began Jim's path to opening Ice Sculpture Inc.

Jim and his team create, deliver, and retrieve designs that include everything from ice bars and vodka ice luges to logos and all types of art. To ensure his carvings meet the highest standards, Jim makes all of his ice on site and employs green practices whenever possible.

With an exceptional range of experience in his past—including carving with hand tools and robotics, molds and machines—Jim loves the challenges that ice presents. And he certainly has passed on the passion for and the knowledge to approach those challenges to his team, many of whom have worked with Jim for numerous years.

For a 16-minute show at Opera Atlanta, two guys and I carved 300-pound blocks of ice with chainsaws and ended the show literally with a bang—the venue's nitrous burst system gave off a stunning display as the final design was revealed.

Photograph courtesy of Ice Sculpture Inc.

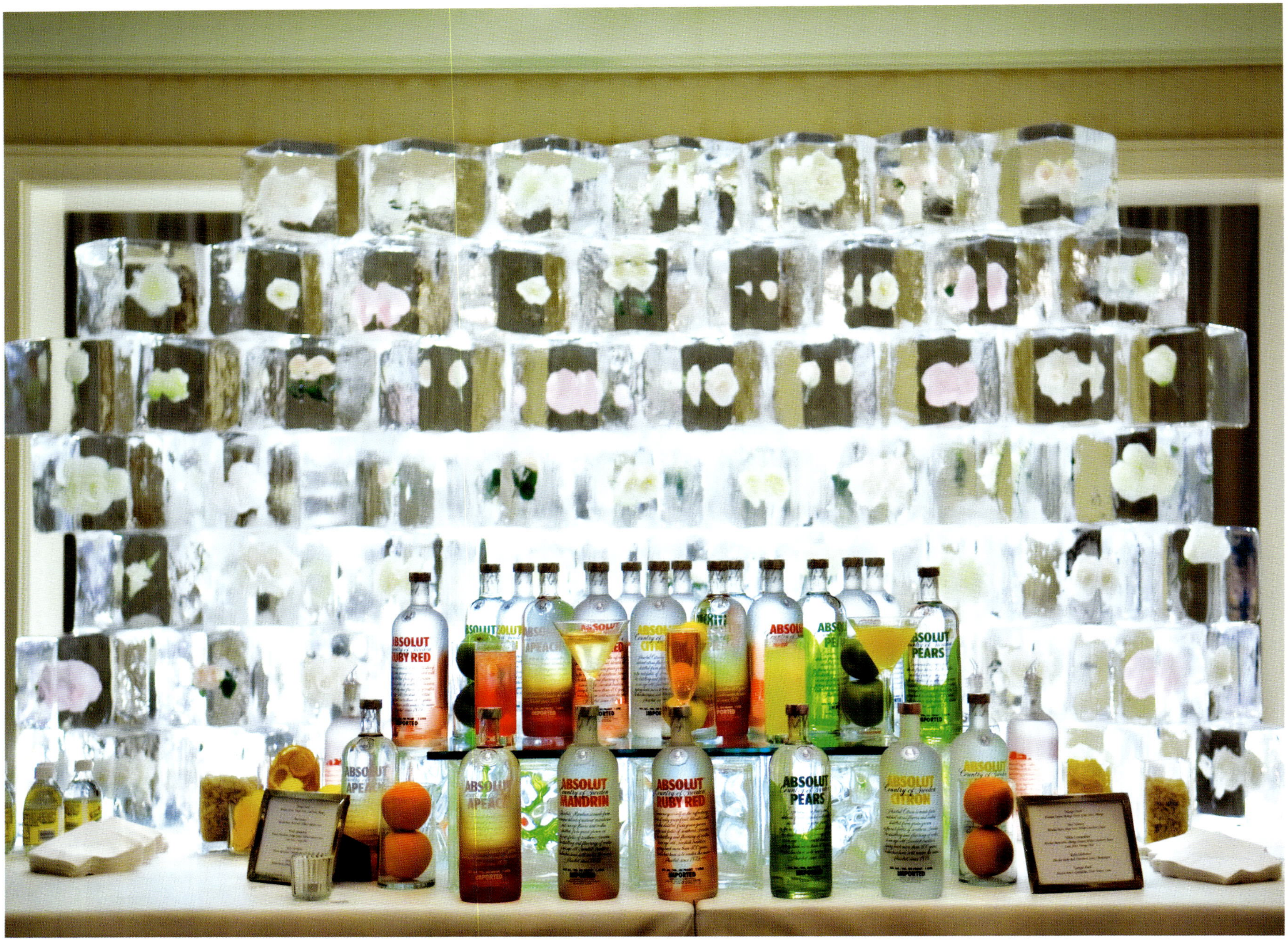

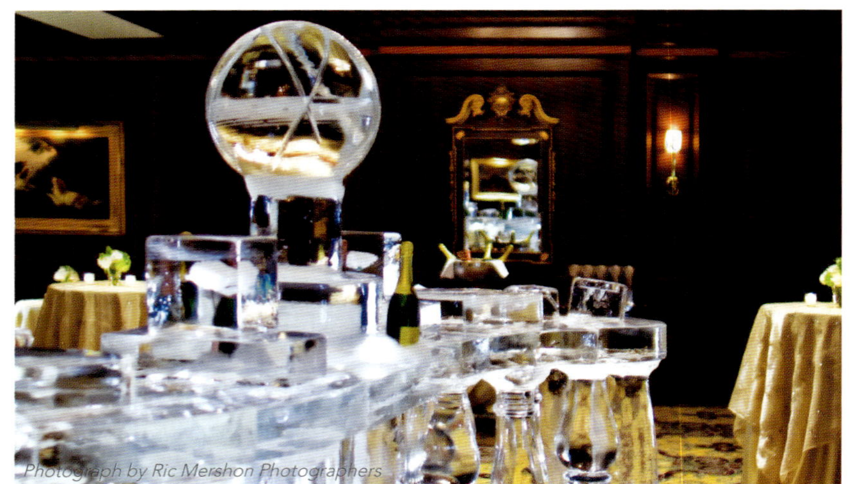

Photograph by Ric Mershon Photographers

Photograph by Ric Mershon Photographers

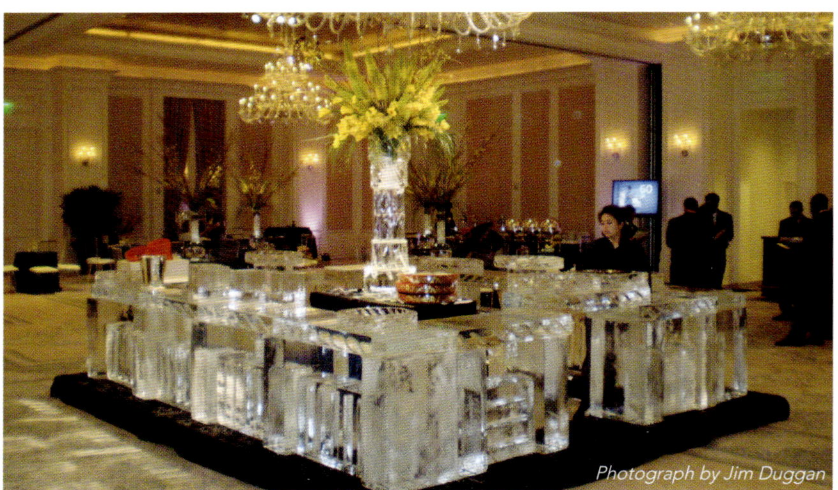

Photograph by Jim Duggan

Right: Safety is always a top priority; therefore placing four, 11-foot hockey players on three-foot risers at a pre-party for the National Hockey League's All-Star Game was a logistical challenge. The dramatic effect was perfect, with each player pointing toward a central ice display featuring the Stanley Cup.

Facing page top: Because we make our own ice, we can incorporate inclusions, such as real flowers, into our sculptures. The flower wall was created with 300, nine-inch blocks of ice.

Facing page bottom: Functional ice bars are always a popular item for guests. While most bars are straight, some up to 40 feet long, we occasionally soften the ambience with a double-sided serpentine bar. Event hosts often incorporate food service into the bar, with cuisine such as caviar, crab, lobster, sushi, and assembled platters. We can even reuse the bar, serving appetizers first, then placing new tops and resurfacing the bar for dessert service.

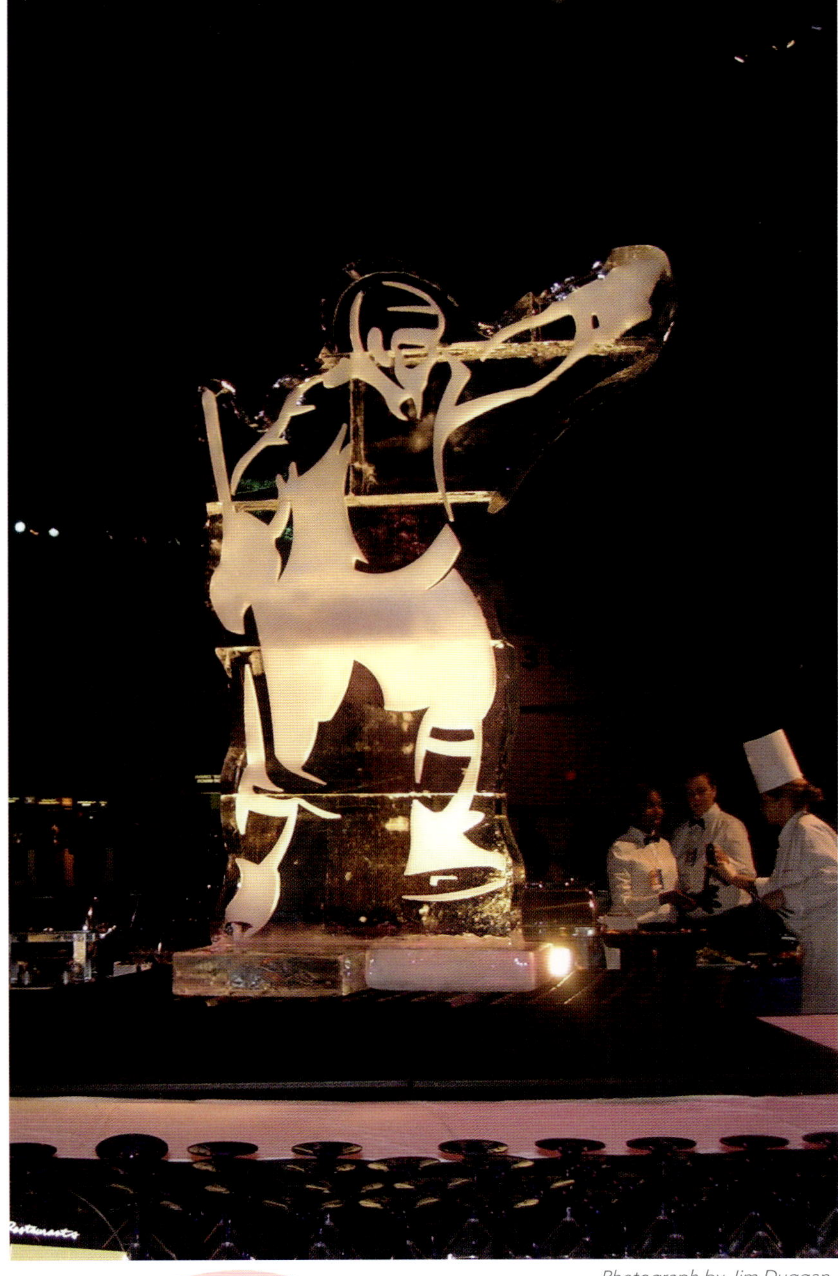

Photograph by Jim Duggan

views

Allow the sculptor to be the paintbrush. By giving the sculptor artistic freedom through general guidelines instead of specific details, the end result is often more creative and stunning.

Kimberley Cary Event Design

KIMBERLEY ICHTER

No element stands alone in its impact on an event's ambience. Whether it's the floral, lighting, furniture, or linens, they all must work together in flawless harmony. For Kimberley Ichter, this philosophy embodies a central focus at Kimberley Cary Event Design.

With an original passion for flowers—and an impressive education under the famed Paula Pryke in London—Kimberley at first concentrated on floral design but quickly fell in love with other event elements. Creating a seamless look by coordinating everything from furniture and linens to floral and lighting became her ambition. Through each event's style, modern or chic, traditional or themed, a cohesive feel underscores every decision.

Regardless of which element she's working with, Kimberley strives to bring out an overwhelming style that will sweep guests off their feet. By interjecting various surprises throughout an event—perhaps a lively cocktail hour followed by a more formal ball—Kimberley maintains the guests' attention and ensures they have a wonderful time. And to make certain the event host is more than pleased, Kimberley is involved throughout each step of the process, all the way until the final guest has departed. This ensures her vision is carried out correctly and allows her to participate in what she really loves—seeing others enjoy her designs.

Changing the colors and overall feel for an after-dinner lounge creates new exhilaration that keeps guests entertained. At a Big Brothers Big Sisters event at the St. Regis Hotel, the ballroom featured a palette of green and ivory with varying shades and textures. To spice up the mood, I punctuated the terrace in stunning red tones, beginning with two red carpets leading out onto the space. A jazz band and lounge seating captured the chic essence, and orchids, roses, and tulips established softness.

Photograph by Eric Wittmayer Photography

Photograph by Ben Vigil Photographers

Photograph by Abby Smith Photography

Photograph by Eric Wittmayer Photography

"An event should lead guests in a journey of the soul by prompting certain emotions throughout the celebration."

—Kimberley Ichter

Right: To animate the traditional look with a bit of an edge, I intertwined glass pillar bases with tall acrylic centerpieces to look like a sea of glass. I carried that feel into the custom acrylic chuppah and expanded it into a calm color palette of blush and white.

Facing page top: The host wanted a clean look that was elegant but not fussy, so I embraced a modern feel with black tones and multiple centerpiece styles. The existing gold drapery in the ballroom was covered in blue fabric to add additional splashes of color.

Facing page bottom left: The Atlanta History Center provided the perfect foundation to create an evening of Hollywood glamour. Live 'Oscars'—gold airbrushed models—and palm trees along the red carpet complete the look.

Facing page bottom right: At a rehearsal dinner, the groom's family was of Cuban descent and wanted to accentuate their heritage. I used a Cuban cigar as inspiration and brought in brown tones for a warm feel. Cognac taffeta linens embraced the tables and allowed several hundred roses in blush hues to lighten the room.

Photograph by Denis Reggie Photographers

views

When talking with a planner or designer, be sure that they discuss details about the event. Specific ideas should be expressed and exact costs—not estimates—should be explained so there is no guesswork involved. Steer away from someone who uses broad strokes and concepts because there's no guarantee the final result will be what you had in mind.

Parties To Die For

KATHY RAINER | TRICKY WOLFES

Like a flower's natural desire to express from bud to full bloom, Kathy Rainer and Tricky Wolfes have blossomed into their beautiful business. These passionate women began as volunteer floral designers and event planners serving numerous Atlanta charitable groups with rave reviews, so the sorority sisters decided to go pro in 1992. With flair and high energy, Kathy and Tricky design some of the most prestigious fundraising soirees and private weddings in historic venues, luxury hotels, and country clubs, making their mark on Atlanta's elite social scene. "One seed of an idea inspires the creative process…a theme, a color, a season, a wish," says Kathy. But what makes event planning and execution so enthralling to the dynamic duo is watching the party evolve far beyond initial expectations to unexpectedly delight guests.

Creative flower arranging is the firm's hallmark, yet exquisite details in the form of custom invitations, tabletop décor, drapery, lighting, and linens highlight its full-service capabilities. From concept stage through celebration day, partners Kathy and Tricky work hand-in-hand with clientele, assuring stress-free success with their personal touch. Each event offers more than meets the eye. The philanthropreneurs founded Rebloom, a floral ministry with the mission to save and recycle fresh flowers from each fabulous fete. Volunteers craft new arrangements to bring joy to people in hospitals, homeless shelters and social-services groups. Active members of the Garden Club of America National Speakers Bureau, the two florists also love sharing design tips at educational seminars, engaging audiences with their comic "Lucy and Ethel" repartee.

Our Bell'acqua "beautiful water" theme for the Atlanta Botanical Garden gala created quite a stir. Shades of cobalt blue wash the room aglow with candlelight and crystal chandeliers. Fluid fabric swaths soften the space and a custom dance floor offers guests a twirl on illusion pools of water. The floral story unfolds with 3,000 dendrobium and phaelenopsis orchids, accented by blue delphinium, hydrangeas, fragrant roses, and lilies in tinted glass vessels.

Photograph by Jim Fitts

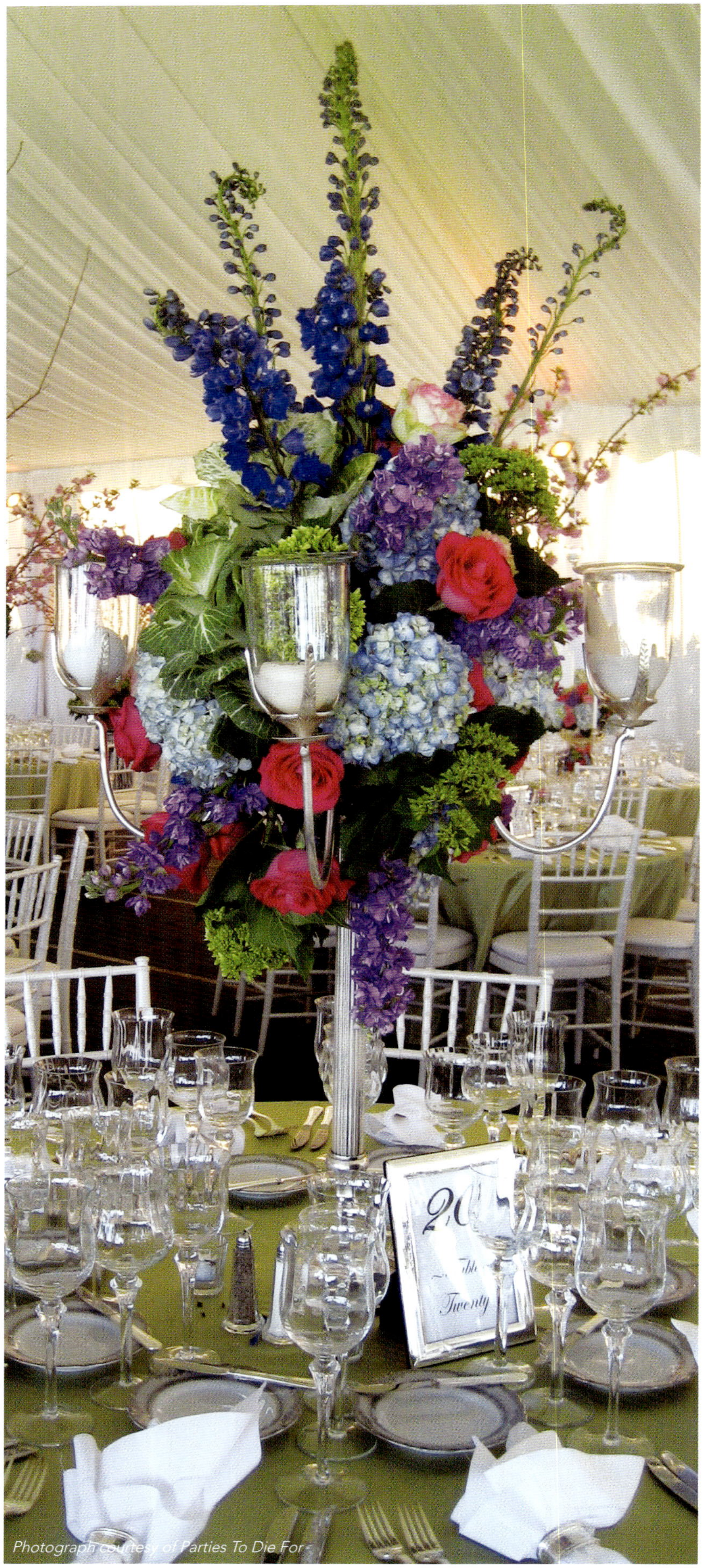

Photograph courtesy of Parties To Die For

Photograph by Jim Fitts

Photograph by Kristen Alexander

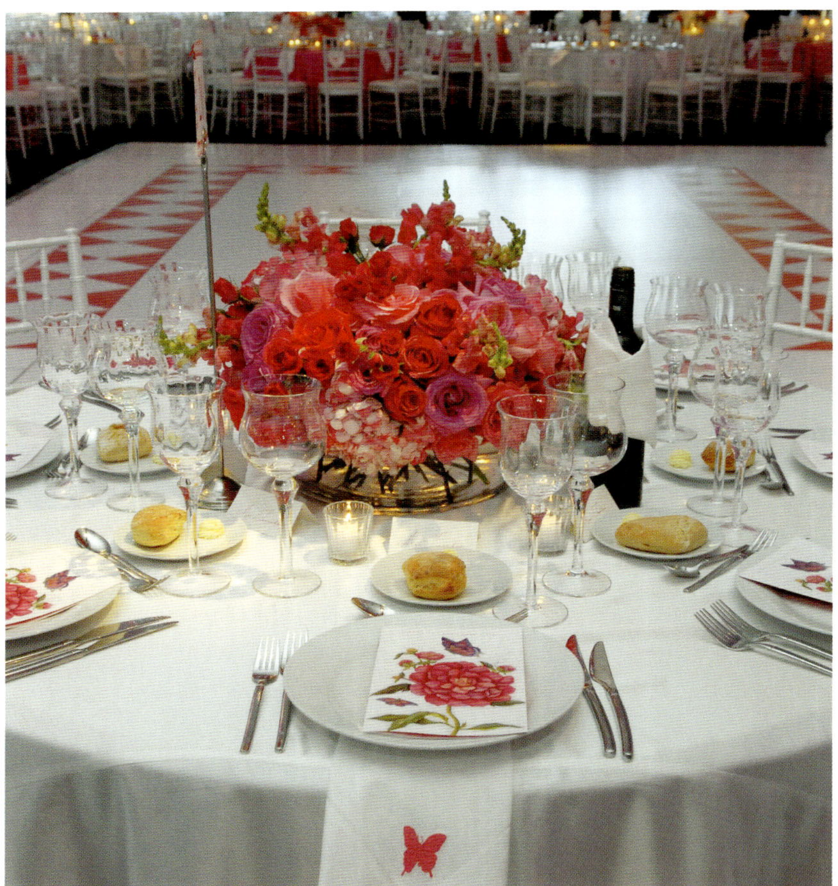

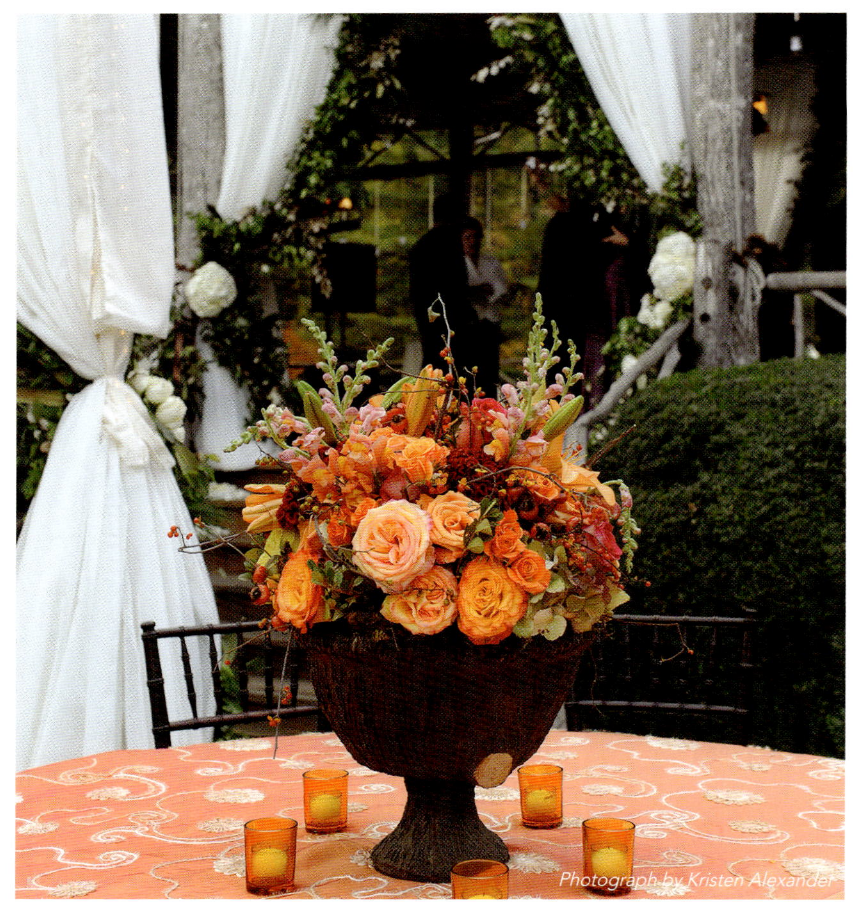

"Anything worth doing is worth overdoing."

—Tricky Wolfes

Right: We dressed the Garden of Eden silver anniversary ball in luscious Tiffany blue. Beaded chargers, mirrored tables and silver cones with flatware are brilliant accents. Silver pedestal bowls, epergne, trumpet vases, and candelabras hold cream-colored hydrangeas, tuberose, freesia, lilies, and roses; dramatic hand-built trees boast 1,000 dendrobium hybrid orchids.

Facing page left: A South Georgia plantation surrounded by Spanish moss and native oaks inspired us to design a tent of refreshingly green details with lavish spring bouquets, striped fabric, and oak tree crests embroidered on napkins.

Facing page top right: The power of pink appears everywhere: pop-up invitations, hand-painted peony murals, and butterfly sculptures artfully crafted with carnation petals. We designed a pink patterned dance floor and 30-foot building banner to extend the happy theme.

Facing page bottom right: The Chattooga Club venue was all ablaze in autumn colors. Our nature-inspired designs included pew markers and garland-adorned drapery panels. We used seasonal berries and local floral materials for décor: Pinecones, nuts, grapevine stands, and bark bowls complemented arrangements of snapdragons, rose hips, orange mambo rose sprays, green hydrangeas, and bittersweet.

Photograph by Jim Fitts

views

Premium flowers take any event to another realm. Choose a florist that sources the best blooms that are fresh and conditioned well. Be open to the creative process and rely on the support of your professional event designer. Relax. Start with one idea and layer on as you go. Enjoy the whole experience as it evolves and watch it grow into something bigger and better.

Savannah Special Events by Ranco

KENDALL WAYNER

The words disaster or impossible are just not in the vocabulary for Savannah Special Events. Regardless of the situation, owner Randy Childs and his team find a way to pull off a fabulous event. If the situation is something simple but isn't necessarily part of Savannah's job description, such as moving flower pots to assist the event host, the team is more than happy to help. And if a more complex problem arises, such as a torrential downpour the week before an annual gala that results in water seeping up from the ground under a well-prepared tent, the Savannah team pulls together to vacuum out the water and provide flip-flops to arriving guests. Whatever it takes, Savannah Special Events accomplishes its goals and meets challenges head-on.

First started more than 25 years ago by Randy and his brother, Tommy, as solely a tent rental company, Savannah Special Events now offers full service party rentals with everything from linens and tables to tents and dance floors. The team, led by Kendall Wayner, enjoys the variety of each event and strives to create a once-in-a-lifetime occasion for the host. From the first point of contact through the tear down after the event, the team inspires creativity and a genuine love of life that brings a smooth, enjoyable experience.

A simple but elegant style was captured in Savannah Square through our attention to details at a winter reception. The monotone color scheme allowed the green of nature to emerge while the different levels of seating added variety. Simple candles and other décor maintained the minimalist style with a warm atmosphere.

Photograph by Donna Von Bruening

Photograph by Christine Hall

Photograph by Christine Hall

Photograph by Christine Hall

"Joy is found in creating a large-scale
version of an idea or image."

—Kendall Wayner

Right and facing page: The tent design itself can dramatically alter the ambience of an
outdoor event, and that's just the beginning of the design. A draped fabric ceiling adds
warmth and formality while a clear tent offers clean lines and a more natural outdoor
experience. The additional details, such as the colors of the linens, the lighting, and the
décor can easily build on the original tone set by the tent. By bringing in personal touches,
such as a plaid tablecloth made by the host's family to coordinate with their Scottish ties,
the event then takes on a life of its own.

Photograph by Donna Von Bruening

views

An inclement weather plan is essential if any part of the event will
be outdoors—even down to how guests will get inside without
getting wet. If a significant part of the event will be held outdoors
and at least a 40 percent chance of rain exists, we encourage hosts
to have a tent set up in advance.

WILDFLOWER LINEN
YOUNGSONG MARTIN

Even as a child, Youngsong Martin was known for her keen style sense and passion for dressing with flair. Those instincts, and formal design school training, led to her successful career as a designer and nationwide marketer of namesake lines of upscale women's apparel. Then one day, Youngsong volunteered to help plan a niece's wedding. Unable to find suitable table linen rentals, she tapped her design expertise and knack for entertaining to craft just the right look for her niece's nuptials.

The satisfaction Youngsong derived from that experience soon inspired Wildflower Linen, which she founded in 2001 to showcase her innovative lines of designer table linens and chair covers for event rentals. That new career direction immediately brought Youngsong critical acclaim from noted event planners, celebrity caterers, and wedding hosts.

Since Wildflower Linen's inception, Youngsong has redefined the rental linen field with her company's couture quality and attention to customer care. Meanwhile, she launched four design showrooms throughout California and became a prestigious provider nationwide and abroad.

In addition to lavish weddings and large-scale society and corporate banquets, Wildflower Linen creations have been featured at the post-Oscars Governor's Ball and Vanity Fair after-parties, aboard charter yachts, in noted resorts and country clubs, at several presidential library events, even at the gala party for a DreamWorks premiere at the Venice Film Festival in Italy. However, Wildflower's extensive inventory of fashion-forward and traditional event decor has attracted hosts of even the most intimate of functions.

I require that each item in Wildflower Linen's distinctive Isabella line be hand-sewn to ensure the highest quality. The subtle textures of the ruffles add allure to the soft, neutral color palette.

Photography by Barnet Photography

Right: To reflect the beauty and drama of Latin cultures, I used bold colors and traditional fabrics in this design, one of many in Wildflower Linen's broad inventory of themed table linens and chair covers.

Facing page top left: In a break with tradition, I went to opposite ends of the design spectrum to marry rich dupioni silk with shiny leather floral appliqués, imparting a feminine, sophisticated look.

Facing page top right: Inspired by Dale Chihuly's blown-glass creations, I gave my Lilybelle line of chair covers a transparent, delicate floral effect that dazzles party guests.

Facing page bottom left: Color plays an indispensable role in any event's overall look, so I used multiple complementary tones to give an alfresco wedding a post-impressionistic feel.

Facing page bottom right: Like the apparel world's "little black dress" fashion staple, my design for this engagement party's chair covers has a chic, tailored simplicity that complements the understated table linens.

Photograph by Imagery Immaculate

views

Wildflower Linen's team emphasizes choice in catering to hosts' tastes and objectives. Event planners are encouraged to give free rein to their imaginations by exploring the breadth of our exclusive fabrics and styles to make their functions memorable. Party hosts should think of design vendors as their partners and collaborators.

Your Event Solution

LINDA BAGLEY | CATHY TAYLOR

Whether it's a chic soirée, a sizzling theme party, or an energetic meeting, Linda Bagley and her team at Your Event Solution partner with Cathy Taylor from UniqueWorks Catering Concepts and Larry Oley at Elite Exhibits to turn events from ordinary to extraordinary. Firmly rooted in developing a relationship with the event host, the team strives to be an invisible tool that allows a vision to be brought to life.

After gleaning the overarching information, the team gathers in the event space. Here is where the inspiration takes flight—from the venue itself. While considering each event's goals and desired style, Linda and her team experience the ambience of the space—the lighting, color, mood, and functionality—and then develop a fusion of the venue with the event's characteristics. After the inspiration is set in motion, designer Ed Wignall produces the event's polish, logistics, and final flair.

While each space has constraints in size and existing décor, the thrill is in the freedom to design and create from scratch. The partnership with Larry enhances this liberty with his ability to build nearly any structure and add graphics to almost any component. In perfect collaboration with the creative side are the responsibilities of ensuring the event is more than just fluff. Just like a builder must construct a solid foundation, Linda and Ed along with their team ensure everything is set for the right party in the right space with the right elements.

For a two-hour reception, we wanted to keep guests excited as they walked through Georgia Aquarium, even as they were standing in line at the bar. Two aerialists were suspended from the ceiling over the bar and plexiglass tubes bubbled with water and changed colors throughout the evening. We based the design on the venue's existing feel and played off of the ceiling waves and overall colors.

Photograph by Patrick Williams Photography

Photograph by Patrick Williams Photography

Photograph by Patrick Williams Photography

Photograph by Patrick Williams Photography

Photograph by Patrick Williams Photography

Right: A custom focal point situated in the center of the room provided a place for entertainment with five aerialists and helped with traffic flow.

Facing page top and bottom right: For an international group in a large space, we designed a European theme specifically featuring France, Italy, and Germany. From the ceiling we suspended an aerialist who poured French wine for the arriving guests. We turned an existing fountain into a living statue for entertainment and added café tables and various food stations to give the feel of walking down a street in Florence. To utilize an existing arbor, we transformed it into a Germanic beer garden.

Facing page bottom left: With only two weeks to plan a nontraditional Halloween party, we created a gothic feel with black draping and deep red accents. Customized sparkling elements on the drape, nearly a thousand candles, and lighted bars lifted the mood just a bit.

Photograph by Patrick Williams Photography

views

Don't forget to engage guests while they are waiting in line at the bar, for food, and for the valet. Whether you involve actual entertainment or just interesting décor elements, keep those attending the event from getting bored or wishing they were somewhere else.

Eat, Drink &

Be Merry

A Legendary Event

TONY CONWAY

President and owner Tony Conway has always had a special relationship with food. As a young boy, Tony learned the farm-to-table process firsthand on his great-grandparents' farm. It was there that he also learned valuable lessons such as the importance of not wasting food as well as food selection techniques like how to choose an egg or tomato. By 17, Tony had already begun his career in the hotel industry, first trying various positions but always being drawn back to the food and beverage service.

In addition to his childhood experiences, Tony's passion for catering grew out of its diverse day-to-day, even hour-to-hour, activities. After working with The Ritz-Carlton during the 1996 Olympic Games in Atlanta, Tony decided he should venture outside the hotel ballroom, so he started his own catering service.

With over a century of experience, Legendary's core culinary team is expert at blending the art and science of food preparation and presentation. Holding temperatures steady while preparing a large amount of food, creating innovative plate compositions, and extracting certain flavors while merging menu aromas with noncompeting floral scents are all part of the culinary process. With service on par with The Ritz-Carlton, Tony continues to cultivate a fantastic culinary team that treats every event like a theatrical performance.

To accommodate a kaleidoscope theme, we created an interactive, buffet-to-order menu that incorporated a range of flavor combinations and placed our guests in the driver's seat in terms of selecting ingredients.

Photograph by Willward C. Hughes

Photograph by Willward C. Hughes

Above: Salmon continues to be a popular year-round request. Regarding flavor and eco-consciousness, we usually select Alaskan Wild Salmon and Farmed Arctic Char.

Above right: A traditional, New England clam bake is an ideal way to celebrate summer. To encourage a relaxed mood, we have guests check their shoes at the door and don a pair of flip-flops for the evening.

Right: Low Country stew with Carolina shrimp was one of the Southern-inspired dishes at the 2008 High Museum Wine Auction. Each year, we work with several guest chefs to create a unique four-course menu, which renowned vintner guests pair with fine wines.

Facing page: Chef Christy Campbell builds each guest's dish according to the nuances of his or her palate.

Photograph by Greg Mooney

"We eat first with our eyes—the food has to both look spectacular and taste amazing."

—Tony Conway

Left: The beautifully composed sushi served atop a lighted bar jived with the stylistic, elegant ambience of *The Atlantan* magazine's Men of Style event.

Facing page top: Simple heirloom tomatoes have been styled with attention to create beautiful art that looks as delicious as it tastes.

Facing page bottom: As people have returned to healthier eating, we've experienced more requests for salads. Our chef loves utilizing farm fresh vegetables, especially with the buzz for micro green salads. Introducing additional ingredients like fresh figs, grown from trees right on our property, in a pomegranate reduction with mini goat cheese cones dramatically enhances the flavor and presentation of a salad.

Photograph by Lauren Rubinstein

Photograph by Lauren Rubinstein

Photograph by Lauren Rubinstein

Photograph by Dawn Brewer

"Whether serving 10 or 10,000 guests, the key to a tantalizing meal is restaurant-quality cuisine."

—Tony Conway

Right: A festive poolside setting is the perfect backdrop for a sophisticated alfresco menu of grilled soft-shell crab and lobster with a choice of salsas to match everyone's palate.

Facing page: With our roots in Texas, we love to prepare chili with a variety of fresh chili peppers. Although fall is the traditional season for chili, we love to serve it year-round with one twist—substituting a cup of water with a cup of locally brewed beer.

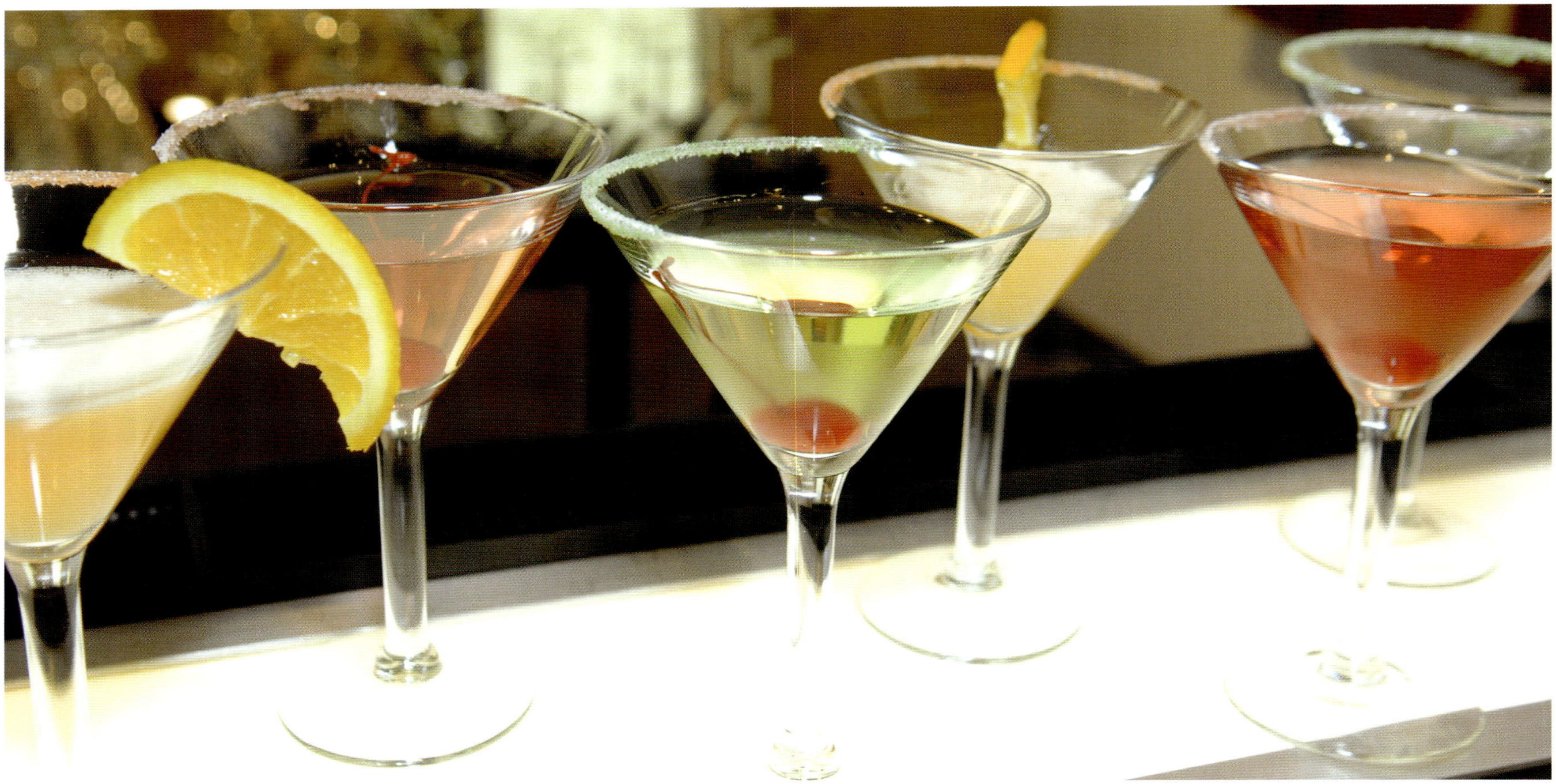

Photograph by Lauren Rubinstein

Photograph by Lauren Rubinstein

Above: Whether it's a pink cosmopolitan garnished with a cherry or a sour apple martini with a sugared rim, we love serving cakes and cocktails together. It's unexpected and twice as sumptuous.

Left: The presentation doesn't have to be over-the-top to set the right mood. With lit candles, chilled champagne, and waiting flutes, the moment just before the guests arrive is filled with anticipation.

Facing page: For a classy birthday party, each guest received a unique, whimsical cake at the end of an elaborate meal that included several types of caviar and Cristal champagne.

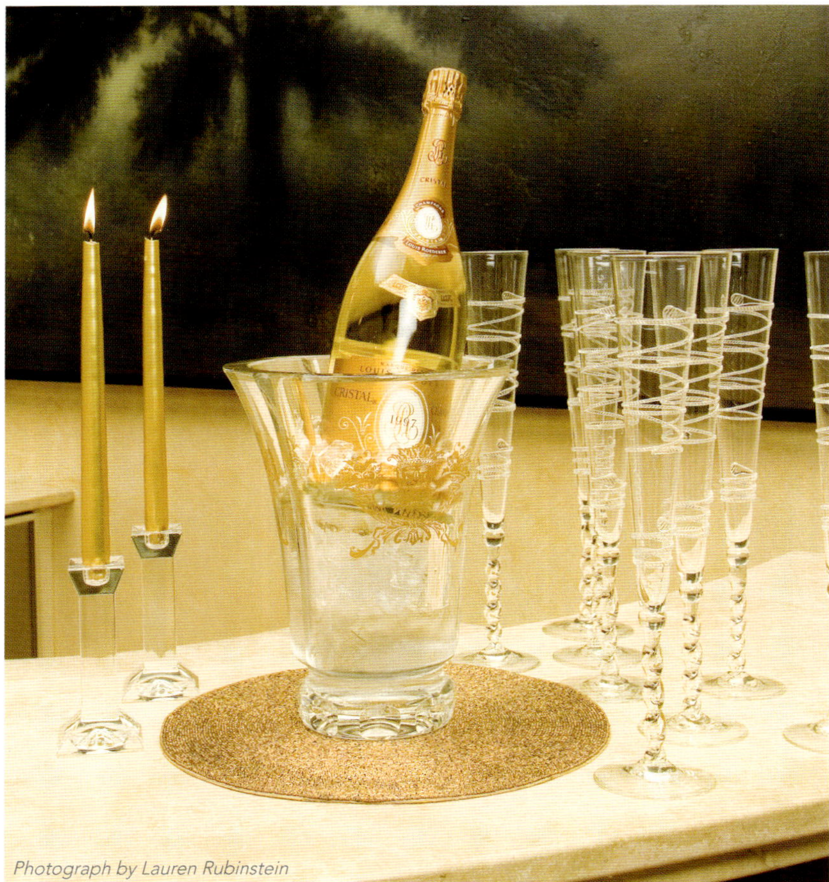

Photograph by Lauren Rubinstein

Photograph by Ric Mershon Photographers

Photograph by Jim Fitts

Photograph by Greg Mooney

Photograph by Lydia Dull

Right: Bite-sized portions seem to fly off the trays, and the gourmet mini Kobe beef, ahi tuna, and seared foie gras sliders were no different.

Facing page top left: The 350 guests at the Atlanta premier screening party for "Julie & Julia" loved the tiny crème brûlée dessert spoons.

Facing page top right: For an annual fundraiser, we coated the dining table in thick milk chocolate and created placemats, chargers, and place cards from the same batch. We used all chocolate-colored décor for a bold, delicious feel.

Facing page bottom: Using seven main dessert selections, including flourless chocolate torte, lemon pound cake, pumpkin cheesecake, and apple dulcé torte, the pastry team combined each with a choice of seven sauces and 18 garnishes to create a seemingly infinite number of combinations for the guests.

Photograph by Lauren Rubinstein

views

When choosing culinary offerings for an event, comfort food with an element of excitement is always a safe bet. But don't go past the point at which people feel the food is too exquisite or surprising to eat. Find the balance.

A Divine Event
KENDALL COLLIER | TERESA DAY | ALAN SOUZA

At first, divine and **wicked don't** appear to be the most compatible descriptions. Yet A Divine Event has flawlessly melded the two concepts in its mouthwatering cuisine. Partners Kendall Collier, Teresa Day, and founder Alan Souza have successfully combined divine inspiration with devilish desire—all in the name of fare that is wickedly delicious.

Spurred on by a passionate love affair with food, the team at A Divine Event excels in artful design, smooth organization, and attentive service. But it is the food that keeps everyone coming back. Set apart by a focus on fresh, local ingredients simply prepared, A Divine Event's culinary treats rival the best restaurants and delight the most discerning palates.

A Divine Event watches over every event like a band of guardian angels. Although no one there has wings, what they do have is decades of catering experience, a shelf full of culinary and event design awards, both local and international, and an appetite for excellence that is never satisfied. As food culture continues to move from the 3,000-mile Caesar salad to more sustainable, farm-to-table options, A Divine Event leads the charge.

To create a more sophisticated look for a Cinco de Mayo celebration, silver, turquoise, and coral inspire the color palette for a series of buffets offering *pequeño* plate pairings. We handcrafted an innovative shadowbox table with a recessed top to accommodate a variety of materials producing looks capable of emulating many styles.

Photograph by Jessica Horwitz

"If preparing wickedly delicious food is wrong, then I don't want to be right."

—Alan Souza

Right: Classic French Tarte Tatin excites the taste buds when unexpectedly coupled with Berkshire pork nestled in roasted root vegetables and topped with a Southern favorite—spicy sautéed greens.

Facing page: At A Divine Event, food is our passion, from decadent lobster mac and cheese to luscious fresh fruit cobbler. Southern-inspired and internationally influenced, the cuisine is just too tempting to resist.

views

❖ Never settle for what's expected in theme, food, or décor.

❖ No matter how humble the ingredients, foods perfectly paired can elevate a dish to the sublime.

❖ Keep it market fresh and simple to allow the natural flavors of the food to speak for themselves.

Susan Mason Catering

SUSAN MASON

At ease in governors' mansions and world-renowned venues as well as in her own Savannah kitchen, Susan Mason has become synonymous with fine Southern hospitality that embodies mouthwatering cuisine and exquisite presentation.

Once just an idea inspired by a Martha Stewart book, Susan Mason Catering now boasts a legendary nationwide reputation. Susan has served as the featured chef at the James Beard Foundation in New York, catered on yachts, barges, and private jets, created menus for numerous celebrity events, and developed her own cookbook. With a philosophy based on perfection and abundance—and a hands-on approach that includes meeting with every host, designing every menu, and attending every event—it's no wonder Susan was selected as the best caterer in Savannah for five years in a row.

Susan's talent in the edible realm does run in her blood—both her mother and grandmother were gifted cooks—but she has also poured her heart and soul into injecting ingenuity and excellence in every menu. Cooking has taken center stage in her career and certainly spills over into her life. She peruses magazines and cookbooks until the wee hours of the morning. When queued up in theater or museum lines, she'll ask complete strangers if they have any new food ideas. She even hosts her own dinner parties at home—all evidence that her passion is in the culinary arts. Combined with her warm personality, this enthusiasm has led Susan to become a sumptuous testament to high style and Southern entertaining.

For an unpretentious, beautiful dessert, I love to serve Bosc pears poached in Port wine with crème anglaise and fresh mint for color.

Photograph by Evan Saunders

Photograph by Christine Hall Photography

Photograph by Evan Saunders

Photograph by Evan Saunders

Photograph by Christine Hall Photography

"If you anticipate that something is going to taste good because of the delectable presentation, then it will be delicious."

—Susan Mason

Right: The ambience at a film festival party held in a cemetery was just amazing. Thousands of candles forged a stunning environment; I supplemented with a chilling menu of cooled corn soup with lobster tail, cold beef tenderloin with tarragon mustard sauce, wild rice salad, cherry tomatoes Provençal, and chocolate mousse with crème anglaise and raspberries.

Facing page top and bottom right: In the South, seafood and grilled entrées are common requests. I love to enhance delicious food with refined presentation, such as adorning each plate with the lobster shell, constructing a magnificent spread of shrimp on an ice-topped table, or infusing brilliant color into a dish of grilled quail.

Facing page bottom left: Provided by my mother as an after-school snack, tomato sandwiches hold a special place in my heart. Much to my delight, this delicious, comforting treat has become my trademark.

Photograph by Dan Saelinger Photography

views

❖ Every menu should be created not based on the trends and popular choices but on what springs forth from the hearts of those planning the event.

❖ The recipe for a successful party includes a good mix of people and a plentiful spread of delicious food.

Sail with
Away Us!
Please reply before
October 31st

ACCEPTS WITH PLEASURE
DECLINES WITH REGRET

It's All in t

TODD'S 40th Wine Tasting
SHHH... IT'S A SURPRISE! AN EVENING TO CELEBRATE TODD'S 40TH BIRTHDAY
COCKTAILS • DINNER • DANCING
FRIDAY, MARCH 27, 2009
SEVEN-THIRTY SHARP
10 WEST
ATLANTA, GEORGIA
KASEY ASARCH
YOUR PRESENCE IS TODD'S BEST GIFT
ACCOMMODATIONS
GRAND HYATT • BUCKHEAD
THE FUN CONTINUES
CASUAL DINNER
SATURDAY
BRUNCH SUNDAY
TODD'S 40TH

Let's help Feather their nest!
Please join us for a
Cocktail Party and Shower
in honor of
Nicole Pickert and Josh Cobb
Saturday, April 12, 2008
seven-thirty
at the Clare's
2697 Mabry Road • Atlanta • 30319
Amanda and Chris Clare
Amy and Daniel Edwards
Dabney and Mark Junell
Scott Letson
Heather Smith and David Ansari
Sherry and Donald Tomberlin
Ashley and Nelson Vinson
Rebecca and Den Webb
Alexandra Whiddon

the Details

Paces Papers

JACKIE GARSON HOWARD

Stationery and invitations are personal statements of style that capture the details of the most important, historic events of our lives. Jackie Garson Howard, the mastermind of Paces Papers since 1974, values creativity in all forms and has surrounded herself with a team of talented designers, including longtime friend and colleague Kathy Davidson. The team offers a fresh perspective on the fine details of event planning and wedding consultation. Each designer gives her undivided attention to a project, determining the best way to achieve the desired look. Sometimes it's through a custom design; other times it's from one of the 30 lines that Paces Papers carries, including Crane, Pendragon, and Vera Wang. Articulating the look they want to achieve can be a challenge for people, but the designers are experts at drawing out every client's uniqueness, every occasion's magical qualities. Through casual conversation, the designers gain an understanding of what needs should be accomplished in the stationery, announcements, invitations, programs, thank you cards, hospitality bags, or other materials.

The designers are especially passionate about the texture and aesthetic of handmade paper, sourcing from as far away as France, Spain, Italy, and the Czech Republic. They feel that engraved or letterpress invitations are the epitome of tradition and elegance. In their design studio and boutique, they enjoy introducing people to a variety of papers, concepts, styles, and choices for printing. Letterpress or engraved, funky or sophisticated, monochromatic or boldly colored, elaborate or simple, each paper creation is a personalized work of art that makes an unforgettable impression.

Our earth-toned look reflects the couple's passion for nature; they are owners of an animal sanctuary. The rustic and elegant design suited their unique farm wedding. We created stationery of kraft paper with mixed textures and organic suede ribbon. Save-the-date announcements, programs, and favor tags were thermography printed, and invitations were engraved. Design and illustration by Sara Haskew.

Photograph by Sara Haskew

TODD'S 40th
Wine Tasting

SHHH...IT'S A
SURPRISE!
AN EVENING TO CELEBRATE
TODD'S 40TH BIRTHDAY
COCKTAILS·DINNER·DANCING
FRIDAY, MARCH 27, 2009
SEVEN-THIRTY SHARP
103 WEST
ATLANTA, GEORGIA
KASEY ASARCH
YOUR PRESENCE IS TODD'S BEST GIFT

ACCOMMODATIONS
GRAND HYATT · BUCKHEAD
404.237.1234
THE FUN CONTINUES
CASUAL DINNER
SATURDAY
BRUNCH SUNDAY

TA

TODD'S 40TH

Photograph by Tara McRae

Photograph by Michele Keeney

Photograph by Ashley Stephenson

Above: Invitations delight partygoers of all ages. An "afternoon at the zoo" child's birthday invitation has a charming vintage animal tag embellished with baker's twine. The engaging piece was flat printed.

Above right: Theming is everything. A retro French "cirque du" design showcases a red glitter envelope lining, custom playbills, and hand-drawn big top invitations announcing the backyard circus event to young guests. Illustrations by Emmi Braselton.

Right: Our save-the-date for a farm wedding features artwork based on an old woodcarving from the homestead's entrance gate. Letterpress printed with apple green hand-painted edges, a giclée image of the outdoorsy couple is on the reverse.

Facing page: For an avid golfer, we created a surprise party invitation design that is sophisticated, masculine, and contemporary. Envelopes are hand lined with the classic argyle pattern. A personal logo decorates cigar match boxes and hot-stamped cocktail napkins. The invitation is engraved. Hand-lettered table flags are by Maria Thomas.

Photograph by Ashley Stephenson

"Stationery is a reflection of who you are."

—Jackie Garson Howard

Above: The wedding program on Italian deckle-edge paper completes the elegant wedding paper trousseau. A subtle, hand-dyed silk ribbon accents the piece for a destination wedding held at the bride's family ranch in Colorado. Calligraphy by Maria Thomas.

Right: Oversized and opulent, the design captures attention. Handmade deckle-edge European paper is hand lettered. We chose heavenly pastels and metallic inks to create a truly original fantasy invitation. Calligraphy by Cynthia Tyler.

Mr. and Mrs. William Meyer
request the honour of your presence
at the marriage of their daughter
Elizabeth Kate
to
Mr. Brett J. Pomerantz
Saturday, the twenty-seventh of September
Two thousand eight
half after seven o'clock in the evening
The Temple
Atlanta, Georgia
a reply is requested
th of September
Regrets

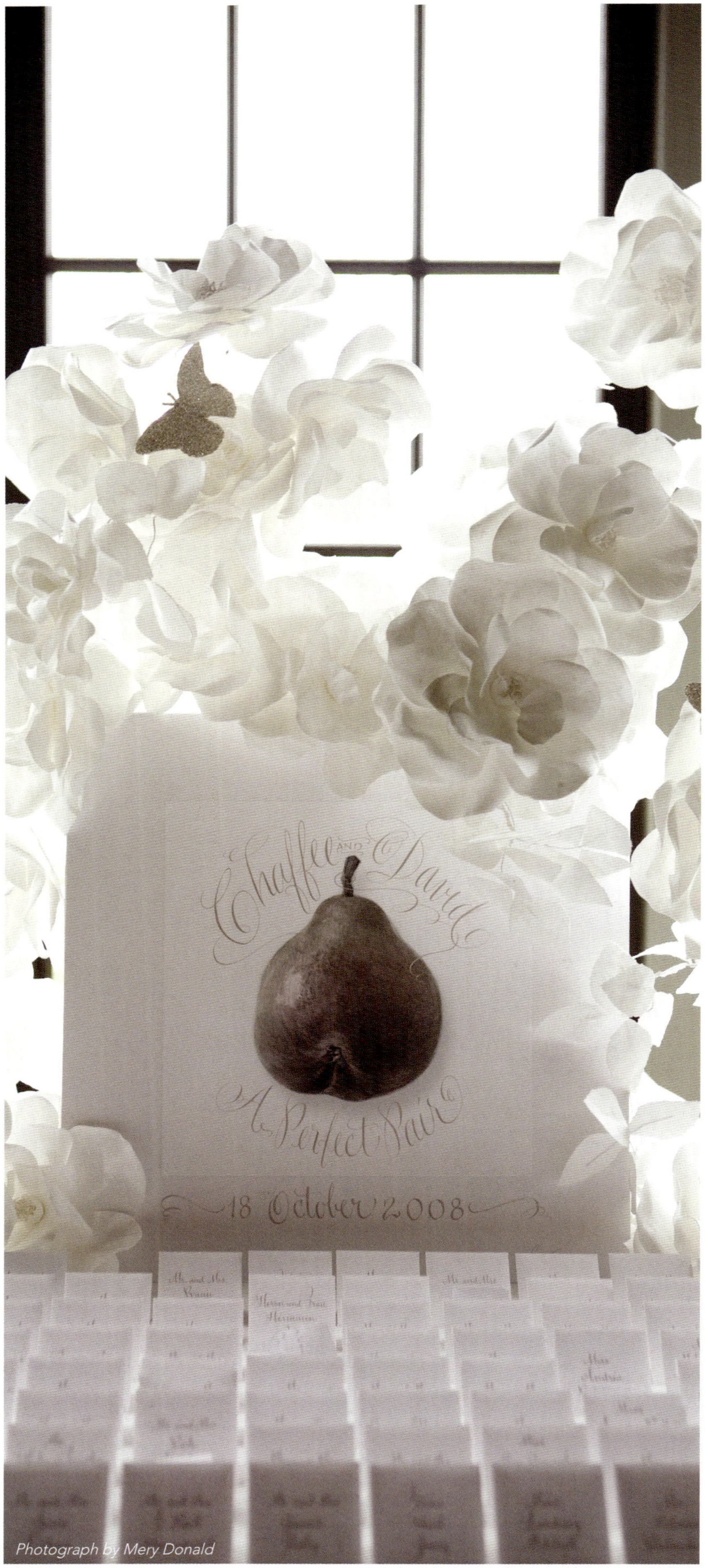

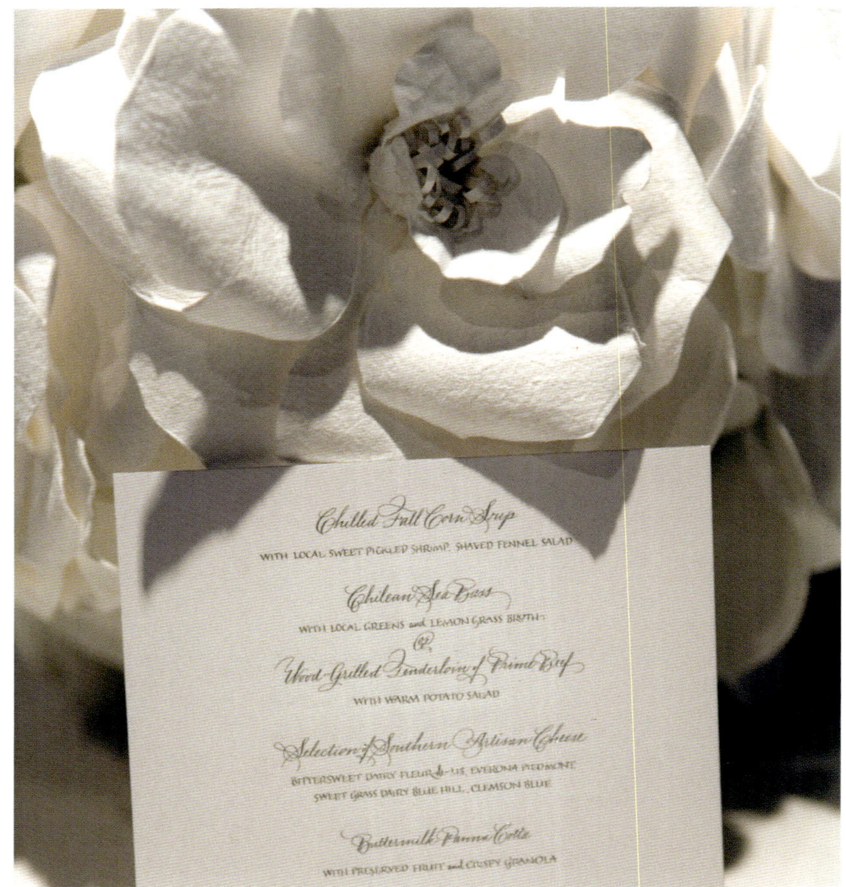

Photograph by Mery Donald

Photograph by Mery Donald

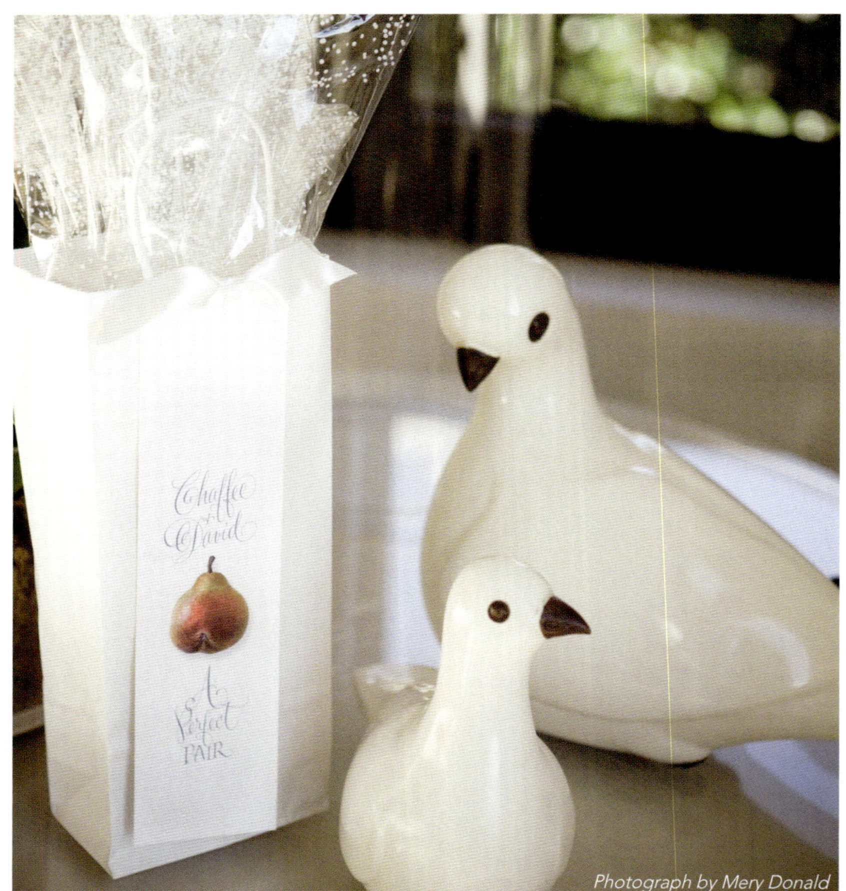

Photograph by Mery Donald

Photograph by Sara Haskew

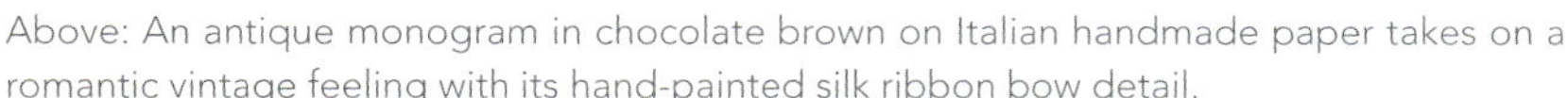

Photograph by Ashley Stephenson

Above: An antique monogram in chocolate brown on Italian handmade paper takes on a romantic vintage feeling with its hand-painted silk ribbon bow detail.

Above right: Our navy blue background with white engraving creates a crisp image on seven-ply, pure cotton Crane paper. Hand lettering, custom postage stamps, an original monogram, and small elegant programs perfectly fit the quintessential Southern country club wedding. Calligraphy by Cynthia Tyler.

Right: Textured bamboo paper is letterpress printed for special delivery in pattern-lined, matching envelopes. Our updated formal design is a lovely prelude to the destination wedding in Jackson Hole. Calligraphy by Smock.

Facing page: The modern bride desired a series of contemporary squares for her "perfect pair" stationery. We designed the pieces to complement a clean white-on-white theme accented with gold and silver ink on very heavy card stock. Hand-lettered place cards, engraved menus, and flat printed hospitality bag tags have a fresh look. Pear artwork by Maria Thomas.

Photograph by Emmi Braselton

Photograph by Tara McRae

Photograph by Sara Haskew

Photograph by Ashley Stephenson

Right: A young girl's precious rite of passage is softly honored with sage and blue-grey colors. Our custom bat mitzvah design includes cards and envelopes that are layered and stepped. The subtle blind embossed folder is in Hebrew, while the interior text is thermography printed.

Facing page top left: A clever "feather the nest" theme for the bridal shower is echoed in the design. We used natural wood pulp paper trimmed in genuine peacock feathers.

Facing page top right: Our invitation for an alfresco rehearsal dinner incorporates real twigs with a punch of color, so it reads casual, yet sophisticated.

Facing page bottom left: Spanish handmade paper combines with flowing circular text inviting guests to the rehearsal dinner in wine country. We commissioned original grapevine drawings and a custom monogram, all printed in rich purple raised ink.

Facing page bottom right: Our spring engagement party invitation features a nostalgic hot air balloon illustration that brings the couple's love of travel to life. Calligraphy and artwork by Maria Thomas.

Photograph by Michele Keeney

views

Invitations set the tone for the entire celebration, so choose a design that is in keeping with the theme or your own personal style. Guests should have six to eight months notice with save-the-dates—even more if the event is over a holiday weekend—and invitations need to be sent two months prior, so plan ahead to allow time for the creative and production processes, addressing, and assembly. Be sure to have each envelope hand-canceled at the post office so that your invitation will arrive beautiful and clean.

DecoMarj

MARJORIE PRUITT

On the surface, a forensic scientist has almost nothing in common with an invitation designer. But Marjorie Pruitt has drawn a parallel between the two and proven that science and art may have more in common than most people think. How so? It takes a hawkish eye for detail, honed observation skills, and a purely perfectionist approach. With a strong creative drive, Marjorie merged these two worlds when she made a dramatic career change almost 15 years ago, stepping out of the lab and into the artist's role. From engraving to letterpress, thermography to flat printing, Marjorie's work has garnered peer recognition with a number of industry honors, including the Allie Awards. Beautifully printed invitations, masterfully detailed cards, and whimsical favors reveal just how much a scientist's training can offer printed art.

DecoMarj began in 1997 and has spread across the Southeast through the approval of satisfied hosts and hostesses. With a highly focused nature and a keen ability to listen, Marjorie dedicates herself to bring a distinctive style to invitations, programs, place cards, and other event accessories.

Capitalizing on a hot trend, a bride chose a peacock theme for her wedding, which I used to design her stationery suite. Instead of the more traditional royal blues and brilliant green hues associated with peacocks, we integrated her wedding colors, teal and eggplant, to maintain the event's color scheme. The cohesive use of colors and images on the invitations, cocktail napkins, and wedding programs coordinated beautifully with her wedding-day décor.

Please reply before
October 31st
ACCEPTS WITH PLEASURE
DECLINES WITH REGRET

For your listening pleasure
SAIL AWAY WITH US

Photograph by Shari Zellers Photography

Sail Away with Us!

Photograph by Shari Zellers Photography

If you need some flats,
please take a pair!
Sizes: Xs, Sml, Med, Lrg
MARCIE MATTHEW

Photograph by Big Day Photography

Dr. and Mrs. Marshall Nash
Drop in on "Big Black"

Photograph by Ben Vigil Photographers

"The strongest inspiration comes from knowing party hosts on a deeper level. Capitalizing on their comments and unspoken reactions, hidden details are revealed, which I express in design."

—Marjorie Pruitt

Right: We went with a family's coat of arms for a rehearsal dinner. When the mother of the groom spoke of her husband and son's proud Scottish ancestry, I knew we had stumbled upon the perfect theme. I pulled in hues of gold and claret to keep with the occasion's colors.

Facing page top: The key to finding a theme isn't always obvious; sometimes the client needs a little coaxing. For a rehearsal dinner, I pulled inspiration from the venue and the couple's hobbies. Set in a dining room overlooking a river, the event featured a sailing theme; I used a striped blue and lime green grosgrain ribbon as the color inspiration. Miniature sailboat favors carrying theme-colored jellybeans sported a striped flag with guests' names, serving both as an edible favor and as a place card. Glass sailboat votive candleholders, which sailed around the tabletops, served double duty as festive décor and as mementos for guests. Because double duty items save time, money, and space they have become popular assets for party planners.

Facing page bottom left: Mimicking the invitation style, I designed custom-printed flip-flop sandals with the couple's signature floral pattern and monogram. Since the reception took place on the family farm, with a recommended "hats and flats" dress code, the sandals served as useful footwear for any ladies wearing uncomfortable heels on the rough terrain.

Facing page bottom right: When a skate enthusiast celebrated his bar mitzvah, a skateboard themed party inspired me to create whimsical party favors that reflect his hobby. I used miniature rolling skateboard keychains to serve as both a souvenir for future drivers and an escort card holder. The silver cards directed guests to their tables—in skater lingo, of course. The table signs were skateboard shapes and named after different skate vendors.

Photograph by Shari Zellers Photography

views

Family heritage and traditions work well as a strong theme for parties, dinners, or ceremonies. Celebrate the past and the present by offering your guests a get-to-know-our-family atmosphere. If you don't know much about your lineage, it's a good reason to do some research and find a meaningful, personal motif for an important event.

The Electronic Pencil
Gwen Ware

For Gwen Ware, owner of The Electronic Pencil, paper is more than just a product for printing. It's a spectacular medium that offers limitless possibilities, as seen in her work for the Atlanta Historical Society's Titanic-themed gala. Armed with creative prowess and intense historical research, Gwen crafted a six-page newspaper complete with the event's program and menu, as well as news articles that she wrote as if it were 1910.

This is just one of hundreds of clever ideas that Gwen has dreamed up since her start in 1991. Summoning knowledge from her Bachelor and Master of Arts degrees, teaching experience, technological interests, and sales and marketing skills, Gwen relies on a strong relationship with the event host. To solidify this connection, a private section on The Electronic Pencil's website allows collaboration with the host regarding preliminary designs, magnified fonts, paper samples, and more.

With the belief that an invitation is a marketing piece and the other elements are part of the event's mood, Gwen generates ideas that often include found objects, especially from nature, or something that requires the guest's participation. Designed to obtain that wow factor, Gwen's materials take guests into another world, into a place where they forget everything else and simply enjoy the event. By using little vignettes or adding personal touches, Gwen creates exclusive paper products that will intrigue the guests and make a lasting impression.

A strong theme throughout every printed piece can draw guests into the experience. For a destination wedding at Oheka Castle on Long Island—where "The Great Gatsby" was partially inspired—I wove a 1920s feel of speakeasies, Art Deco, and ritzy dinner parties through the materials. The colors of seal brown, cream, and silver coordinate with the event's ambience, while black ice Swarovski crystals and dupioni silk ribbon exude sophistication.

Photograph by Ann Hamilton

Photograph by Ann Hamilton

Photograph by Gwen Ware

Photograph by Gwen Ware

Photograph by Gwen Ware

"You can basically hang everything, from the save-the-date to the menu card, on the feelings you want your guests to experience."

—Gwen Ware

Right: To accommodate a request for a boxed invitation that would be hand delivered, we personalized wrapped boxes with a red bow and gold corrugated cardboard.

Facing page top and bottom right: Whether it's a gilded wooden binding, nature-inspired materials such as corrugated board and a mulberry twig, or pre-worn jeans cut to showcase the pocket and silk-screen printed with information, unusual materials can make the best invitations.

Facing page bottom left: We were challenged to create a piece that reminded guests of modern art but also had a sense of humor. With precise planning, the variation on a pop-up card design was a big hit.

Photograph by Gwen Ware

views

Cheap doesn't necessarily mean bad, and expensive doesn't always equate to quality. At first, don't even look at the monetary value. Just determine what catches your eye and what kind of impression you want to give. Then figure out how to create that image in a way that meets the budget.

Capturing the

Moment

Priscilla Wannamaker Photographer

PRISCILLA WANNAMAKER

Priscilla Wannamaker has had a lifelong passion for photography. Even as a young child, she recognized how a photograph could bring back a special memory. This passion grew into her profession, and Priscilla has received international acclaim for her photographic art.

Priscilla uses each photograph or group of photographs to relay a story that will strike a chord with each person who views the images. To achieve this narrative, she remains observant and reacts correctly to the unfolding events. Her awareness comes straight from her heart and her emotional response to the moment. Priscilla's hope is that each image will bring this response for others, too.

As with any art, experience and tools are certainly important components of the work; however, telling a story with images is not a static process. Priscilla utilizes her understanding of the equipment, as well as her instinct for movement during the photography process, which involves knowing when to pull back for a shot and when to approach.

The couple's love, the light, and the overall setting came together to help create a perfect moment.

Photograph by Priscilla Wannamaker

Photograph by Priscilla Wannamaker

"Photographs hold life's experiences and become treasures."

—Priscilla Wannamaker

Photography is one of the most universal languages around, and you don't have to say a word.

Photograph by Priscilla Wannamaker

Photograph by Priscilla Wannamaker

Photograph by Priscilla Wannamaker

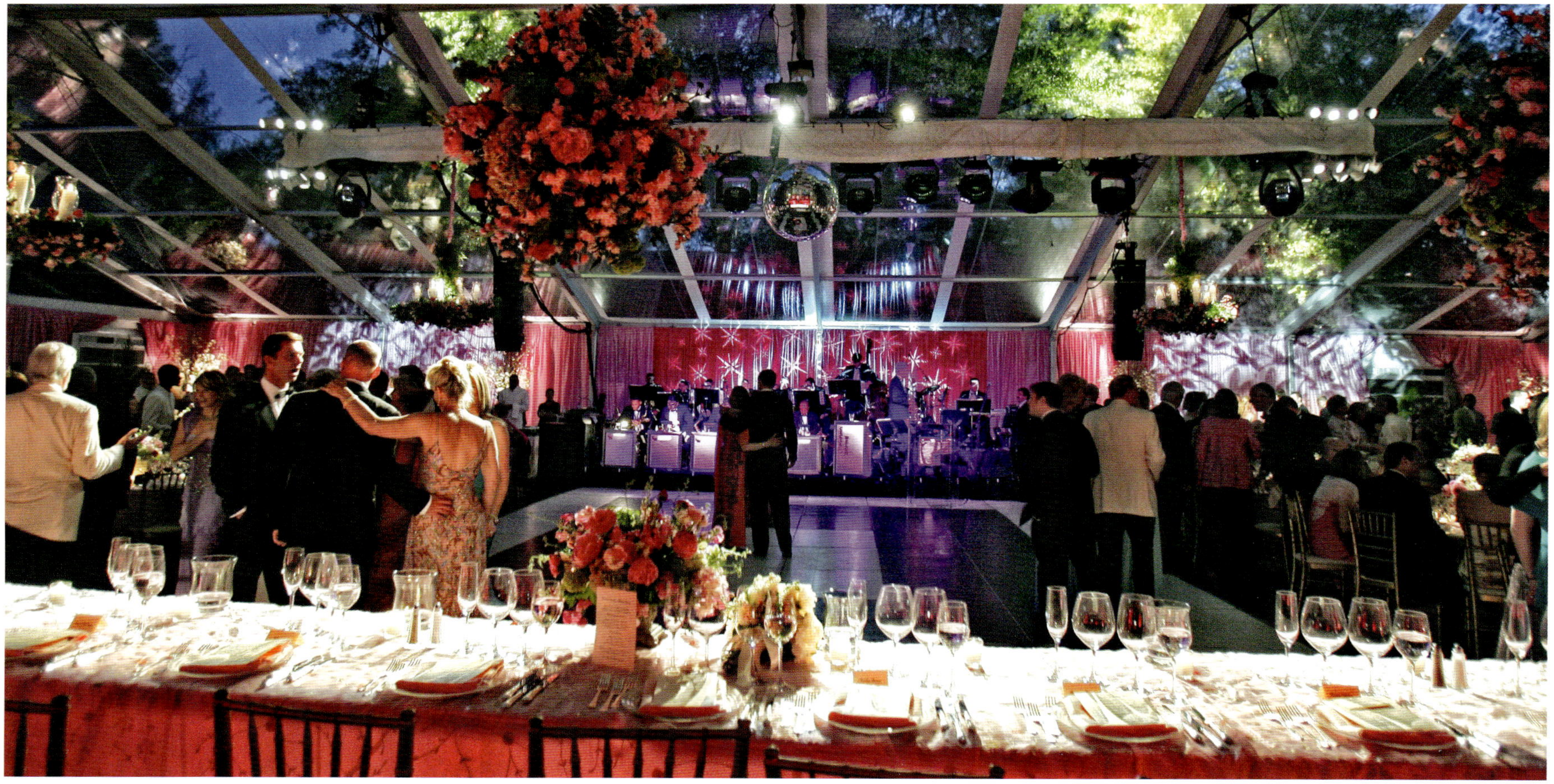

Photograph by Priscilla Wannamaker

Photograph by Priscilla Wannamaker

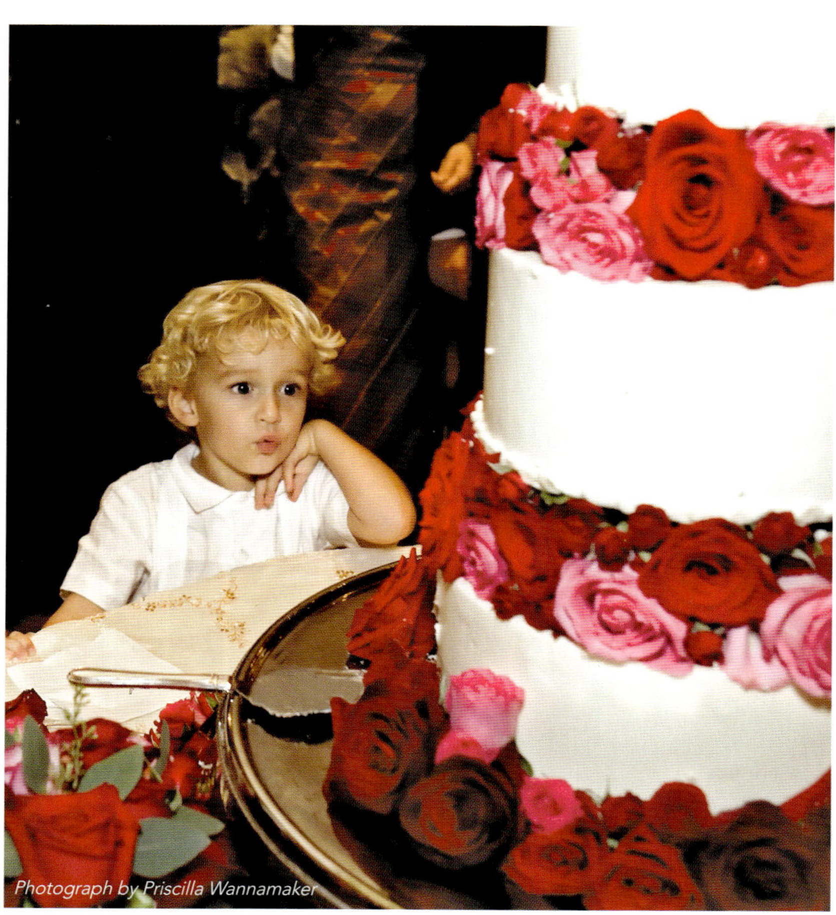

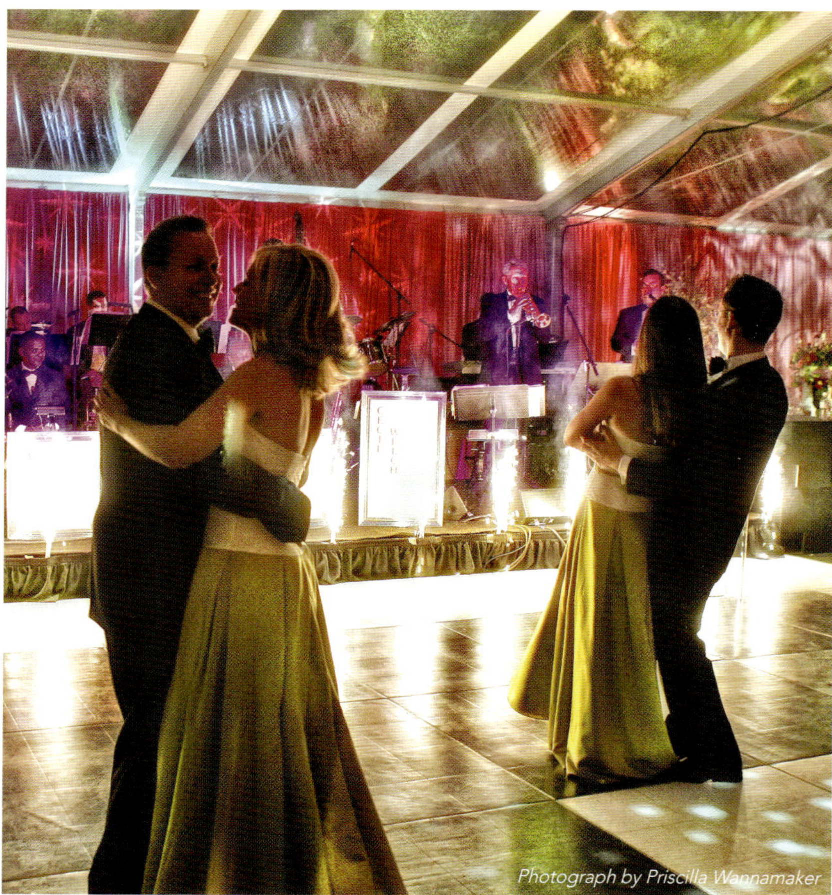

Photograph by Priscilla Wannamaker

"It never ceases to amaze me how a photograph has the power to take you right back to a moment in time."

—Priscilla Wannamaker

Through all of my photographs, my goal is to show a true moment in time without adding to the setting or being distracting.

Photograph by Priscilla Wannamaker

views

My inspiration often comes from Ansel Adams, who said "Photography, as a powerful medium of expression and communication, offers an infinite variety of perception, interpretation, and execution."

EASTCOAST ENTERTAINMENT

In 1988, EastCoast Entertainment opened a major branch office in Atlanta. The experienced producers there combine a love of music and entertainment with business acumen. Today, the entire company produces over 400 celebrity entertainer concerts and issues nearly 10,000 contracts each year.

EastCoast's large network, long history, and national and global experience allow the EastCoast Atlanta team to offer a variety of proposals that include both the traditional and the unique. From celebrities such as Lionel Richie to exclusive local groups like Party on the Moon and Anita, EastCoast works with a huge variety of celebrations, people, and budgets.

Booking entertainment isn't the only focus. On the contrary, EastCoast is the only agency in Atlanta to combine entertainment booking with large-scale artist representation and production integration. By representing a number of entertainers, EastCoast can better pair them with the right events based on style and budget—a win-win for all involved. EastCoast's specialty of incorporating the production requirements of the entertainment aspect—such as the lighting and audio technology—with video technology and other elements to support the program, also has its advantages in preventing duplicate equipment and cutting expenses.

Team Atlanta takes great pleasure in its ability to help event planners narrow their focus, choose the right entertainment, and produce spectacular events.

Some elegant events require a bit of high-energy fun to create just the right ambience. We brought in a high-tech, costumed dance band and coordinated phenomenal lighting and effects for a well-integrated event.

Photograph by Lila Events

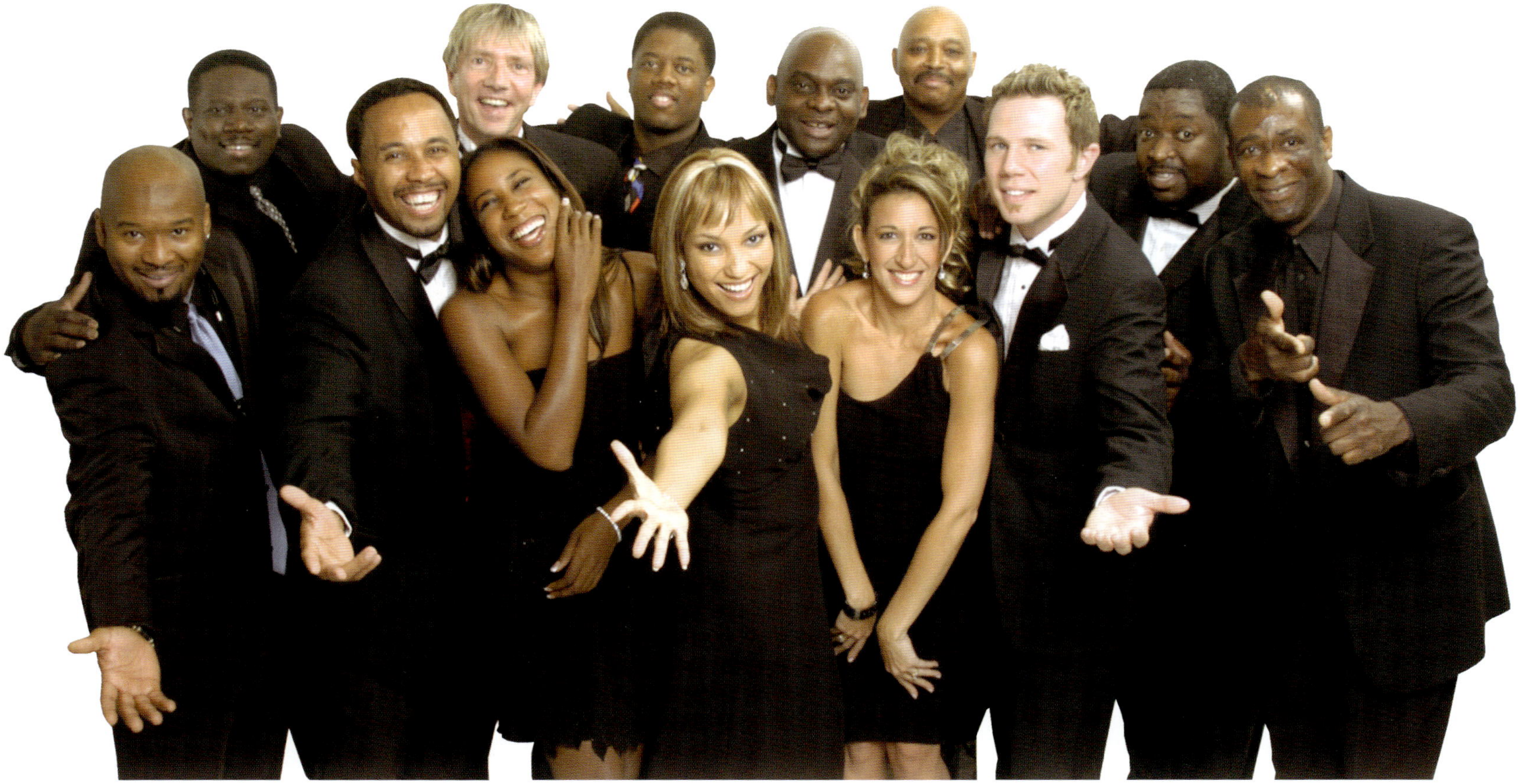

Photograph by FITZ Studios

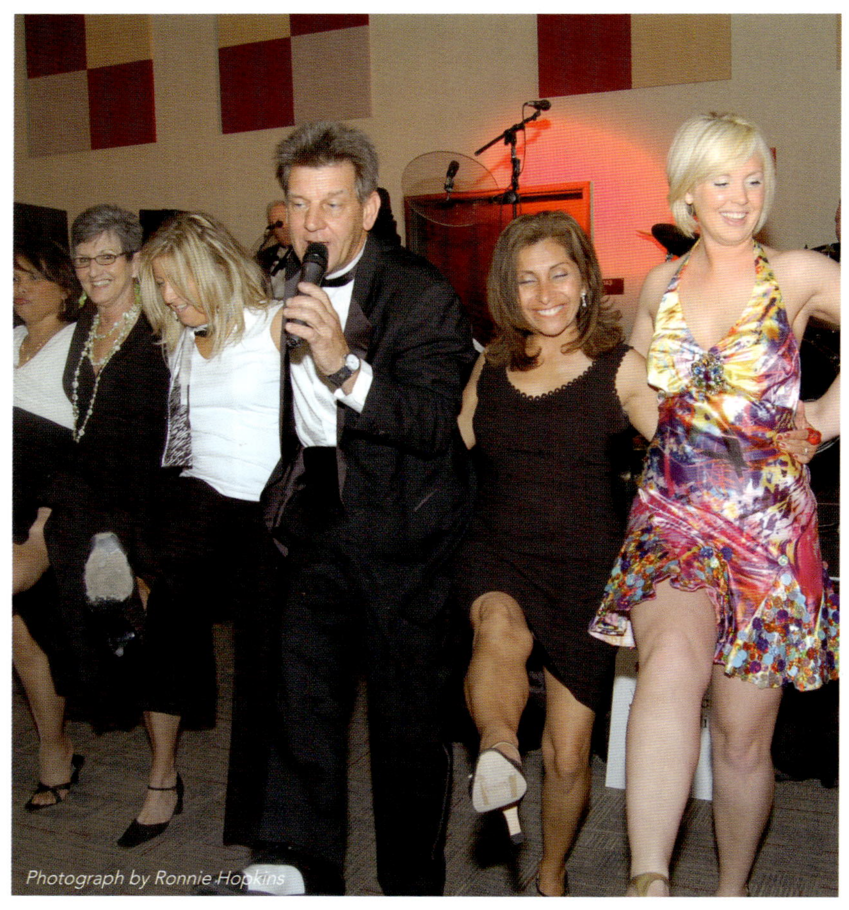

Photograph by Ronnie Hopkins

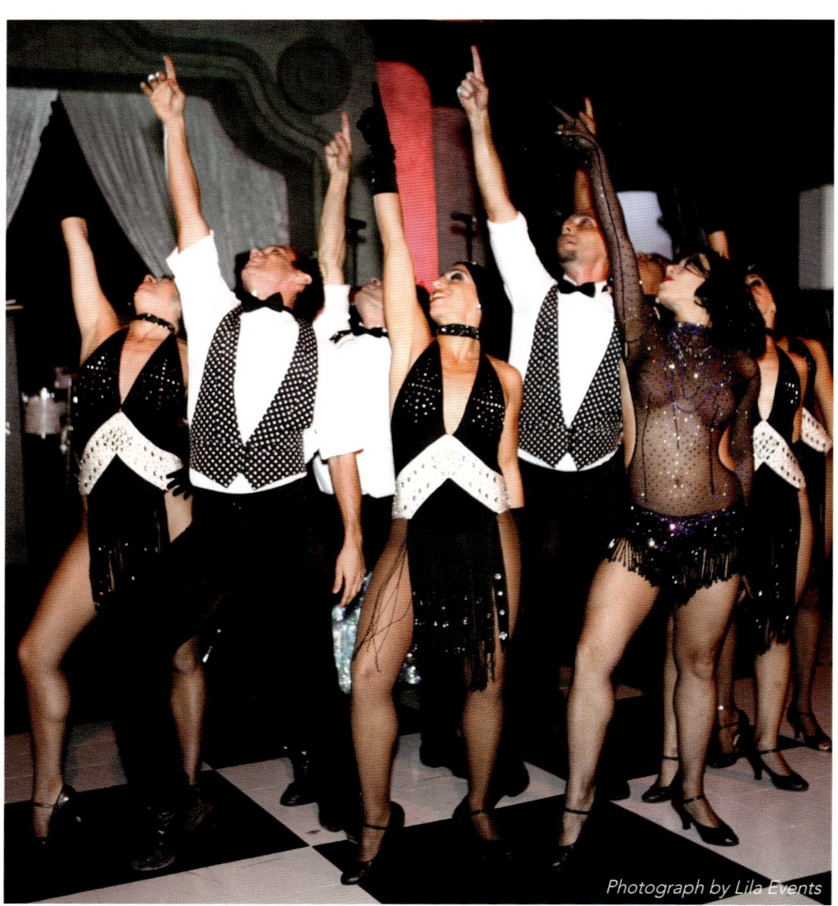

Photograph by Lila Events

"Thinking even just a little outside the box, say an '80s-themed band at an elegant reception, can add an interesting twist to the life of the event."

—Steve Thomas

Right: We work with not only dance bands and concert acts, but novelty entertainment of all types.

Facing page top: Party on the Moon is a high-energy, well-known group in Atlanta. They've performed at everything from President Obama's Inaugural Ball to Eli Manning's wedding in Cabo San Lucas. They are exactly the kind of top-shelf talent we are proud to represent.

Facing page bottom: Interactive programs can be especially important for certain events. We draw from an assortment of options, including DJs, MCs, and fabulous dancers.

Photograph by Lila Events

views

Choose an entertainment consultant to represent the vision and goals of the event planner, instead of the planner talking individually with multiple entertainment acts. The consultant will have the knowledge and relationships to significantly cut down on the time and money associated with searching for entertainers.

Paula M. Gould Photography

PAULA M. GOULD

Photography is more than just a career; it's an avenue of insight into a person or a group of people. Likewise, taking good photographs requires more than just a camera, but also an understanding of how people think and an ability to smoothly become part of the group. These are the ideas that Paula M. Gould embraces. Matched with her personality as a people-person, degrees in sociology and commercial photography, and a confidence in her capability to capture memories, this philosophy weaves throughout each event Paula covers.

As far back as Paula can remember, photography has been one of the major loves of her life. With a grandfather who had his own studio and darkroom and a father who enjoyed taking pictures, Paula was immersed in the wonder of still photos from an early age. She remembers staging photo shoots with her father when she was in high school.

For Paula, this enthusiasm for photography translates into a complete absorption in her work. Each family and individual she works with becomes a sort of extended family—her involvement in their lives and participation in their celebrations provide a unique connection. Paula's work is enhanced by her photo assistants' perspectives and photos as well as the technical aspect after the actual shot is taken. After the shoot, she ties all of the elements together on the computer to create images that express her patience and passion.

As a boutique photographer—one who gives specialized time to each client, event, or product—I first shoot exactly what is desired. I then incorporate various effects, including those done in camera as with the belly dancers and those done on the computer, to provide an assortment of images. While these special effects may not be requested initially, they are often a wonderful surprise.

Photograph by Paula M. Gould

> "A black and white image with a pop of color is like taking a step back in time with a modern twist."
>
> —Paula M. Gould

Whether I'm shooting a bar or bat mitzvah, a wedding ceremony, a product for advertising, or a corporate party, I capture a little bit of everything—the details, the feelings of those involved, the ambience of the room, and even a few surprises.

Photograph by Paula M. Gould

views

When choosing a photographer, ask the right questions: how many events they've photographed, what happens if the photographer is sick, what they do if the camera breaks, etc. Then, actually call the references and take time to browse the portfolio. Ultimately, decide if the photographer's personality will mesh with yours.

RIC MERSHON PHOTOGRAPHERS

RIC MERSHON | BARRIE MERSHON

Born out of change and adversity, Ric Mershon Photographers was created when Ric and Barrie Mershon followed their hearts. After circumstances forced them to consider their future careers, Ric and Barrie at first struggled with the idea of starting a business but unanimously decided to strike out on their own to do what they had always loved.

Nearly 10 years later, Ric Mershon Photographers epitomizes what drew Ric and Barrie into photography in the first place—the honor of recording the emotion and the celebration of family events. Focusing on weddings and b'nai mitzvah celebrations, Ric and Barrie add their personal experiences and flavor into their work. Their love for and friendly banter with each other eases the nerves of soon-to-be-married couples. An immense respect assures families they will receive priceless heirlooms that preserve the planning and emotion of the celebration.

Embedded deeply in their philosophy is the need to connect with the family and determine some of the details that make the relationship unique. In addition to relaxing the family, this relationship also provides Ric and Barrie with indispensible information. This knowledge allows them to create beautiful images by avoiding conflict, helping keep the event joyous, and capturing what the hosts feel is truly important.

Occasionally lighting can be a challenge, but the best images occur when we can use the ambient lighting in the room without manufacturing a mood. The candles hung in Georgia Aquarium provided just enough light in the foreground while the purple hues in the ceiling and background produced a nice contrast.

Photograph by Ric Mershon Photographers

Photograph by Ric Mershon Photographers

Photograph by Ric Mershon Photographers

Photograph by Ric Mershon Photographers

Photograph by Ric Mershon Photographers

"Discovering the nuances that
make a relationship or event special
helps tremendously to preserve the
emotions and occurrences of the day."

—Barrie Mershon

Right: We try to take a creative approach to the details. For example, we shot the image from the opposite side of the light to give the centerpiece a dreamy glow.

Facing page: We always capture the broad view of a room and then focus on the beautiful details. Because we are in attendance both as professional photographers and as spectators, we bring a unique viewpoint to the setting. We vary our shots from the close-up of centerpieces or chairs to the overall feel of the space.

Photograph by Ric Mershon Photographers

views

Photography is all about understanding the use of light. This component is best incorporated as part of the planning process so that it complements the décor and mood. Adding uplight around the room can create a nice ambience and will provide a beautiful background for the eye and the camera.

Art of Celebration

GEORGIA TEAM

EXECUTIVE PUBLISHER: Phil Reavis
GRAPHIC DESIGNER: Ashley DuPree
EDITOR: Jennifer Nelson
MANAGING PRODUCTION COORDINATOR: Kristy Randall

HEADQUARTERS TEAM

PUBLISHER: Brian G. Carabet
PUBLISHER: John A. Shand
PUBLICATION & CIRCULATION MANAGER: Lauren B. Castelli
SENIOR GRAPHIC DESIGNER: Emily A. Kattan
GRAPHIC DESIGNER: Kendall Muellner
MANAGING EDITOR: Rosalie Z. Wilson
EDITOR: Anita M. Kasmar
EDITOR: Michael McConnell
EDITOR: Sarah Tangney
EDITOR: Lindsey Wilson
PRODUCTION COORDINATOR: Maylin Medina
PRODUCTION COORDINATOR: Drea Williams
PROJECT COORDINATOR: Laura Greenwood
TRAFFIC COORDINATOR: Brandi Breaux
ADMINISTRATIVE MANAGER: Carol Kendall
CLIENT SUPPORT COORDINATOR: Amanda Mathers

PANACHE PARTNERS, LLC
CORPORATE HEADQUARTERS
1424 Gables Court
Plano, TX 75075
469.246.6060
www.panache.com
www.panachecelebrations.com

INDEX

THE PANACHE COLLECTION

CREATING SPECTACULAR PUBLICATIONS FOR DISCERNING READERS

Dream Homes Series
An Exclusive Showcase of the Finest Architects, Designers and Builders

Carolinas
Chicago
Coastal California
Colorado
Deserts
Florida
Georgia
Los Angeles
Metro New York
Michigan
Minnesota
New England

New Jersey
Northern California
Ohio & Pennsylvania
Pacific Northwest
Philadelphia
South Florida
Southwest
Tennessee
Texas
Washington, D.C.

Perspectives on Design Series
Design Philosophies Expressed by Leading Professionals

California
Carolinas
Chicago
Colorado
Florida
Georgia
Great Lakes

Minnesota
New England
New York
Pacific Northwest
Southwest
Western Canada

Spectacular Wineries Series
A Captivating Tour of Established, Estate and Boutique Wineries

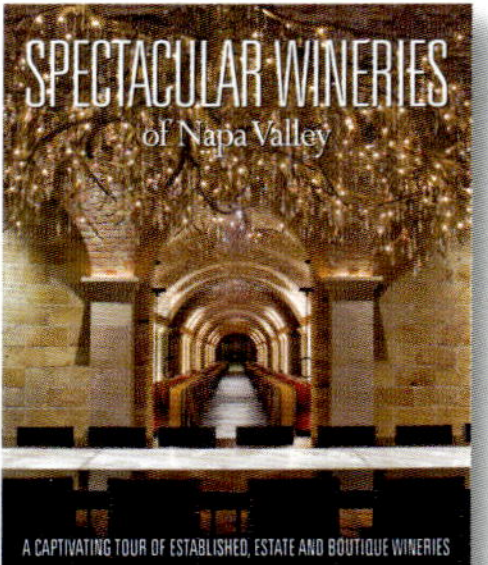

California's Central Coast
Napa Valley
New York
Sonoma County

City by Design Series
An Architectural Perspective

Atlanta
Charlotte
Chicago
Dallas
Denver
Orlando
Phoenix
San Francisco
Texas

Spectacular Homes Series
An Exclusive Showcase of the Finest Interior Designers

California
Carolinas
Chicago
Colorado
Florida
Georgia
Heartland
London
Michigan
Minnesota
New England

Metro New York
Ohio & Pennsylvania
Pacific Northwest
Philadelphia
South Florida
Southwest
Tennessee
Texas
Toronto
Washington, D.C.
Western Canada

Art of Celebration Series
The Making of a Gala

Chicago & the Greater Midwest
Georgia
New England
New York
Philadelphia
South Florida
Southern California
Southwest
Texas
Toronto
Washington, D.C.
Wine Country

Specialty Titles
The Finest in Unique Luxury Lifestyle Publications

Cloth and Culture: Couture Creations of Ruth E. Funk
Distinguished Inns of North America
Extraordinary Homes California
Geoffrey Bradfield Ex Arte
Into the Earth: A Wine Cave Renaissance
Spectacular Golf of Colorado
Spectacular Golf of Texas
Spectacular Hotels
Spectacular Restaurants of Texas
Visions of Design

PanacheCelebrations.com
Where the Event Industry's Finest Professionals Gather, Share, and Inspire

PanacheCelebrations.com overflows with innovative ideas from leading event planners, designers, caterers, and other specialists. A gallery of photographs and library of advice-oriented articles are among the comprehensive site's offerings.